"In order to be truly successful, you must be phys[...] healthy. *The Power of Positive Fitness* by John Ro[...] gives you the 'why' and the 'how' along with an ea[...] get there. I loved it and I know you will too!"

—TOM ZIGLAR, proud son of Zig Ziglar

"To be totally fit and to enjoy life to the fullest, you need to be both physically and spiritually fit. In this book, John Rowley gives you a plan of action to help you achieve this goal so that you can live a long, healthy, and inspired life. But remember—fitness is a journey, not a destination, and must be continued for the rest of your life in order for you to have the energy to serve the world with your God-given talents."

—KENNETH H. COOPER, MD, author of the classic work *The New Aerobics*, *Faith-based Fitness*, and many other books

"John knows that energy is a big part of the fuel for personal restoration. This is a powerful guide to filling your tank."

—DR. KEITH ABLOW, author, TV personality, and human behavior expert

"It doesn't do any good to become rich and successful if you aren't healthy enough to enjoy it. In fact, it would be DUMB! Don't be dumb; read this book and do what John tells you to do—you owe it to yourself!"

—LARRY WINGET, television personality and five-time *New York Times/Wall Street Journal* bestselling author, including *Shut Up, Stop Whining & Get a Life*

"This book shows how, when you nourish your body, mind, and soul, you are better equipped to travel the road from success to significance. A healthy lifestyle combined with a focused mindset allows you to serve the world with your talents, abilities, and skills."

—DR. NIDO QUBEIN, President, High Point University

"John inherently understands that the link between health, fitness, and powerful success goes beyond balancing the physical, mental, and spiritual. How fortunate for all of us that he also knows how to teach it! Read John's *The Power of Positive Fitness* and go beyond inspiration . . . to transformation."

—KRISTI FRANK, diet & fitness expert from NBC's 'The Apprentice' & featured on 'Oprah,' 'The Today Show,' 'MSNBC' & 'The View'

"In order to live a healthy, energetic life full of vitality and well being, fitness has to be a major part of your lifelong commitment. The big shift mentally for people that I come into contact with is changing from *having* to work out to *wanting* to work out. When that change occurs, people make it part of their lives and this is where John really delivers in this book. He shows you how to transform your life by transforming your lifestyle."

—MITCH GAYLORD, 1984 Olympic Gold Medalist, motivation speaker & fitness celebrity

"In his refreshing, matter-of-fact tone, John cuts through the clutter and helps us connect the dots between physical, mental, and spiritual health. He delivers a comprehensive roadmap to enhance the journey of our lives."

—KAREN JAMES, author, inspirational speaker, widow of Mt. Hood climber Kelly James

"Freedom and liberty when handled with integrity is a tremendous blessing to you, your family, and your nation. It all begins with personal responsibility and living your life in such a way that you maximize your God-given talents, abilities, and skills. In this book, John gives you the tools that will get and keep you physically, mentally, and spiritually fit so you can live out your purpose in life!"

—CONGRESSMAN BOB McEWEN, six-term member of the U.S. House of Representatives from Ohio

"As a husband, father, former professional athlete and CEO of a growing company, it would be impossible to achieve any level of success without having the proper balance in life. In *The Power of Positive Fitness*, John Rowley has laid out a complete physical, mental, and spiritual plan that will help you in being all you were created to be."

—LEE LABRADA, IFBB Pro Bodybuilding Hall of Fame, CEO Labrada Nutrition

"Energy, passion and purpose are tools that are universal to success in every area of your life. They are the tools I used to build my NFL career as well as my business. I am pleased that John is giving you the tools that will have you operating at peak performance and being on top of your game in every area of your life. "

—KEN HUFF, Baltimore Colts, 1975–1982, Washington Redskins, 1982–1985; owner, Ken Huff Builders, Chapel Hill, NC

"In this book John gives you the tools to be prepared so you can conquer your circumstance. John's brilliance prepares you physically, mentally and spiritually to conquer your world and have the energy left over to enjoy the fruits of your labors. Stop messing about, making excuses: lock yourself in a room, put a DO NOT DISTURB on the door, and drink in the brilliance that John Rowley shares with you page after glorious page!"

—DŌV BARON, The Elite Mind Strategist and creator of The CORE Affluence System for Leadership

"One key to success in every area of your life is to find your passion and purpose. And to follow a set of principles that keeps you centered. Like John, I believe we experience the best in life when we are physically, mentally, and spiritually fit. John gives you a fitness plan that will affect every area of your life in a positive way."

—DOYLE YAGER, Crown Ambassador, Amway

"I love the great books about health and fitness. I also love the great books about personal development and success. The only thing even greater is one book that teaches you both. John's *Power of Positive Fitness* does exactly that. It gives you the keys to being well-rounded and achieving that rare life balance everyone is after: a sound mind and spirit in a sound body."

—Tom Venuto, natural bodybuilder & author of *The Body Fat Solution*

"John has mentored me from cover to cover on how to achieve optimal results with all spiritual, mental, and physical areas of my life! Most definitely a must-have book on life's essentials."

—Aaron Yager, social entrepreneur and 4th generation Amway business owner with the Yager family

"Much lip service has been given to living a well-rounded life, but this book actually achieves it. A must read for anyone striving for success. Get it, read it, do it!"

—Rick Frishman, bestselling author; founder & publisher of Morgan James Publishing

"Sculpting a lean, muscular physique requires setting goals and being disciplined in the achievement of those goals. You can use these same tools to sculpt a successful life. John lays out a life plan that will keep you physically, mentally, and emotionally fit. This is a must read!"

—John Basedow, fitness celebrity, YouTube.com/JohnBasedow

"John is revealing the secret that has been hidden to many. Physical fitness is not only essential to good health but is the springboard to a rewarding and fulfilling life."

—William Dabish, co-founder, Powerhouse Gyms International

"John get's it. John teaches it. Will you use it? That's the question. John straight talks what it takes to live life to your fullest potential. Make a positive change in your life...turn the page, read, and put into action today."

—Ewell Smith, Executive Director, Louisiana Seafood Promotion and Marketing Board; producer, Great American Seafood Cook-off

THE **POWER** OF **POSITIVE** **FITNESS**

THE **POWER** OF
POSITIVE
FITNESS

MAXIMIZING PHYSICAL,
MENTAL & SPIRITUAL
HEALTH

JOHN M. ROWLEY

LEAFWOOD
PUBLISHERS

THE POWER OF POSITIVE FITNESS

MAXIMIZING PHYSICAL, MENTAL & SPIRITUAL HEALTH

Copyright 2011 by John M. Rowley

ISBN 978-0-89112-292-0
LCCN 2011027712

Printed in the United States of America

Scripture quotations, unless otherwise noted, are from The Holy Bible, New International Version. Copyright 1984, International Bible Society. Used by permission of Zondervan Publishers.

LIBRARY OF CONGRESS CATALOGING-IN-PUBLICATION DATA
Rowley, John M.
 The power of positive fitness : maximizing physical, mental & spiritual health / John M. Rowley.
    p. cm.
 Includes bibliographical references.
 ISBN 978-0-89112-292-0
 1. Physical fitness. 2. Mental health. 3. Spiritual life. 4. Well-being. I. Title.
 GV481.R684 2011
 613.7--dc23

                                                                            2011027712

Cover design by Thinkpen Design, Inc.
Interior text design by Sandra Armstrong

Published in association with Rosenbaum & Associates
Literary Agency, Brentwood, Tennessee.

Leafwood Publishers
1626 Campus Court
Abilene, Texas 79601
1-877-816-4455 toll free

For current information about all Leafwood titles, visit our website:
www.leafwoodpublishers.com

11 12 13 14 15 16 / 7 6 5 4 3 2 1

Dedication

To my beautiful wife, Cathy, who has walked with me through the fire that has led to our life's work. Thank you for always being there for me and believing in me, even when I didn't believe in myself. I love you so much!

To my children, Jim, John, Jessica, and Jacqueline. God has redeemed my life through you! You are all the good that God intended in my life, but I fell short. I rejoice and delight as I watch with great but humble pride as you conquer and contribute to this world. To my daughter-in-law Jocelyn, I love having you as our third daughter. You have brought a dimension to our family that we never knew was missing. To Jennifer and Jacob, how my world has changed since you became my grandchildren. I love being your Papop! I love you all in a way that no words can express!

To my parents, Jim and AnnMarie Rowley, who taught me values and a strong work ethic, and who suffered through my tragedies in a way I could never understand until I was a parent. What you taught me as a child saved my life as an adult! I love you both

To my in-laws, Jim and Judy Rafferty, who raised the most incredible person I have ever known. You instilled love, integrity, perseverance, and joy into Cathy that has in turn changed my life for the good and forever. I love you both

To God for blessing me with all of the above, especially Cathy, and for giving me a second chance to serve you and to become the man you intended me to be! Please let me finish the work you gave me and one day stand before you and hear "well done good and faithful servant."

To all who are embarking on the *The Power of Positive Fitness*, thank you for allowing me to serve you with the passion that God has burning in my heart.

Contents

Appendices

Foreword

The way you become a great football team is by bringing your best to practice every day. Then on game day it is second nature to perform at your best and expect to win. Winning is a habit and so is losing. Living an un-compromised life is a habit, and so is accepting compromise in your life. Allowing the day's challenges to overwhelm you is a habit, but so is looking those challenges straight in the eye and getting down on your knees to thank God for these wonderful opportunities. Your daily life is the culmination of your daily habits and this book helps you develop habits that will empower your life.

Every day people are counting on you to contribute to their lives. The talents, abilities, and skills you have are God's gift to you, but what you do with them is God's gift to the world. Every day, if you aren't jumping out of bed excited to face the day, then you don't have goals that are in alignment with the purpose God has for your life.

In this book, John shows you how to get into top physical, mental, and spiritual shape; but more importantly he challenges you to seek out God's purpose for your life. Once you know your purpose, he brings you through the "Lifestyle Restoration Cycle." This cycle has you identify your purpose in every area of life and then helps you put a plan of action together that guides your habits, which in turn transforms your life one habit at a time.

Yes, this book will help you win; but more importantly it will bring you from success to significance. Significance is when you help other people to be successful—in order to do that you must be at your personal best physically, mentally, and spiritually. In this book, you will not only be given a plan of action but many examples of how to implement the principles into your life. John has sought out over thirty busy people from all walks of life to share with you how they structure their lives in order to assist you in designing your own Power of Positive Fitness Lifestyle.

This book gives you a powerful play book for your life. Read it, enjoy the funny and inspiring stories, and soak in the simple-to-implement principles—but most importantly use it! Act on these principles and bring God's gift to the world.

Coach Lou Holtz

Acknowledgements

This book, like everything else in my life, is the result of the help of many people. I extend my deepest and most heartfelt thanks to:

Rachel Owen for encouraging me day in and day out for months to write this book, even when I didn't want to hear it! Then at crunch time you blessed me and Cathy when you became part of our editorial team. Without you this book would still be a dream.

Doyle and Holly Yager, you have been a true blessing to us. You have sown into our lives in every way possible and have given us an incredible example of the way Christ wants us to selflessly love and bless others.

My agent Bucky Rosenbaum for catching the vision the Lord gave me and making it a reality.

Gary Myers and Leonard Allen at Leafwood Publishers for embracing our vision, opening our eyes to new possibilities, and then running with it.

Pastor Chad and Darla Harvey, thank you for the integrity you exemplify through your lives. You are treasured friends.

Brian McLaughlin, my friend who has been through every tragedy in my life as well as the victories and continues to walk the path God puts before us. Thanks for always being there!

Mitch Mayer, my friend who walked through this book with me one hundred times before the words were ever written and encouraged me every step of the way. *"This is how it happens"* was the mantra you spoke to me during the development of this book and over the past twenty plus years of friendship.

Bill Roettger who made me laugh when all I wanted to do was cry, and who knew just the right time to call with an encouraging word. I have known Bill since we were in diapers and he will be a trusted friend until we are in them again at a ripe old age.

Pastor Danny Collins, Pastor Chris Connell, Mike Cason, Rob Marrin and everyone at Raleigh First Assembly of God.

Chris Mangum for being a faithful friend and prayer partner. I am not sure you would have signed on if you knew where we were going, but you never let go!

A close and trusted friend who has been praying with and sowing into Cathy's and my life for many years. You know who you are even though you choose to remain nameless.

To Laurie Magers for praying for me and encouraging me when I needed it most.

To all the warriors out there who are unwilling to settle for anything less than God's best. You are willing to lay it all on the line because God breathed the inspiration of a dream into your spirit and you are unwilling to bend your knee to anything or anyone but God. You are my inspiration and this is your story!

Introduction

The original title for this book was The Peak Performance Lifestyle, then it evolved to The Great American Challenge. Both titles well describe the journey we are going to take together. This book is indeed a guide to live an empowered lifestyle which is a tremendous challenge that I feel America desperately needs to embark on. NOW!

The Power of Positive Fitness is much more descriptive of this book's message. My desire is to see you completely whole and living the life you were designed to live. This book is about living a holistic lifestyle, encouraging physical, mental, and spiritual fitness in the correct balance. It is no mistake that I used the words "positive fitness" in the title. Anything taken to an obsessive extreme is unhealthy and therefore will have a negative impact on your life. Yes, even too much of a good thing can be unhealthy if it throws your life out of balance.

I look forward to embarking on this wonderful journey together. I have a passionate desire to see you restore your life to the original splendor that God intended for you. *The Power of Positive Fitness* will help you overcome the fear and self-defeating habits that may stand between you and your dreams. At any moment you can decide to change and alter the course of your life forever by simply altering your lifestyle. We call this *lifestyle restoration.* Your lifestyle is the way you live minute to minute; it is made up of the habits and behaviors that guide the direction of your life. *The Power of Positive Fitness* will help you to be physically, mentally, and spiritually healthy and fit and in turn to restore your life.

Before We Start, Tell Me Just One Thing—
Who's Better Than You?

Even though I currently live in the south, it is very difficult to miss my New York accent. I was raised in an ethnic area which was mainly Italian and Irish. Growing up it was like *The Little Rascals* meets *The Sopranos*, if ya know what I'm talkin' bout. Everyone—and I mean *everyone*—was a peak performance expert. We didn't have seminars, CD's, or even great books like this. What we *did* have, however, was the *front stoop* and the *curb*.

I remember one day walking down the street as a kid. I was a little down. You know the look: mopey, head hanging low, really dragging down the block. Then I heard a shout from Mr. Roettger who was sitting on the stoop.

"Who's better than you, Johnny boy?"

"Well, you know Mr. Roettger, Joey just beat me up and . . . ."

"NO, NO, NO!" shouts Mr. Roettger. "That doesn't matter. Come over here kid and sit on the stoop with me. Now tell me, Johnny boy, who's better than you? And say it like you mean it kid!"

"No one is better than me, Mr. Roettger," I stated in a less than enthusiastic voice that he chose to ignore.

"That's right and don't you ever forget it, kid! Always remember. You're from 10th Avenue. I don't care if you are getting beat up by Joey or in the business world when you get older . . . you never let it beat you! You get up, brush yourself off, and keep on going. That's how we do it!"

Then a few days later, I'm walking down the street again, head hanging low like I just lost my best friend, and there he is again. "Who's better than you, Johnny boy?"

"Well you know Mr. Roettger, we just lost the game and . . . ."

Mr. Roettger just laughs, walks out to the street with me and says, "Pull up a curb, Johnny boy." So we both sit on the curb and he looks me dead in the eyes and says, "Who's better than you, kid? And say it like you mean it."

Then I said with enough passion that I almost believed it, "No one is better than me, Mr. Roettger."

"That's right, kid. You're from 10th Avenue. You may lose now and again, but you come back stronger and harder the next time. You may get knocked down, but you never stay down. That is how winning is done and 10th Avenue only grows winners! Got it, kid?"

This went on my whole childhood and it wasn't just for me; it was for all the kids on 10th Avenue. We thought 10th Avenue was the best place on earth. My point is, no one is better than you. God planted the seed of greatness in you and this book will help nurture that seed so that it grows into the life you deserve! The very life God intended for you!

Now, go look in the mirror—yes, you—and say, "Who's better than you?" Now go find your spouse, co-worker, or friend and say, "Who's better than you?"

Have that person answer with passion and then have him ask you the same question. "Who's better than you?" And keep doing it until you both believe that no one is better than you. Now . . . I want to ask you a question. Yeah! I'm tawkin' to you! Dat's right YOU! *Now who's better than you?* And tell me like you mean it!

You are exactly right. No one is better than you. God planted the seed of greatness in you and no one else was given what he gave you! You are a priceless gift to this world, one of a kind. This book will encourage you, give you tools, and challenge you to be all you were created to be.

Over the coming months you are going to "work out" your body, mind, and spirit. Every week you will make small changes that will incrementally bring you closer to your goal. This is your book so write in it, highlight it, mark it up, and most importantly, use it. If you are anything like me, you are anxious to improve, so you rush through a book and excitedly try some things, but never take the time it takes to change. You can certainly scan through the book to see where you are going, but I heartily encourage you to read each day and implement the little nuggets as we move along. Before you know it, those little nuggets will turn into a strong, solid foundation that will support your life.

My Story and Why You Need This Book

When I opened my eyes flames were licking my face. I tried to take a breath and couldn't. I was crushed behind a curtain of metal. I was all alone. You will never know what your reaction to certain death is until you are in the midst of it. Mine was to fight. I didn't think or reason, I just entered the fight of my life, for my life.

It was the summer between my freshman and sophomore years of college and was a turning point in my life. I was a collegiate athlete who up to that point had put all my effort into training. I realized I couldn't run forever, so that summer I was determined to dig in at school and prepare myself for the future. I was working long, hard hours for my dad as a janitor in a New York City school and really enjoying it. My dad always made a point of hiring my buddies, so we worked and played hard. In the evenings, I got together with my friends from high school and in between worked out on the track and in my garage with a full weight room. Life was good!

One night I was getting ready to go out with some friends and my dad told me to stay home. "You're burning the candle at both ends," he said. I decided to go out to the movies with my friends anyway and told dad that I would come right home. Which I did. I was so tired that I slept through the movie. When I got out to my car I threw my cowboy boots that I acquired at college in Kansas into the back seat and headed straight home just as I promised.

Driving down Stewart Avenue in Garden City, I realized just how tired I was. As I neared Nassau Boulevard I saw a million stop lights careening across the intersection. I knew it was only one light and that I was so tired everything was becoming a blur. At that very moment I decided to pull over and take a nap.

Then the explosion! I was heading straight toward a house. Without thinking I cut the wheel, saw two trees immediately in front of me, thought I could steer between them, then it went pitch black. Everything ended. It was over. A bad dream. I didn't see that cool white light people talk about; all I saw was black.

Then it all came flooding back as the flames licked my face. Somehow I fought my way out of the car. My left foot was pinned between the tire and metal and my right arm was twisted around the steering wheel, the dashboard, and the engine and I couldn't breathe. I was crushed. I just kept kicking, pulling, and pushing at raw metal and glass until I fell into the street and was able to fill my crushed lungs with air.

My initial reaction was to run away. Just run home and get into my safe bed. I took a step and realized that nothing moved. I looked down. My left foot didn't look like a foot. It had a hole through it, it was the size of a football, looked like chopped meat and was full of blood. My attention was taken off my foot when I saw a fountain shooting into the street. The "fountain" was blood shooting out of my face with the rhythm of my heart. I grabbed my face to stop the blood but I couldn't because it was from my nose. It was gone and the only thing left was a hole in my face. I also realized that my right arm wouldn't move so I looked down and my hand was back by my elbow. Breathing was impossible because every rib was broken and my breast bone was split in half and separated by a few inches.

Soon, a car light broke the trance I was in and a woman stopped to see if she could help me. Before she could speak she vomited on herself. Then everything went black again. I remember waking up on a stoop, surrounded by horrified onlookers. They gave me a huge blanket to cover my face but it was instantly soaked in blood. I took a shallow breath and said, "I can only say this once. Call my mom and dad and tell them to come here. Please tell them I am alive."

My dad turned the corner, got very weak kneed, and softly said, "I thought you were dead . . . when we saw the car. . . . I left mom in the car." All I asked my dad was, "Did I hurt anyone?" "No." "Did I kill anyone?" "No." Okay, I thought, I can deal with this now. At the hospital they didn't think I would make it initially. I overheard a few say, "Why bother, he won't make it." But the warrior nurses and doctors didn't listen and kept diligently working through the night and into the morning. These memories took a few years to return to me and I am still not 100% sure of accuracy, but this is how I remember it. They later told me that I probably fell asleep back by the light, with my eyes open and was aware enough to steer for a while. After that, everything went blank for a while.

This is where the real fight began. I had to rebuild my body and my life. My dreams were crushed along with my body; but I was alive and decided not to look back. Through this very long, extremely painful, and lonely process I realized the value of a healthy, strong body. A focused, unwavering mindset. A faith that can move mountains.

Often I'm asked in interviews if faith played a role in my recovery. The answer is a resounding NO, if you are talking about a faith outside of my own abilities and willingness to survive. But a faith in God? Absolutely not.

Thirty years after my accident, my father and I briefly spoke about it—a conversation we had avoided for three decades. Overlooking his beautiful pool in Florida, I took this unique opportunity to thank him for holding my hand while I was in the emergency room. "That is what got me through," I said. My dad then told me he wasn't allowed into the emergency room, that it wasn't him. For thirty years I believed that my father was holding my hand giving me the strength to live. In an instant I realized that it was my Father in heaven who gave me comfort and the strength to live.

Throughout this book I will share with you what I have learned over the thirty plus years since that pivotal day. The tools to crawl out of a fiery crash and rebuild a body, life, and career from the ground up may be just what you need. I didn't know what to do so I sought out the people who did. I became an unrelenting success detective, uncovering the clues to success. Yes, success does leave clues—you just have to mine for them like buried treasure; when you find them they enrich your life.

Over the years I have become friends with some of the brightest minds in real estate, business, fitness, nutrition, bodybuilding, the media, medicine, and entertainment. What follows is the knowledge that I gleaned from many who were willing to share their lives with me, and that I now share with you. But don't worry, the rest of the book will be upbeat and fun! The only reason I told you about my accident is because tragedy has a way of defining who we are.

I'm Not Just the Author . . . I'm Your Guinea Pig! I'm nothing special. I am just a regular guy, from a regular New York neighborhood who wanted to achieve the extraordinary and would settle for nothing less. I believe you are holding this book for a reason, so dig in and enjoy. God has planted the seed of greatness in you and together we will turn that seed into the life that you deserve!

Life's a Balancing Act

As we begin I want to let you know what this book isn't and what it is! The purpose of this book isn't to prepare you to be the cover model of a fitness magazine, although it could. It isn't to make sure you look fabulous on the beach, although it can. It certainly isn't designed to put your primary focus on you and how you look! No, the purpose of this book is to ensure that you are vibrant, fit, and healthy enough to fulfill your purpose in life. To help you to be the best you, you can be. To restore your life to the original splendor that God intended it to be!

This book takes a holistic look at your life. We are not only going to focus on physical fitness. We are going to look at you as a whole person and make sure you are physically, mentally and spiritually fit. In my opinion, that is why most diets, exercise programs and self-help books fail to deliver on the intended result. They are only focusing on one aspect of the person. Working on only one aspect of your life is like putting cheap gas in your car, never doing any maintenance, and expecting it to never break down or lose its value. That is ridiculous for a car and even more ridiculous for a human being.

❧ ❖ ☙

A Little Background

A couple of years ago my wife Cathy and I went to Columbus, Ohio with friends Jim and Kay Hansen to attend the Arnold Sports Festival after roughly ten years away from the bodybuilding scene. While at Arnold Schwarzenegger's incredible event, a couple of things struck me. The first was the number of spectators who were out of shape, even though they obviously loved the sport of bodybuilding and being around it. The second was how narrow the world was for many of these people. I saw people with great bodies but not much else. Now keep in mind I am not talking about everyone. But there were enough people like this to make it jump out at me.

As I walked through the Arnold, I would see person after person I had known for years who didn't recognize me until they heard my voice or I told them my name. "Okay, I haven't seen you for ten years and I *did* shave my head since you saw me last," is what I kept thinking until I heard someone yell, "JOHNNY!!!!" from half-way across the convention center. It was my old friend, Jimmy Pellechia, whom I also hadn't seen in ten years. He ran up to me, picked me up, and gave me a great big bear hug. After we chatted for a while, I asked him how he recognized me when no one else had. He told me in his deep, charming New York accent, "How da heck can any of doze guys see ya when dey are so busy lookin' in da mirra!" We both got a great laugh out of this. Jimmy is the best! Whenever we see each other, it's like the old days.

Not long after seeing Jimmy, I ran into some other friends, who are among the great bodybuilders. They were champions who admitted to having a hard time with relationships, finances, or both. Then I ran into my childhood hero and lifetime friend, Lou Ferrigno. He is one of the best bodybuilders of all time. He and his wife Carla have a great relationship with an incredible family life, plus they are very successful in several business arenas. He is an actor, trainer to the stars, an author, and motivational speaker, to name a few. Louie and Carla could find balance. My friend Larry Scott, the first Mr. Olympia, could find it, as could my good friends Lee Haney, Lee Labrada, Tom Platz, and Samir Bannout. They are living life to its fullest. But many, it seemed, couldn't. Now this really got me thinking and looking for answers. Especially since this came on the heels of two eye-opening trips.

A few years before I attended the Arnold Classic, I traveled to China and Kazakhstan on mission trips to serve the people in these areas. The days were long and the work was hard. It was physically, mentally, and emotionally draining. Everything started off status quo on both trips for the first few days, but then it happened. Tempers flared. People who others were looking up to as spiritual elders or mentors "lost it" once they got tired. This really threw me for a loop at first. But then I realized that God created us as body, mind, and spirit. Our mind and spirit are housed in our body. When your body gets weak, your mind and spirit will surely follow.

Pat Teague, the associate pastor at our church at the time, was an example of true fitness on one of my trips. Pat's visible example of being of sound body, as well of sound mind and spirit, was the whole reason I decided to become involved in that church. On this trip, Pat worked harder than most and he acted the same, day in and day out regardless of how hard we worked or how tired we got.

Pat grew up as an athlete. He played football for North Carolina State University and then for the NFL with the Tampa Bay Buccaneers. He was physically, mentally, and spiritually fit. In fact, Pat was one of my early mentors and is one of the few people I know who really lives The Power of Positive Fitness. His well-balanced life reflects it. Pat is successful in every area of his life. He is living the life God intended for him. When he goes to the gym, he calls it "temple maintenance." And as big and strong as he is, no one would dare argue with him.

Full Circle

My experience on those two mission trips, and then later at the Arnold Classic, got me thinking about what a balanced life looks like. It really got me pondering. I was particularly thinking about the three types of people just mentioned: the ones who love being around bodybuilding and fitness but are out of shape, the ones who are in fantastic physical shape but not well-rounded as a person, and the ones who are in great spiritual shape but are letting weak bodies drag them down.

Then it dawned on me. It is all about lifestyle. People just need help in realizing that being fit in all areas of their life requires a few lifestyle changes. I think that each of these three types of people are afraid that the process of seeking balance will consume their lives and cause neglect in areas where they have excelled.

So they never start. *The Power of Positive Fitness* will help you to live a balanced and rewarding life, empowering all the areas of your life. It will not take time from you. Rather, it puts time back into your day by giving you the energy to utilize it properly. Most people don't have a problem with having enough time; the challenge is having enough energy to utilize the time they have more effectively.

The Power of Positive Fitness is divided into four sections. Section one covers physical fitness; section two, mental fitness; section three, spiritual fitness; but section four is where the power is! Section four shows you how to effectively implement what you learned in the first three sections into your lifestyle. It sounds simple. It *is* simple. The power is in the simplicity.

Scrabble

I recently consulted with someone about my business. He compared my business to a game of Scrabble. In playing Scrabble you take all the letters, put them in a cup, and then scatter them all over the board. You then organize the letters in such a way that you can make words. He told me, "You have all the letters, they are just scattered all over the board. We have to organize the various pieces so that your business operates as a healthy, profitable endeavor that is lifestyle friendly."

Many people treat their lives like a game of Scrabble. They put their God, family, business, mental and physical health, relationships, and personal responsibilities into a cup, shake it up, and then scatter it all over the board of life. The self-help, diet, exercise, and spiritual communities have added to this disconnectedness by only focusing on one aspect of the person and addressing their piece of the puzzle as if it were the most important piece. It can get confusing very quickly and have you living completely out of balance, which is very frustrating. As in Scrabble, you need to look at all the pieces of your life and put them together in such a way that you live a healthy, rewarding life. The *Power of Positive Fitness* is all about physical, mental, and spiritual fitness and "The Lifestyle Restoration Cycle" will help you transform your life by making small adjustments to your lifestyle.

The Lifestyle Restoration Cycle

Throughout this book, I am drawing on more than thirty years of pursuing physical, mental, and spiritual fitness with a passion. I am going to leave out the filler and just give you the things you can implement, so you can live *The Power of Positive Fitness* in an easy but powerful way. At the end of each section we will work through a portion of the "Lifestyle Restoration Cycle."

I have discovered that success in every area of your life becomes effortless once it becomes part of your lifestyle. At one point in time, tying your shoes was an effort. Later in life, getting to work without directions would have been impossible. At work you had a learning curve while you were introduced to your new duties. Once you learn these things and do them on a consistent basis, you do them without much effort. When was the last time you had to concentrate while tying your shoes? Have you ever driven home from work and you were supposed to stop by the grocery store but forgot until you were in your driveway and had to face your spouse? Of course, we all do that. We are on auto pilot. How about your responsibilities at work? You can do a lot of them without thinking now, can't you? Welcome to "The Lifestyle Restoration Cycle."

4 Simple Steps of the Lifestyle Restoration Cycle

1. Find your "why," which is your purpose in life.
2. Put a plan together.
3. Identify disempowering habits.
4. Replace disempowering habits with empowering habits on a regular basis to close the loop on The Lifestyle Restoration Cycle.

Habits Are the Foundry of Success!

To simplify and help automate the process, we have a cutting edge, online tool called Habit Foundry that can be found at http://habitfoundry.com.

A foundry is a factory that produces metal castings. Metals are cast into shapes by melting them into a liquid, pouring the metal in a mold, and removing the mold material or casting after the metal has solidified as it cools.

Habits are the foundries that "cast" our life!

Empowering Habits lift our lives to incredible heights.

Dis-empowering Habits destroy our lives.

Many have said it takes 21 days to form a habit. I think that works for smaller habits but to make permanent lifestyle changes that really transform your life, it can take a bit longer. 21 days, 30 days, or 60 days—no one really knows how long it takes because that is individual. What I do know is that it takes consistency and that is what HabitFoundry helps you with. I chose 30 days simply because it gives a full month and then if you are solid in the foundation of this new habit you can start a new one. It simply fits on the calendar better. This is an online tool that will change your life forever!

PART I

SUPERCHARGE YOUR BODY

Chapter 1

TAKING THE CONFUSION OUT OF EATING

You Have to Eat!

Don't you like the way we are starting off? You don't have to starve yourself. Eating too little will damage your metabolism! I am going to help you make some simple changes in how you eat so you can stimulate your metabolism. You will begin to lose unwanted fat, tone and tighten up, gain sleek muscle, be more vibrant, and become healthier.

Do you realize that by this time next year you will be all new? No, you can't trade yourself in for a new model and I'm not talking plastic surgery, but you can create a better you. All of the cells that make up your body will be gone and new ones will take their place. Your organs, skin, and muscles will all be new, regenerated cells. Do you think your re-generated cells will be healthier if you spent your time sitting on the couch eating food your body can't use effectively, or by investing in yourself by exercising and feeding yourself properly? Sounds silly when it's put that way, doesn't it? The fantastic thing is you have the opportunity to re-create yourself starting today. We will start off by eating and exercising properly.

Eating Shouldn't Be Confusing

Let's get this straight right from the beginning. You have to eat in order to be healthy, lean, fit, and energetic. The simple act of eating has turned into a firestorm of controversy. God gave us food to enjoy and nourish us, not to have misleading marketers confuse us for selfish gain. As we start, I want to state just a few of the questions I hear all the time and that you may have, too.

Which diet should I be on?

High carb and low protein?

Protein only and no carbs?

What *is* a carb—and what is protein?

Should I count every calorie that goes in my mouth or only eat prepackaged food from the diet plan I am on?

How about fat? Can I ever eat fat or do I eat only good fat?

What the heck is a good fat?

Not long ago they said all fat is bad. Is fat really bad?

Do I fast and drink only that new fasting weight-loss drink or should I eat every two or three hours?

Do I eat only grapefruit or live on those new miracle diet pills?

That celebrity is doing this diet and he/she looks incredible. Oh, wait—now he/she is fat again!

Should I do what they are doing in Hollywood? Manhattan? South Beach? Miami? Russia? China? Japan? France or the Mediterranean?

This celebrity is doing great on the chocolate diet. That sounds delicious.

Or how about that newly discovered berry everyone is talking about?

How about that book that has all those incredible "before" and "after" pictures? They seem too good to be true.

This doctor wrote that book and everyone is following it; but the doctor really doesn't look like he is in that great of shape. Shouldn't he be in great shape if he is doing what he is teaching others to do?

Should I watch my total carbs or just my net carbs? What exactly is a net carb?

And my all time favorite (drum roll here) . . . Is sugar a carb?

If you are feeling as if you just read something out of an insane asylum, you wouldn't be too far off. Welcome to the diet industry. This is just a very brief overview and IT IS INSANE! The diet industry has confused people so much that people aren't even sure what a carb is anymore. They do this for a reason. Money! The diet industry alone is a *$100 Billion a year business*. This is very simple: it pays to confuse you.

Are All These Diets Really Working?

"The second day of a diet is always easier than the first. By the second day you're off it." —Jackie Gleason

The proof that all these diets aren't working is all around us. Too many people are being gripped by epidemic levels of physical disaster: skyrocketing rates of preventable illness—obesity, diabetes, heart disease, depression, and cancer. It is not only costing the individual but the country as well! The cost of medical care for obesity in the United States in 2008 was $147 billion and rising![1] Fad diets wreak havoc on your metabolism. The typical order of weight loss from these fad diets is water weight, then fat, and finally, muscle mass. When you lose muscle mass you damage your metabolism. The more muscle you have the more calories you burn, even at rest. When dieters lose muscle weight, they have also lost the ability to burn as many calories because they have less muscle. To make matters worse, most dieters eventually return to their old pattern of eating and tend to gain back all the fat weight they lost. Most will find that they have gained even more fat weight. This has happened because they have less muscle available to burn calories. So they then go on another incomplete diet program, lose more muscle, creating an even higher body fat ratio, and the cycle continues. That is, until the person finally gives up, often being much fatter than when they started. Isn't this insane?! *The Power of Positive Fitness* will put you back in control of your body and your life once and for all.

Eat the Weight Off!

Did you know that eating stimulates your metabolism? If you are overweight, eat the weight off, don't starve it off. When you don't eat often enough, your body goes into starvation mode. This is a protection mechanism that allows your body to store calories as fat, so they can be used later in the event that you don't eat again for a long time. Is it any wonder why most people who diet get fatter, flabbier, and more discontent with dieting?

I find it really interesting that when I speak to one of my friends in the fitness industry who wants to get leaner for a photo shoot or something else, they inevitably say, "Man, I need to start eating more! I really need to lean out." To average people this makes no sense because if they want to lose weight, they stop eating. To the seasoned athlete this way of thinking is second nature—you eat the weight off.

What to Eat

The key to eating properly is to know what you can eat and what you can't eat. You need protein, carbohydrates, fats, and water. Let's take a look at each of these

Protein

Protein is your friend! Protein feeds your muscles so that they can become strong and shapely. Most people simply don't get enough protein. In fact, increasing protein is even more important than cutting carbs. One day I was counseling with someone about her training routine and nutrition. I told her the first thing she needed to do was increase her protein. She was severely malnourished—though she was at least 150 lbs overweight. When I told her she needed more protein, she looked me straight in the eye and said, "No John. I get plenty of protein. I have a sausage with my biscuit every morning." No lie. I stood up and went into the other room looking for Ashton Kutcher. I thought for sure I was being punked for his TV show! Sadly, I was not being punked and this woman was digging her own grave and using her fork to do it. I come across this constantly all over the world. People do not eat enough protein and it is killing their metabolism. This lack of dietary knowledge does not just afflict the average Joe. I have doctors consult with me regarding proper nutrition all the time because many of them don't know how to eat properly.

If you are looking to stay or get lean, energetic, strong, and healthful, protein should be on your shopping list. Protein allows your body to heal itself. Protein is also what makes your muscles grow. And muscle is what keeps you lean. You need lots of protein to build and maintain muscle. I will show you just how much protein you need and an easy way to keep track of it on the next page.

One more thing! I recommend that you eat primarily low-fat protein choices like fish and poultry. Plenty of research says that you can eat higher fat foods and have no ill effect. But there are also studies backing up anything you want to back up! Also keep in mind that high-fat salmon contains a different type of fat than eating bacon, so use your head as you fill your grocery cart. My grandmother and grandfather ate basically the same way and had very similar lifestyles, yet my grandfather passed away at the age of 65 and my grandmother lived to be 104 years old. Obviously they each had genetic dispositions that made them respond differently to the same lifestyle choices. My recommendation is to stay with healthier types of fats most of the time such as fish, lean cuts of beef, chicken, and turkey breast.

How Much Protein?

Now I want to show you how much you should eat. The rule of thumb is at least one gram of protein per pound of body weight per day. For example, a 100 lb. person would take at least 100 grams of protein. This is a unisex rule. It doesn't matter if you are a man or a woman. It is still one gram of protein per pound of body weight. Use your current weight, not your goal weight! It's that simple.

Okay, I can hear you now. "*I don't know how, nor do I want to go around measuring my protein every time I eat.*" Don't worry; you don't have to be meticulously exact. It is very easy. In fact, I will show you an old bodybuilding trick and give you a chart to make it simple. Twenty grams of protein is a serving. A twenty gram serving of meat is approximately the size of a deck of cards. Usually one scoop of protein powder will be approximately twenty grams of protein, but read the label because some companies use smaller scoops and that means smaller portions. You can get that information from the nutrition label on the protein container.

So let's go back to our examples. A 100 lb. person would need at least five servings of protein during the day (100 pounds = 100 grams of protein, divided by twenty grams of protein = five portions). Now, just divide these servings among the meals you are eating. This 100 lb. person would have one serving of protein with every meal if he/she were eating five meals a day. Below is a simple chart that will help you. You don't need to go crazy counting your protein intake. Just use this as a guide and do the best you can. Making this easy for you will allow you to focus more time on the passions that God has put in your life.

Daily Protein Requirements

Body	Protein		Body	Protein	
Weight	Grams	Portions	Weight	Grams	Portions
100	100	5	260	260	13
110	110	6	270	270	14
120	120	6	280	280	14
130	130	7	290	290	15
140	140	7	300	300	15
150	150	8	310	310	16
160	160	8	320	320	16
170	170	9	330	330	17
180	180	9	340	340	17
190	190	10	350	350	18
200	200	10	360	360	18
210	210	11	370	370	19
220	220	11	380	380	19
230	230	12	390	390	20
240	240	12	400	400	20
250	250	13			

The above portions are based on body-weight. For many years, I told people to throw their scales away because body weight is not an accurate portrayal of your fitness level. Since muscle is heavier than fat, you could be getting in better shape, but be heavier. Now, I tell people to get out the scale to help determine what their protein requirements are.

Fiber

We need to consume at least 25 to 30 grams of fiber a day. The average person is lucky if he gets twelve grams of fiber per day. According to the American Heart Association (AHA), fiber is important for lowering cholesterol and body fat, as well as for the health of our digestive system. Both the AHA and the National Cancer Institute recommend that we consume 25 to 30 grams of fiber a day. This is just the minimum. You would be better off with 50 grams of fiber a day. With today's eating habits and lack of true fiber in our diets this is very difficult, but not impossible. I use psyllium husk in my protein drinks to supplement my fiber intake.

Carbohydrates: The Dr. Jekyll and Mr. Hyde of Foods

Carbohydrates are a bit like Dr. Jekyll and Mr. Hyde. You have to know which one you are getting ready to face or the result may not be pleasant. Like Jekyll and Hyde, carbohydrates have their good side and bad side. Unfortunately today, it is very vogue to despise *all* carbs and make them the fall guy in our quest for health and fitness. Many diets promote a high protein diet with little or no carbs. If God didn't want us eating carbs he wouldn't have created them and this is a good point to make right now. For the most part, if God made it, in other words if you can find it in nature, it is okay to eat. If you can't find it in nature, stay away from it.

You'll find the Dr. Jekyll or good carbs in your fruit, vegetable and whole grain sections of your grocery or health food store. Raw or slightly cooked vegetables will leave you satisfied for hours and it's almost impossible to over eat them. Fresh fruit and starchy carbs will require some caution if your intent is to lose fat. As you will see on the food chart, I classify fruits and healthy starchy carbs as cautious carbs.

Healthy vs Physique Transforming

A lot of confusion enters the picture with regards to carbohydrates. Fruits are good for your overall health but contain fructose, which is a sugar. Fructose, although better for you than table sugar, still burns extremely fast and you will want to stay away from or limit fruit when you are trying to lose fat. I have never known anyone to get fat eating fruit, but if you already have a weight challenge you will want to severely limit fruit until you are at your ideal weight and pay attention to how your body responds.

Healthful starchy carbohydrates such as brown rice, sweet potatoes, and Irish oatmeal also need to be eaten in moderation. Although they are slow burning carbohydrates, they are calorie dense. Serving sizes should be no more than 3/4 of a cup. While you are in the fat reduction phase, you should cut these off no later than 3:00 PM. Your meals after 3:00 PM would consist of lean protein and vegetables. The key to eating properly is to pay attention to how your body responds to various foods, even when you are at your ideal weight, so you don't put the weight back on.

We don't want to mess with Mr. Hyde. We don't need much reminding of what bad carbs are. They are the highly processed ones that are low in fiber and deliver a quick jolt to your blood sugar levels. Once your blood sugar levels plummet, usually an hour or so later, you start craving more and more carbohydrates. It's this never-ending cycle that causes people to overeat.

Let's start with public enemy #1: wheat, and yes, whole wheat counts. There are many reasons for this, but the main one is that most people respond poorly to gluten in one way or another. Getting into the the nooks and crannies of wheat and gluten is beyond the scope of this book, but my recommendation is to stay away from wheat or anything containing gluten.

Bad carbs are easy to pick out in a line up. Bad carbs are usually white: white bread, white rice, white potatoes, any dessert made with white flour, and many of the starchy carbs. I know many people who have simply cut out all starchy carbs (cautious carbs) from their diets and lost a ton of weight and are able to stay lean year round. They eat protein, vegetables, fruit, and no starchy carbs, and have no problem staying lean. I want you to learn how to eat properly, not just go on another diet. In order to be successful you must be aware of how your body responds to certain foods and take responsibility for what goes in your mouth.

These are the basics of eating healthy, but I always want you to be aware of how your body responds to certain foods and take responsibility for what you eat. I personally limit starchy carbohydrates. I may have half a yam or a ½ cup of forbidden black rice after my weight training to replace my glycogen and help with recovery and depending on what my goals are, one-third of a cup of Irish oatmeal in the morning, but not much more then that. I do this for weight control and health reasons. You can't go wrong with lean protein, vegetables, and fruit. Everything else either eat sparingly like a condiment or stay away from completely. I can't emphasize enough paying attention to your response to foods.

Fats

My research on fat started for personal reasons. I had some health issues that were directly related to my genetics and diet. I have a genetic predisposition for high LDL cholesterol and low HDL cholesterol. I was shocked when my doctor wanted to put me on statins to control my cholesterol because I had been following a typical "good" diet of high protein, moderate carbohydrates, and very low fat. I requested thirty days to try to turn my numbers around using nutrition. This led me to contact my friend Jerry Brainum, one of the writers at *Ironman Magazine*. Jerry is immensely knowledgeable about diet and nutritional supplements and is always helpful. Jerry gave me a list of some nutritional supplements to take and told me to greatly increase my good fats by eating more fish, taking a fish oil supplement, and putting olive oil on everything. My intake of good dietary fats had been way too low. By making these simple changes, my blood lipid profile greatly improved in only thirty days. I had fallen prey to the low fat conspiracy!

To emphasize this point, my doctor, Dr. Cara Davis, told me to go on the sticky note diet. Dr. Davis' patients started calling this diet the sticky note diet because Dr. Davis would write all allowed foods on a sticky note. Protein, good fats, low glycemic carbs, and water. Dr. Davis tries to make healthy living very simple to fit into her busy patients' lifestyles. She is one of the few doctors whose focus is on wellness and prevention through a healthy lifestyle.

We need good fats in our diet for many reasons. Fats protect our organs. It protects and repairs the walls of our cells, regulates our body temperature, keeps skin and hair healthy, and leaves us feeling fuller after a meal. Vitamins like A, D, E, and K cannot be absorbed by the body without the right fat in our diet. My diet is moderate in fat, but I get my fats from good sources like fish, olive oil, avocados, almonds, and fish oils. Keep in mind that fat is also a good source of energy for your body.

Most people pay more attention to the kind of oil they put in their cars than what kind of food they put into their own bodies! Understanding the differences among the three types of fat (monounsaturated, polyunsaturated, and saturated) will allow you to make intelligent food choices when eating. Here's the skinny on fats.

Monounsaturated fats are the MVP (Most Valuable Player) in the fat world! Monounsaturated fat can lower harmful LDL cholesterol, as well as total cholesterol, leaving the beneficial HDL cholesterol unchanged. Olive oil, canola oil, avocados, and most nuts are high in monounsaturated fat. Did you know that the people in the Mediterranean regions have a very low occurrence of coronary artery disease despite the fact that they do not eat low fat diets? In fact, olive oil is a staple of their diet. Do like they do back in my old neighborhood or as the Mediterranean's would and make this one of your primary fats.

Polyunsaturated fats may also help lower blood cholesterol levels. Polyunsaturated fats have omega-6, omega-3, EPA, DHA, and CLA. The heavy hitters as far as health goes are the omega-3 fats, EPA, and DHA found in cold water fatty fish. They protect you against everything from heart disease to depression. They inhibit the storage of unwanted body fat and also have anti-inflammatory effects on the body as well. CLA, found in red meat and dairy, is also very beneficial. It can improve body composition by helping your body build muscle and burn fat. It also fights cancer.

The omega-6 fats are the ones you have to watch out for. They are found in candy bars, chips, crackers, and many other process foods. A higher intake of omega-6 can lead to inflammation and promote arthritis, cancer, heart disease, and obesity.

Saturated fats have the reputation of wreaking havoc on your blood cholesterol levels which, in turn, increase your health risks. This is the reason why the American Heart Association gives it a major thumbs down. Saturated fats, however, are critical for testosterone production and research shows that saturated fats may only be bad if you are also eating a high carbohydrate, high calorie diet. I would say as long as you are eating a low carbohydrate diet, you are okay to get your saturated fat from beef and poultry along with the monounsaturated and polyunsaturated fats listed earlier. Be responsible with your health and get regular blood tests to make sure all of your blood lipids are in order.

Transfats raise the bad LDL cholesterol. They may also lower the good HDL cholesterol. Stay away from everything made with vegetable oils that have been hydrogenated or partially hydrogenated. Food manufactures love this cheap fat because it extends shelf life and adds to their bottom line. But, they will shorten *your* shelf life! So stay away from them. One important thing to remember is that even good fats have calories. Use your good fats in moderation and always choose monounsaturated and polyunsaturated fats over saturated fat.

Water

How important is water to our bodies? Your body can survive approximately forty days without food, but only seven days without water. Amazingly, the body can lose up to 50% of its protein, while a loss of even 10% of its water causes severe physical problems. A 20% loss of water may even cause death.

The body uses water to help rid itself of fat, remove toxins, aid in circulation and joint lubrication, and increase energy. Water helps regulate your body temperature. It is important for transferring oxygen throughout your body. It helps in the distribution of vitamins, minerals, and other nutrients throughout your body. Water may be the only true "magic pill" for permanent weight loss, better health, and vibrant energy. You need to drink at least half your body weight in ounces each day. It might sound like a lot, but considering that your brain tissue is made up of 85% water and your body is approximately 65%, it's crucial that you're giving your body what it needs for a vibrant life.

The Million Dollar Question—How to Lose Fat

Losing fat is simple once you know what you're doing. Body fat is stored fuel. Just like gas in your car. When you want the car to move, you push on the accelerator, which pushes gas to the engine for fuel. The bigger the engine the more fuel that is used for energy. A bit simplified, I know, but it makes my point.

Your body is similar. When you exercise your body uses available fuel. The more muscle you have the more fuel it uses. Unlike a car, your gas tank is sequential. First it looks for fuel in your blood stream, which is where it would find glucose or blood sugar. If your tank is "full" with glucose it doesn't have to look any further. A full tank equals no fat loss. The only way to lose fat is by running your tank of glucose low so your body has to go find more fuel in the form of fat.

The key to fat loss is to eliminate "cautious" carbohydrates and eat your veggies which release less glucose into your blood, protein, and a little fat. There is no way to burn fat while you have glucose running around. Your body prefers glucose to body fat. If you want to lose fat you have to lower your carbohydrates. Simply put: Fat control = Carbohydrate control.

This is all pretty simple. Eat your protein, Dr. Jekyll carbs, good fats, and water, and pay attention to how your body responds to the foods you eat. Keep an eye on this and you can eat a lot—and often. All while getting into the best shape of your life and becoming more vibrant! Now that you know what you can and should eat, let's Mangia.

Chapter 2

Mangia—Let's Eat!

"Mangia!" *"Let's eat!"* in Italian (pronounced *monja*). I grew up in an ethnic New York neighborhood that was mostly Italian. Whenever you went to someone's house, it sounded something like this:

"Johnny boy! Howza you Mama anda you Daddy?"

"Oh, dey ah great, danks fa askin'."

"Come on, Johnny boy, sit down and eat sumthin'."

"Oh, I'm not hungry, I just ate."

"Oh, that's a great, how mucha do ya want?"

In my neighborhood, the word "no" just meant you didn't have enough information to make an intelligent decision. And you had to eat! So . . . we ate.

The Power of Positive Fitness encourages you to eat, probably more than you are eating now, so you can be lean, healthy, fit, and vibrant. You are encouraged to eat at least five or six meals a day, dividing your protein, fats, and carbs among those meals. In addition, we are going to include a Victory Day or meal. On Victory Day you can eat whatever you want! Allowing yourself to splurge a little is good for your head and body. Immigrants have been eating this way for centuries. Let's go back to the neighborhood and take a peek at how they ate.

Back to the Neighborhood for a Victory Day

In the neighborhood, Sunday was the big feast day. Relatives came from near and far to sit and eat together. The men told their war stories from the previous week's activities—some were even true—while the ladies made and cooked homemade pasta, gravy (or spaghetti sauce, as the rest of the world calls it), meatballs, and sausage. Oh man, I have to stop! I'm getting hungry! You get the point. They ate all day long together to celebrate the week. This was their Victory Day. The rest of the week they ate a pretty high protein diet with tons of fresh vegetables and good fats from imported olive oil. Even the pasta they ate was from true whole grains and natural imported ingredients.

Key Components to Healthy Eating— Lessons from the Neighborhood

Fish and poultry are the primary protein sources. Eat primarily plant-based foods, such as fruits and vegetables, whole grains, legumes, and nuts. Replace butter, margarine, and other unhealthy fats such as vegetable oil with healthy fats such as olive oil. Use spices and herbs instead of salt to flavor foods. Red meat is limited to no more than a few times a month. Drink plenty of water.

A good lesson from the neighborhood is that everyone recognized the importance of enjoying a good meal with family and friends. This is a good example for us today. We should start spending more time together on a regular basis and sharing a meal is a wonderful way to do this.

Getting Started Is as Easy as 1—2—3!

1. You will be eating five or six small meals per day, instead of three large meals. Never go more than two and a half to three hours without eating if you are awake—you must keep your metabolism stoked high so that it is continually burning calories.
2. You will eat lean protein, carbohydrates, and some healthy fats throughout the day.
3. Drink at least half your body weight in ounces of water a day to flush out your system and to keep feeling satisfied and hydrated.

Smart Eating

I tend to eat the same foods. I have done this for most of my life and I find most people are the same way. When I was working in Manhattan, I would eat out at the same restaurants on a regular basis. My favorite was, and still is, the Post House on East 63rd between Madison Avenue and Park Avenue. When Jacko seated us, he made sure we were not only seated at the same table, but before we even opened our mouths he already had a pretty good idea of what we were going to eat. "Mr. Rowley, will it be the filet tips with fresh vegetables or a porterhouse today?" He would go around the table in a similar manner for all the regulars.

Sure, every once in a while we would surprise him with something new, but not often. The next time you are in Manhattan make sure you go to the Post House and be sure to tell Jacko that John sent you.

Every time I speak with nutritionists, they insist that consistency and simplicity are essential in controlling body weight and living a healthy life. I agree. This is one of the reasons most diets fail. It's not all the dieter's fault. It's just that most diets are either too difficult to follow or too narrow to be enjoyable. We are not going to discuss a one-shot-Charlie, quick fix diet, but a way to eat that is enjoyable, healthy, and simple to incorporate into your life.

Mangia Several Times a Day

That's right, let's eat several times a day. I think the smartest way to eat is to have three meals and two or three snacks a day. This is one constant that I see in people who stay in great shape year round. They eat often and keep eating simple. Three good meals will give you the fuel to power you through the day and the snacks will keep your blood sugar levels up, keeping the edge off your hunger and your energy revving high all day long.

All of your meals and snacks should include a quality source of protein. Protein stimulates your metabolism, keeps blood sugar stabilized, cuts down on cravings, and feeds lean muscle tissue. This puts protein at the top of your shopping list. Carbohydrates in moderation are good as well.

Carbohydrates come in the form of vegetables, fruits, and complex carbohydrates. Vegetables are great because they are full of fiber, which keeps you feeling full longer and keeps your system clean and healthy. You can eat these all the time with no worries of putting on fat. Fruits and complex carbs—in the right amounts—are important for good health as well, but the key is moderation. While you are trying to lose fat, I recommend not having more than two pieces of fruit a day and be sure to stay within the recommended guidelines for complex carbs. If you are not losing as much fat as you like, you should cut back on the complex carbs until the fat starts melting away again. If it is still slow going with losing fat, cut back on your fruit. A healthy rate to lose weight is around one to two pounds per week. You may lose more the first couple of weeks because of water weight loss, but one to two pounds a week is a good, healthy goal.

The chart on the next page will give you a good baseline on how much protein, carbs, and cautious carbs you should eat each day for your specific goal. The chart is simply a guide to get you started. You will still want to pay attention to how your body responds to the different foods and amounts you are eating.

I can't stress this enough: this is just a starting point. You *must* pay attention to how your body responds to various foods and the amounts of those foods.

Daily Protein & Carbohydrate Guideline

Body Weight	Protein		Cautious Carbs (grams)		
	Grams	Portions	Burning Fat	Lean Muscle	Maintenance
100	100	5	50	100	150
110	110	6	55	110	165
120	120	6	60	120	180
130	130	7	65	130	195
140	140	7	70	140	210
150	150	8	75	150	225
160	160	8	80	160	240
170	170	9	85	170	255
180	180	9	90	180	270
190	190	10	95	190	285
200	200	10	100	200	300
210	210	11	100	200	300
220	220	11	100	200	300
230	230	12	100	200	300
240	240	12	100	200	300
250	250	13	100	200	300
260	260	13	100	200	300
270	270	14	100	200	300
280	280	14	100	200	300
290	290	15	100	200	300
300	300	15	100	200	300
310	310	16	100	200	300
320	320	16	100	200	300
330	330	17	100	200	300
340	340	17	100	200	300
350	350	18	100	200	300
360	360	18	100	200	300
370	370	19	100	200	300
380	380	19	100	200	300
390	390	20	100	200	300
400	400	20	100	200	300

* This is a baseline to guide you. You MUST pay attention to how your body responds to the amounts of and various nutrients you eat. This is only a guide to get you going!

The 3³ Eating Technique

This is very simple. Eat **three** meals a day. Eat **three** snacks a day. Divide your plate into **three** sections when eating.

We have already discussed eating three meals and three snacks a day. Now I want to show you how dividing your plate into three sections makes it easy to remember how much food to eat. This is a good way of eyeballing your meals. One third of your plate is for your protein, one third of your plate is for vegetables or salad, and one third of your plate is for a complex carbohydrate. Remember this is just a rough eyeball. Be sure to stick within the portion sizes for your protein and carbs from the chart in the previous chapter.

Food Staples

Below is a list of basic foods that you can eat while you manage your weight and stay in top shape. As you learn how your body responds, you can add other foods to this list, but the key is simplicity.

APPROVED FOODS					
Protein	Vegetables	"Cautious" fruits	"Cautious" carbohydrates	Fat choices	Condiments
Chicken Breast	Broccoli	Apples	Steamed Brown Rice	Olive Oil	Salad Dressing (<3 grams of sugar per serving)
Turkey Breast	Lettuce	Apricots-dried, fresh	Sweet Potatoes	Canola Oil	Mayonnaise (Low Fat) Olive oil, Safflower Oil, etc
Seafood	Cabbage	Blueberries	Yams	Enova Oil	Hot Sauce
Eggs (mostly whites)	Cauliflower	Cantaloupe	Steel Cut or Irish Oatmeal	Grapeseed Oil	Salsa
Veal	Green beans	Cherries	Fiber One Cereal	Safflower Oil	Soy Sauce
Lean Steak	Mushrooms	Grapefruit	Kellogg's Extra-Fiber All Bran	Avocado	Steak Sauce
Buffalo/bison	Onions	Grapes	Ezekiel bread	Guacamole	Worcestershire Sauce
Lamb	Asparagus	Kiwi	Whole grain pasta	Almonds	All spices that contain no added sugar
Lean game meats like venison	Cucumber	Mangoes	Macadamia Nuts	Broth	
Lunch Meat (fat free or low fat)	Spinach	Oranges	Extracts (almond, vanilla, or others)		

Protein	Vegetables	"Cautious" fruits	"Cautious" carbohydrates	Fat choices	Condiments
Fat free cottage cheese	All forms of peppers	Peaches	Horseradish sauce		
Greek Yogurt	Zucchini	Pears	I Can't Believe It's Not Butter! Spray		
Cheese (low fat or fat free)	Snow peas	Plums	Butter Buds		
Turkey Bacon	Celery	Strawberries	Lemon Juice		
Protein powder	Pickles	Figs	Lime Juice		
Lean Pork	Collard Greens	Dates	Fat Free Sugar Free Pudding		
Lean Ground Beef	Radishes	Prunes	Mustard		
Lean Ground Turkey	Sauerkraut	Pineapple	Ginger		
	Sprouts, Alfalfa	Grapes	Garlic		
	Pepper				

Enjoy a Victorious Weekend

I've noticed that when anything is too restrictive, it won't work for long because we will rebel against it. Eating good is only good for so long. Eventually we want that burger or a slice of pizza. I start my Victory Day on Saturday afternoon so I can eat a burger with fries, go wild with some ice cream, grab a sandwich in front of the TV, or even get some sushi. Then on Sunday morning, I feel free to eat some waffles with my children and grandkids or even go to brunch with some friends after church—complete with some desert if I want it. But by Sunday afternoon I am sick of my freedom and I am craving to go back to my healthy eating.

The Victory Day is not only a mental break but is good for your body as well. Your body gets used to anything if you stick to it long enough. Eating the same way day in and day out can have a slowing effect on the metabolism. When you shock your system with the occasional influx of calories at one time, the body's metabolism increases to kick start your "furnace" into high gear once again. This will help keep your body off balance which will make it easier to get lean.

Timing Your Meals

A quick note on the timing of your meals. It is very important that you eat throughout the day on a regular basis. Small meals spread over the day allow you to eat fewer carbs at any one meal. Carbs are the chief releaser of insulin. Since our blood sugar levels have to be within a certain range to stay healthy, eating carbs will trigger the release of insulin to ferry the excess glucose to be converted to glycogen. But our bodies will only store just so much glycogen before converting the excess glucose to triglycerides or fat. Although the body limits the amount of glycogen it stores, it will store an unlimited amount of triglycerides. Simply stated, too many carbs eaten at one time will cause an elevated spike in insulin which can contribute to fat storage. Five or six meals spread throughout the day not only provides you with a constant supply of protein for cellular growth and recovery, but smaller meals modify insulin output which will lead to a leaner, more muscular and desirable body. Also, if you are trying to lose fat, have the bulk of your carbs early in the day and taper off as the day goes on. The only exception is your post workout meal. If you are working out later in the day, you can still have your post workout carbs.

Post Workout Meal

It is very important that you have some protein and a small amount of carbohydrates within thirty to forty five minutes of working out or training with weights to refill your muscles with glycogen and to give them the protein needed for repair. Training with weights uses a lot of glycogen. Eating carbs immediately following a workout causes your body to quickly release insulin so the glycogen stores can be replaced for future use. Since these stores must be met before any excess glucose can be stored as body fat, this is a perfect time to carb up. When the insulin levels get elevated after training, it drives amino acids from protein foods into the muscles where they are used to grow new muscle tissue. So, in short, having some of your carbohydrates and protein right after your workout is a good idea. One cup of strawberries is only eleven carbs, but is enough to help me recover from my workout and keep me feeling energetic. Along with this, I also have forty grams of protein powder which helps my muscles recover and improve after my work out. Timing is everything. Another good time to have some carbs is first thing in the morning. Since you have been fasting for eight hours or more, the carbohydrates will go right to filling your muscles up. I recommend steel cut oats; but start out with only a small amount, one-half cup at most, and see how your body responds. Are you putting on fat? How is your energy? It is very important that you pay attention to these things. Everyone responds a little differently. I may be able to eat half a cup of steel cut oats for breakfast and stay lean, whereas some friends of mine can eat a full cup plus berries and still stay lean. Drives me nuts!

A Sample Day of Eating

Now let me give you a sample of what a good day might look like. Of course everyone has different tastes and this will also require adjusting the amounts based on your weight and desired goals. The purpose is to show you how to incorporate my recommendations into your daily life and to help you on your journey of living The Power of Positive Fitness. Mangia! Mangia! Buon appetito!

Breakfast sets you up for a successful day. Don't skip it. If you do, you will be starving by 10:00 AM and you will be tempted to eat something that isn't good for you. Some people think they will lose weight if they eat only a meal or two a day. As you undoubtedly already know, just the opposite is true—missing one meal will usually lead to overeating on the next one. The old saying, "Eat breakfast like a king, lunch like a prince, and dinner like a pauper," is good advice if you want to manage your weight.

Breakfast

Irish or Steel Cut Oatmeal topped with blueberries.
A protein drink or eggs (mostly egg whites)
Coffee or tea

Snack

Since it is essential that you eat every two and a half to three hours, your first snack will be at around 10:00 AM, then another one at 3:00 PM and, if you have three snacks, the last one an hour or so before bed.

Protein pudding
An apple

Lunch

Lunch is always my favorite meal. You can still eat a good bit because it is early enough in the day to be able to work off the excess. It is very important that you have the 10:00 AM snack because, if you don't, you will most certainly overdo it at lunch time.

Grilled Chicken Breast
A large salad with 1/2 sliced avocado with olive oil and balsamic vinegar
A small yam

Dinner

At the end of the day, it is smart to take it easy. You don't have much day left for using food. I suggest cutting back or eliminating starches all together at this meal and just have lean protein and vegetables.

> Grilled White Fish
> Steamed broccoli
> 1/2 cup of brown rice (optional)

Final Snack (if you have one)

The last one should be protein only, like a protein drink or Greek yogurt. My wife and I have Greek yogurt every night; at twenty grams of protein per cup, it is a great protein-packed snack.

❖

Cheers!

You've probably heard that red wine in moderation has a positive effect with certain cancers and heart disease, and can be effective in controlling cholesterol levels. I think it is best to steer clear of the wine until you get your weight under control. If you don't, just realize that it may take you a little longer to reach your goals. Also, if you do have a glass of wine, it may lower your resolve and you may not stick to your eating plan. So drink red wine with caution.

The best thing to drink is water; if you are going to drink other things be sure they have no sugar in them. Diet soda, zero calorie soft drinks, and coffee and tea without sugar are fine as well. It is a good idea to stay away from alcohol while you are trying to get your weight under control. Like red wine, alcohol will lower your resolve but, unlike red wine, alcohol has no positive effect on the body. I know one thing for sure. I don't know anyone who regrets not drinking alcohol and quite a few people who regret ever taking their first sip. Ultimately, the choice is yours. If you know you have an issue with alcohol, I suggest you follow the "no exceptions rule."

The No Exceptions Rule

Before we leave this section on eating, I need to cover one more important point. The "No Exceptions Rule" is critical and one that I learned the hard way. I have read in books to take a off-day and to cheat on my diet. I prefer to call this a

Victory Day and not a cheat day. There are certain things that you do not include in your Victory meal if you struggle with them.

A few months ago, our friends Mitch and Alexis Mayer came to visit. They both told me that I looked like I was in the best shape of my life. I was feeling good! Right after this a pinched nerve in my neck flared up again, leaving my left arm in a lot of pain and very weak. This was right before Thanksgiving and normally I will take Thanksgiving Day as a Victory Day, eating whatever I want to eat. This Thanksgiving was no different. But after Thanksgiving there was a problem. I was not exercising because I was in a lot of pain and I just kept eating. My Victory Day turned into a Victory two months.

I never should have made that exception after Thanksgiving because without my regular routine of exercise and healthy eating, the exception became the rule. I put some pounds on and had to go through additional effort to get it off. Had I stuck to my Victory Day instead of the Victory two months, I could have just gotten back to my regularly scheduled lifestyle. I see this happen to people all the time. They are making great progress, but they make an exception where they shouldn't and the exception becomes the rule. "Oh, I didn't eat well on Monday and Tuesday so I'll take off today too—and the weekend's right around the corner. Anyway, I might as well wait to get back on my eating plan until Monday." Before you know it, it is six months and more pounds than you'd like later.

Keep in mind that we don't get fat, go broke, or ruin relationships by the things we do once in a while. It is what we do consistently that counts. Remember: failure is part of success. If you get into a bad cycle like I just confessed, don't beat yourself up. Just know that in the future you are going to implement the "no exception rule" so you can be victorious. If cheesecake is something that you can't stop eating, don't eat cheesecake. If you have a problem with alcohol, don't drink. The exceptions will become the rule, not the exception. So on the things that you know are difficult for you, don't make that exception . . . ever!

Chapter 3

How to Get the Body You Want

The Power of Positive Fitness training plan is a very targeted, specific program that will get you maximum results in a minimum amount of time. Over the past thirty years I have had the opportunity to try every form of exercise routine under the sun. Some gave me outstanding results and others actually set my progress back. I have had the privilege to work out with, pick the brains of, and observe some of the greatest athletes, doctors, and experts in the world. Not one to keep knowledge to myself, I would try new techniques out on friends, family, and anyone who would listen. My wife is usually about three or four weeks behind me. If I stick with it, then she adds it to her routine. She is the wise one in the family

Always anxious to improve, I have tried everything out on my own body as a sort of testing ground. I try the different routines and techniques and carefully monitor the results. I was curious how changes would affect not only my muscle growth and body-fat percentages, but also my energy levels and mental clarity during the day. How was my ability to focus at work? Did it enhance the rest of my life or take away from it? In short, how did my exercise routine affect my whole life, not just my body?

I've taken everything that I have learned from others, experimented on myself, friends, and family then filtered it through over thirty years of experience to create a program that will work for you regardless of where you are starting. I want to save you over thirty years of trial and error so you can get into the best shape of your life—so you can truly LIVE your life.

Burn Fat Like a Champ

Muscle burns fat! It's as simple as that. The more muscle you have the more effective your metabolism will be. You don't have to look like Mr. or Ms. Olympia for this to be true. When you have more muscle your body utilizes more energy to operate, even at rest. The more muscle you have the more calories you burn. Workout, put on muscle, and watch your body turn from a fat storage machine to a fat burning machine.

Most of us, as we age, become less active, so we are naturally burning fewer calories. This will cause us to put on a little weight, probably fat. Then the problems begin: our metabolism slows down and we get even fatter. Oh, it doesn't end there. We then go from diet to diet and from exercise plan to exercise plan, damaging our metabolism in the process.

We are going to stop this ruthless cycle right now.

Lifting weights is not rocket science. There are certain principles, yes, but it is not as complicated as some books and magazines make it out to be. Remember, people make money by marketing the new solution to your problem. Also remember, there are very few things that are new. Repackaged yes, but new? Not necessarily. Yes, we may have some new equipment or technology, but our bodies work the same today as they did thousands of years ago.

Ladies, This Means You, Too!

This applies for the ladies as well. Yes, you heard me right! Women must concentrate on building muscle, also. You must stop focusing on losing weight and start focusing on building lean muscle. Muscle is heavier than fat, so you might weigh a little more, but don't let that scare you. Who cares, as long as you feel good, look good, and are healthy? There is no reason why any woman should have hunched over shoulders due to weak muscles or flabby upper arms. Weight training is the prescription to these cosmetic concerns that can and will lead to devastating health problems.

"But I don't want to look like a man!" "I don't want all those muscles." Don't worry about it; you won't look like a man. Women can't build muscle the way men can because they don't have testosterone. In fact, most men don't even have the genetics to build huge muscles. I have said it before: muscle burns calories, even at rest. The problem is most women don't build enough muscle when they are young and then as they age they have a very fast decrease in the little muscle mass they do have. This is a major health threat to women and leads to devastating health problems and needless, yet endless yo-yo dieting as women try to get their weight and health under control. Women everywhere are discovering the benefits of resistance training because this stuff really works.

Muscle is also smaller than fat! As a point of reference, imagine a pound of muscle being the size of a handball and a pound of fat the size of a softball. Muscle takes up much less space on your body, but it gets better than that. When you put fat on your body, it usually has its favorite hiding places like the belly, butt, hips, and thighs, whereas muscle will be more evenly distributed throughout the body giving you a more shapely body. Not only does having more muscle help you burn fat, but it gives you a nice, shapely physique.

One Size Fits All Programs

This is not a one-size-fits-all program. In fact, nothing bothers me more than seeing fitness professionals telling people that theirs is the only way to train and get fit. Some say only do weights. Others say forget the weights; you need to do cardio. Yet others get very specific and say you need to do cardio on Tuesday, Thursday, and Saturday and weights on Monday, Wednesday, and Friday. I have news for you. Your body has no idea what day of the week it is. It doesn't know if you are using a machine, barbell, or dumbbell. All it knows is that something is pushing it beyond its previous limits so it has to either die or adjust. The adjustment is you getting stronger and in better shape. Period! Very simple.

You don't need any fancy equipment and forget about the machine that gives you shredded abs in only 90 seconds a week. It doesn't work and the model showing it doesn't even use it. Advertisers think that everyone is stupid. No, I take that back. Advertisers know that people are desperate to take back control of their bodies and their lives once and for all and are willing to try anything. How about the commercials for the various diet pills? They have the before picture with the very fat person cloaked in milky white skin and a hairy body, but in only a few weeks he is not only ripped but sporting a tan and missing the body hair. Come on! Give me a break! It took time to put the weight on and it will take some time to get lean. But it is well worth it.

Appendix 2 gives you various workouts and every one of them is effective. As I said earlier, your body doesn't know anything other than to respond to the stimulus you put on it. Your brain is another thing altogether. Some people can do the same routine week in and week out and stay very motivated. Others, like me, get bored very easily and need to mix things up constantly to stay motivated. Just figure out what works for you, your personality, and lifestyle.

Workouts for Everyone

One thing I have learned over the years is there is no perfect exercise routine. The one that works the best is the one you do consistently. Believe me, I have tried them all. This is your book and is designed to enhance your life by adjusting your lifestyle. It is not meant to impress you with my vast knowledge, exercise kinesiology, or biomechanics, but to break things down to their simplest components so you can implement them immediately.

I know people who lift weights six, five, four, and three days a week and grace the covers of magazines. Some will give you a very sophisticated answer as to why they work out the number of days they do. But most will just say, "That is what I like to do. I like to be in the gym X number of days a week." Doing it the way you like to do it is very important. If you like your routine, you will be consistent and if you are consistent you will get great results.

Yeah, But Which Workout Is the Best?

If I was reading this book the first question I would ask is, "Which is the best routine? I don't mind putting the time and effort in. I just want the best results I can get." Oh, I am so glad you asked! The answer isn't as straight forward as I would like. Every workout listed in this book can be an advanced or a beginning routine, depending on the intensity you put into the workouts. Intensity and consistency are the keys to results. If you go in the gym and just go through the motions and put little effort in, your results will reflect that. But if you go in the gym and put in the effort on a consistent basis, you will achieve great results. I do, however, recommend one routine frequently to people that never fails to get results if they put the effort in.

The Perfect Routine: The Best Results in the Least Amount of Time

I am a big fan of a three-day-a-week weight training program, which combines muscle groups so that you are working each body-part once a week. Then you do cardio at least three days a week on non-workout days. This will get you in very good shape in the least amount of time. This routine never fails because it gives you just the right amount of stimulus and then allows plenty of rest for your body to recover and re-build. It doesn't require a lot of time so people are consistent with it. As I said earlier, there are endless ways to arrange your training schedule. In Appendix 2, I will give you an arsenal of various workout routines and training methods to keep you making consistent gains for years to come.

Make an Appointment with Yourself

My wife and I put our workouts in our schedule just as you would a business meeting which diminishes conflicts that would then make us miss our workout. If you have your workout in your schedule for a certain time each day, that time is carved out like any other important meeting and everyone around you will get used to it.

I know many successful and busy people who never do a business lunch because that is the time they workout. Instead, they opt for a coffee meeting that can be done in a fraction of the time. I was recently invited to a luncheon with Donald Trump at Trump Towers. Although he provided an incredible filet mignon lunch, he didn't eat. Mr. Trump came in before the food was served and we had our meeting. His assistant told me that he seldom has meetings that last more than five or ten minutes. If they go longer than that, something is wrong. He was very gracious with his time but when we were done he left and we enjoyed our lunch. I try to avoid business lunches; I opt for a coffee meeting. An obvious exception is when you get invited by Donald Trump. You need to be flexible and use your head and if something does come up, you can use overflow days to make up a workout or just double up during the week if you miss a work out.

The Workout

Aerobic Training

On non-weight training days do thirty to forty five minutes of aerobic training. First thing in the morning would be best, but if you can't do it then, schedule it for the best time that is good for you.

Resistance Training

You will train with weights three times a week, preferably with a day between each training day. For example, you can train Monday, Wednesday, and Friday or Tuesday, Thursday, and Saturday. Rest sixty to ninety seconds between each set. A *rep* is one complete motion of the exercise. A *set* is a group of the quantity of reps suggested.

Monday or Day 1 (Chest, Shoulder, Triceps, and Abs)

Chest Press	3 sets of 8–12 reps
Incline Chest Press	3 sets of 8–12 reps
Shoulder Press	3 sets of 8–12 reps
Lateral Raise	3 sets of 8–12 reps
Triceps Press Down	3 sets of 8–12 reps
Lying Triceps Extension	3 sets of 8–12 reps
Crunch	3 sets of 10–20+ reps
Reverse Crunch/ Leg raises	3 sets of 10–20+ reps

Wednesday or Day 2 (Legs and Abs)

Leg Extension	3 sets of 8–12 reps
Leg Press	3 sets of 8–12 reps
Leg Curls	3 sets of 8–12 reps
Standing Calf Raises	3 sets of 8–12 reps
Crunch	3 sets of 10–20+ reps
Reverse Crunch/ Leg raises	3 sets of 10–20+ reps

Friday or Day 3 (Back, Biceps and Abs)

Pulldowns	3 sets of 8–12 reps
Seated Rows	3 sets of 8–12 reps
Hyper Extensions	3 sets of 8–12 reps
Curls	3 sets of 8–12 reps
Preacher Curls	3 sets of 8–12 reps
Crunch	3 sets of 10–20+ reps
Reverse Crunch/ Leg raises	3 sets of 10–20+ reps

Cardio Schmardio

Your heart is a magnificent muscle. It takes oxygen rich blood and pumps it through your body. It then takes carbon dioxide laden blood back from the body and pumps it into the lungs, where it is expelled and exchanged for more oxygen. Your heart starts beating before you are born and it doesn't stop until death. Ironically, the heart beats faster and less efficiently when you give it little to do, and works more efficiently when you put regular demands on it. They say that a boat will rust out much faster when sitting idle than when sailing the open seas. The same is true of an airplane. It will wear out quicker sitting on the runway, than when soaring through the heavens. The same is true with you. You must work your heart so it stays strong and healthy. One of the things I hear from a lot of people is, "I am going to take it easy tonight. I am exhausted." Yes, they may be working hard at their job but they are exhausted because they are not feeding and utilizing their bodies properly. They are killing themselves by "taking it easy."

Cardiovascular Exercise

Cardiovascular exercise is a hotly debated topic among fitness experts. Some are adamant that all you need is very brief, very intense bursts of cardio exercise done in a fashion that will work your heart sufficiently. Then others say that you need to go long and slow. I think it is good to incorporate both. Let me explain. Short, intense interval training is a specific period of work, followed by another specific period of rest (e.g., one minute sprint followed by two minutes of walking). This is a great way to strengthen your heart and cardiovascular system, but if you do too much of it you risk burning muscle which will short circuit your progress. If you want to do this type of cardiovascular training I suggest doing it on non-weight lifting days. For our purposes I will call this interval cardio. Many people I know, including myself, don't do this type of cardio but instead opt to move quickly enough between exercises when weight training that it works the cardio vascular system very well. You heart doesn't know the difference—it just knows it is working.

Essential Cardio

I recommend you do cardio training three to six days a week. On non-weight training days I recommend thirty to forty five minutes, first thing in the morning if possible, at the very least. If you can do more I would recommend you add at least twenty to thirty minutes of cardio first thing in the morning on training days or right after your weight training. Please keep in mind this is your program and you have to see what works best for you. One parameter I will lay out is to never do more than an hour of essential cardio during one session because you risk burning muscle at that point.

I can hear it now! "But John, that is a lot of cardio!" I know it is. I know plenty of people who stay in great shape lifting weights three times a week and doing cardio three days a week on non-weight lifting days. I recognize, however, that doing daily cardio is good for your health. Both your mental and physical health. Yes, it burns fat, but it also gets your endorphins going and makes you feel good. It is a great time to just be with yourself, unwind, and think. I get some of my best ideas when I am doing cardio. It is also a great time to talk with someone. Often my evening cardio is when my wife and I catch up on the day's activities and get to spend some uninterrupted time together.

The type of cardio that burns fat best while sparing muscle is performed at moderate intensity. For this book I am calling it *essential cardio*. If you can hold a conversation without gasping for oxygen you are in the fat burning zone. You should be working hard enough that if you are talking to someone you'd feel like you are on the verge of running out of breath. Of course there is an easier way to do this—you can monitor your heart rate.

Heart Rate

It is a good idea to monitor your heart rate to make sure it isn't too high and also to gauge how much more you can push yourself. In the beginning, however, don't worry about putting your heart rate in the correct range. Just do something and progressively work up to getting your heart rate in the correct range.

The formula widely used for the heart rate is to subtract your age from 220 and multiply the result by how hard you want to work. For our purposes I want you to stay in the sixty to seventy percent range.

For example, if you are forty years old it would look like this:

220 - 40 = 180
180 x 60% = 108
180 x 70% = 126

So according to this formula, if you are forty years old, your maximum heart rate would be 180 beats per minute. If you wanted to keep your heart rate in the optimum zone which is 60% to 70% of your maximum heart rate (MHR) you would stay between 108 to 126. Most machines now have heart rate monitors attached to the equipment or you can go to any sporting goods store and buy a heart rate monitor pretty inexpensively.

Here is a handy reference chart that you can use to find your ideal target heart rate. Simply look up your age and it will give you the target heart rate range that will work best for you. As I said before, let's keep it simple.

Age	Target Heart Rate 60%	Target Heart Rate 70%
20	120	140
25	117	136.5
30	114	133
35	111	129.5
40	108	126
45	105	122.5

50	102	119
55	99	115.5
60	96	112
65	93	108.5
70	90	105
75	87	101.5
80	84	98
85	81	94.5
90	78	91
95	75	87.5
100	72	84

What Type of Cardio?

The best type of cardio is the kind that you will actually do. So pick something that you enjoy. I like to ride my mountain bike with my wife and kids but seldom have time to do it. Most of the time, I use my recumbent bike at my home because it is more convenient and I can do it consistently. My good friend John Guelzow gave me a recumbent bike, a spinner like the bikes used in spinning classes, and a rowing machine as a gift and it has made all the difference in the world. I usually do 45 to 60 minutes of cardio first thing in the morning. I also like walking at a brisk pace and do this often when weather allows.

Exercise doesn't have to be boring; just look for ways to stay active that fit into your lifestyle. Also keep in mind that cardio is only good if you DO it. So choose a time when you know you can do it. Of course, there is always the most effective time to do cardio. There are really two times that produce the best results. One is first thing in the morning, before you eat. Your body has been fasting for eight hours or more, so when you are doing your cardio, your body will burn fat much faster than if you did it later in the day after you've been eating. Another very effective time is immediately after you've completed your weight training. The same principle applies—you burn your glycogen (blood sugar) when you are lifting weights and if you do your cardio immediately following, you will begin burning fat faster.

Multi-Tasking

The most important thing is to find a time that works best for you. I don't like doing cardio after my weight training so I do it first thing in the morning before my day gets away from me. I usually watch a sermon on a podcast or take a walk and listen to something. I also love doing an additional session in the evening if I can. I really enjoy this evening session because it is a good way to unwind after a long day. If the weather allows, my wife and I will walk Titan, our 85 pound pit bull, or I will do another session on the bike. Sometimes this second session is more for my head than my body. As I have been saying all along, our head, body and spirit are all part of the same person. You can't separate one from the other.

Rest and Recovery

Learn to relax. Your body is precious, as it houses your mind and spirit. Inner peace begins with a relaxed body. —**Norman Vincent Peale**

This is one area that is too often overlooked. If you're not getting enough rest, you will get over tired, be ineffective in every area of your life, risk getting hurt, and you will not see the results of all the hard work you are putting into exercise and nutrition. "Not fair!" you say. Too bad. This is the way God created you. We are going to talk about rest: rest between sets when you are working out, rest between workouts so you recover properly, and ongoing rest and recovery which is essential for good health, creativity, and effectiveness.

Rest between Sets

Resting between sets should last anywhere from one to two minutes. Rest long enough to catch your breath between sets before you begin your next one. A good rule of thumb is to rest one minute for smaller body parts like arms and abs and about two minutes for larger body parts like back and legs. Don't rest any longer than necessary to catch your breath before doing the next set. You want to make sure you're not out of breath but not breathing so easy that your heart rate is also slowed down as well.

Rest between Workouts

Your muscles should fully recover before training them again. What I am talking about is the recovery between training *sessions* of the same muscle group. It should be the time between one chest workout until your next chest workout. It may be two days until your next chest workout or it may be a week depending on the routine you are following. This is very important for enhancing the muscle growth process. Most training programs have you training way too often. Muscles don't grow in the gym. Muscles grow when they are resting. Muscle must adapt to compensate for future stress by growing. If you don't get enough rest, energy levels will fade, your appetite will suffer, and motivation will disappear. This is called over training.

Ongoing Rest and Recovery

A good night's sleep is every bit as important as eating properly and exercising effectively. Statistics show that seven out of ten adults get six or fewer hours of sleep each night. Too many people think they can do without sleep. They are shooting themselves in the foot.

The average person is trying to get more done, so they spend more time doing things in place of sleep. They are exhausted all the time and can't focus properly because of fatigue, so it takes longer to do these things because they are not effective. It is a never ending loop. You need more sleep in order to be energetic and productive. Most healthy adults need between seven and nine hours of sleep each night. Some need less and some need more, but this is a good starting point.

Find your cycle, stick to it, and see how much your life changes. Your body lets you know when it is tired, so pay attention to it. If you don't, you will get irritable and have problems concentrating or remembering things.

Getting a Good Night's Sleep for a High Energy Day

I recently asked a doctor what was the most important issue that people suffer from, and without missing a beat he answered, "sleep." With more activities than ever before pulling at you, you probably don't even realize how much your poor sleep habits are affecting your health, reducing your productivity, and lessening your enjoyment of life. If you're not well rested, all areas of your life will suffer. Your home life, work life, personal life, and spiritual life are all affected when you don't get enough sleep.

First determine how much sleep you need. You probably have a rough idea of how many hours of sleep you need, so for a few days try to go to bed at a time that allows you that amount of sleep and see how you feel. You may have to experiment a bit, but quickly you will know what works best for you. Once you know how much sleep you need, arrange your regular sleep schedule to give you that amount each night. If you are a "morning person" like me, make sure you go to bed early enough to wake up rested. With DVR's and technology today you won't even have to miss your favorite TV shows. You will thank yourself for this as you find yourself with better health and more daily energy.

Tips for a Good Night's Sleep

- Don't eat large meals late at night. Your last meal of the day should be small; ideally, it should contain "slow" proteins (e.g., meats, Greek yogurt, cottage cheese, or a casein drink, which is just a milk-based protein drink you can get at most health food stores). This will provide a steady supply of amino acids in your bloodstream all night long, helping with muscle growth and fat loss.
- Avoid caffeinated drinks and alcohol in the evening.
- Try to go to bed at the same time most nights.
- Avoid upsetting yourself before bed: Don't watch the late news or review your overdue bills before going to bed. Unwind. Don't check e-mail or think about work related issues for at least an hour or two before bedtime.
- Develop and follow a bedtime ritual. For instance, take a bath or go for a short walk every night before going to bed. It will help you relax and get you ready for bed.
- Eliminate noise and outside light. Make sure that your bedroom is quiet the whole night and that you don't have a street light shining in on your face or a pit bull snoring in the corner like I do.
- Keep the bedroom at a temperature that suits you. Most people sleep better when the room is a little cooler.
- Make sure your bed, mattress, and pillows allow you to get a good night's sleep.
- Read something boring; usually you will be asleep within minutes—which eliminates my books . . . right?
- If you have an active mind and your thoughts are keeping you awake, try keeping a pad of paper next to your bed and write down everything in your head. This way you won't forget it and you can let go of it. I did this for many years with great results.

Time for Yourself

Many people tell me that they can't take a day off from work. I thoroughly disagree. I spent some years as a real estate broker, when I first moved to Raleigh, N.C. Most realtors work seven days a week and never take time to themselves. I knew some who took their laptops and worked deals over the phone even when they were on family outings. I became committed to taking a day with my family for church and to spend time together. I was committed for two very good reasons. Cathy wanted me to be with the family at least one day a week and God commands it. The funny thing was that I immediately realized increased sales. Was it because I was more rested, so I was better able to focus? Or was it God honoring my commitment? I don't know for sure. I think it was a bit of both. What I do know is that I took the time off. I started to produce more and my income went up all while I was feeling stronger, more rested, and more connected to God and my family. There was no downside as I had feared, only upside results.

In order to have energy to fuel your passion, you have to take care of yourself. We now know that you have to eat right, workout, and get some rest. It is one thing to know these things and quite another to actually do it. If you are working seven days a week, you are probably not as effective as you could be during the other six. I challenge you to schedule your upcoming week on Friday afternoon or Saturday morning. Review everything you have to get done and schedule time to get it done. Put a plan together and give your week some thought. Most people spend more time planning their vacation than they do their own lives.

Fartlek Success System©

Okay, so you are an overachiever. You are going to put a plan together and change your life for the good. You are going to really make a difference in this world . . . but then it happens. It may be next week or the week after but it *will* happen. I don't know if it will be on a Monday, Tuesday, or Wednesday, but one day you will be at work and it will ring in your ears: John says I should be energetic and I don't feel like it. Those days happen to all of us, and if anyone tells you it doesn't happen to them don't listen, because they're going to lie about something else, too. Any athlete will tell you that you can't be 100% all of the time, so you have to plan for it.

Because our energy ebbs and flows throughout the day, I developed the Fartlek Success System.© Now say that out loud—I don't want you to forget it. I know it sounds funny but it works. Studies have shown that we have waves of energy during the day, that after 90 to 120 minutes of activity our body begins to crave a period of rest and recovery, and this is where the Fartlek Success System comes into play. Fartlek is a Swedish term which means "speed play."

When I was a runner I would train in the Fartlek fashion. I would run and then sprint between telephone poles and then go back to my pace. Today this type of training is called interval training and most treadmills and bikes in a good gym have a setting for this. *It is basically periods of intense effort followed by periods of active rest.*

When I was in Manhattan real estate I would get up and walk around about every 90 minutes. An Australian secretary from one of the companies I worked at called it "Mr. Rowley's walk about." I would just go walk around one of the floors and say hello to everyone. It gave me a chance to rest, network, and to see what else was going on in the company. If you can't do that you may want to use the down time to do things that require less effort and concentration like answering emails or doing anything that doesn't require you to be in top form. Do these things and not only will your energy soar, but you will look better and you will live a longer, more productive and rewarding life.

Chapter 4

The Lifestyle Restoration Cycle

Your Why

*Know your why and the what and how
will take care of itself.* —John M. Rowley

Your "why" in life is your purpose in life. This is the time to put in a little work and define why you want to do what you are setting out to do. Once you know your why, it will be so much more powerful as you go about implementing the principles in this section. **This section is on Super Charging Your Body!** Knowing why you want to be more physically fit, vibrant and healthy is probably the most energizing revelation you can have.

Step 1

Write down "why" you are passionate about getting into physical shape. Next to each "why" on your list, write a brief paragraph defining why you are committed to achieving the result you are after. "Why" is very powerful. (E.g., I want to get my body-fat down to 10% so I can live a long, healthy, vibrant life and enjoy my family)

1 _____

2 _____

3 _____

4 _____

5 _____

Step 2
This is where we put the plan together.

Take the above list and put together an action list of things you would need to do to achieve them in your life. This is where you formulate your plan. It is easier to put a plan together once you know why you are doing it.

1 _____

2 _____

3 _____

4 _____

5 _____

Step 3
Master your habits or they WILL master you!
—John M. Rowley

For each step in your plan, write down one or more habits you will need to develop and the disempowering habits you will need to get rid of in order to support your ultimate outcome. Imagine if you exchanged six limiting habits for six empowering habits every year. In five years, that would be 30 empowering habits that you do without effort and 30 disempowering habits that don't hinder you any longer. Do you think your life would be different?

List of Disempowering Habits

1 _____

_____

2 _____

_____

3 _____

_____

4 _____

_____

5 _____

_____

List of New Empowering Habits

1 _____

_____

2 _____

_____

3 _____

_____

4 _____

_____

5 _____

_____

List Which New Empowering Habit Will Replace the Old Disempowering Habit

(For example: Replace eating a donut during your coffee break with drinking a protein drink during your coffee break)

1 _____

2 _____

3 _____

4 _____

5 _____

Congratulations! You just defined your first lifestyle restoration cycle! You found your why. Then you put a plan together. You identified disempowering habits that you are going to replace with empowering habits on a regular basis so they become part of your lifestyle, hence closing the loop on The Lifestyle Restoration Cycle.

Now go to http://habitfoundry.com to supercharge your habits. We will check in with you daily by email to see how you did the day before. You can either "Go solo" or "Join a Group" of people who are working on a similar goal as you.

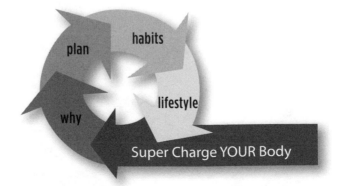

PART II

UNLEASH
THE MINDSET
OF SUCCESS

Chapter 5

What Were You Thinking?

What goes in your head is much more important than what goes in your mouth because one directs the other. Eating because of stress, boredom, habit, or any other satisfying or distracting reason will keep you unfit and unhealthy. I think this is one of the most overlooked aspects of staying healthy and fit. Every area of your life affects every other area. Sounds funny, but most self-help, diet, or spiritual books only focus on the one aspect of the person. I am convinced that you must address the whole person for complete and lasting results. If you are weak and tired because you aren't taking care of your body, your mind and spirit will suffer. If you are mentally weak, your body and spirit will suffer. If you are spiritually bankrupt, your body and your mind will not operate at peak performance. For this reason a holistic approach including physical, mental, and spiritual fitness is the most effective route to living a life that will empower you to fulfill your purpose.

Every action in life is preceded by thought. "We are what we eat" is a much-used quote, but I challenge that statement because we eat based on what we are thinking. Thought is the seed that blossoms into the lives we live. Plant good seeds and you get a good harvest. Plant bad seeds and you get a bad harvest. I am not one of those "believe it and you can achieve it" people, although that does have much merit. For one thing, you have to be careful what you are believing so when you arrive at the intended destination, you are where you should be. Many people have climbed the ladder of success only to discover that the ladder is leaning against the wrong wall. I suggest that, instead of just chanting a mantra of self achievement over your life, rather reflect on God's word and let your mind be influenced by the creator of the universe. Then prayerfully consider your path, listening to the still soft whisper of God's direction, and believe you can achieve it because it is God's will for your life. In other words, have the faith that God is guiding you in the right direction. As you seek his face he will move you along the right path, sometimes even giving you detours along the way, so that when you arrive at the intended destination you are also the person you should be.

Many years ago, I got completely consumed with buying a business. My wife didn't think it was a good idea and quite honestly everyone else around me thought it was not going to work. I even had a partner who dropped out of the deal after we completed our due diligence. But I knew better. I would make this work! I can do it on my own! Notice all the I's? I had more eyes than a ten-pound potato. Man, I knew it all! I didn't need to listen to the people who cared about me the most! So I stopped asking opinions and went about doing this on my own. It turned into one of the most miserable yet rewarding times in my life.

I wouldn't change anything because it helped me grow as a person and as a businessman, but not without severe pain. Winston Churchill once said, "If you are going through hell, keep going." This is exactly what I did. I learned a lot but the business ultimately failed and we lost a lot of money, along with that particular dream, in the process. My point is, regardless of how positive I was that I would succeed and my deep belief that I could make it work, I still fell flat on my face. I did it all—I had a positive vision, didn't give failure a second thought, was 100% engaged, worked long hours, and did everything I could to make this business work, yet it still failed miserably. I even got an outside job to support my family because this business wasn't. At that point in my life I was convinced that if I could believe it, I could achieve it! "If it was to be, it was up to me!" I was a walking, talking cliché. I memorized them all and believed them with 100% of my being and still failed. Regardless of what I was thinking, it didn't work out.

I now hold firm to the truth that if it is to be, God is with me and will direct my path. God will open doors that no one else could and will shut other doors that seem promising but lead to disaster. I have learned that self-effort and good old positive thinking that isn't directed by God and his word will lead to eventual destruction. You may succeed financially, but God looks at the whole person, not just the business person. The business person can be a raving success but the family person, the community person, the spiritual person, the physical person all live inside the same person and God wants the whole person, not just the business person, to succeed. So when you seek God for guidance, he will give you a plan or guide you in such a way that every area of your life will be healthy.

❧ ❖ ☙

*"Most folks are about as happy as they make
up their minds to be."* —Abraham Lincoln

Happiness is a conscious decision. Most people who are happy have just made up their mind that they are going to be happy! But whose choice is it? That's right—the answer is you! Being optimistic and happy is a daily choice. It is not an emotion we wait to feel or something we wait around for so that when the situation is right we can get ecstatic about our lives. In fact, if we let our situations dictate our attitude, our lives will be like an out-of-control roller coaster. We have the power to choose our response to every situation in life—good or bad. So why not choose to be happy? A good friend of our family is Happy Teague. When you are with Miss Happy you can't help but be filled with joy! She is an incredible lady and a blessing and inspiration to everyone who comes in contact with her. I once asked her why everyone calls her Happy. She told me in her charming southern accent, "Well, I had two choices and I didn't like the other one." Like Happy, you have two choices. Which do you want? King David said, "The LORD has done it this very day; let us rejoice today and be glad."[1] He didn't say, "This is the day the Lord has made, let's see what happens. Things aren't looking great so far." What you think and how you respond to life is a conscious decision.

Subway School

Many years ago I finally shoved my foot in the door of Manhattan real estate, by sheer willpower and perseverance. During my first year, I took the subway into Manhattan and had to walk a couple of miles from our home in Queens to the subway station. Getting on the 7 train was like stepping into a human sardine can. I hated starting my day this way but it was kind of ironic. Once at work, I was an executive, but on the way to work I was just one of the sardines. It was very hard to be upbeat and happy when I arrived at work after my "subway" experience, but I wasn't about to let my travel affect my career path. Instead, I decided to make the best use of the trip every morning. I took Zig Ziglar's advice and recorded my "positive" affirmations, reminding myself of everything I was happy and thankful for. I listened to the tape every day on the way to work. I was never without a motivational tape. Once I was done with my affirmation tape, I would pop in one of my "mentors" and have a great time having my own private apprentice meeting with them. My subway trip began to be a very positive experience and something I looked forward to because I turned the sardine can into a classroom. Take the things in your life that you dread and turn them into something positive or productive. We all have choices—choose to take the day that God has made for you and make the most of it.

❖

"Men are not prisoners of fate, but only prisoners of their own minds." —**Franklin D. Roosevelt**

My journey from being a janitor in Brooklyn to conducting business in the real estate boardrooms of Madison Avenue started off as a thought that turned into a dream as I was pushing a broom in Franklin K. Lane High School in Brooklyn. I then intensified the dream by going to the 59th Street Bridge where, while looking at the skyline of Manhattan, I convinced myself that I would conquer Manhattan real estate. And sure, people thought I was nuts and didn't hesitate to tell me so.

Owning R & J Health Studio also started off as a dream that I had while watching the movie "Pumping Iron." Watching Arnold Schwarzenegger and Lou Ferrigno battle it out in Pretoria, South Africa for the Mr. Olympia title, I dreamed of owning "the east coast Mecca of bodybuilding," the Brooklyn gym made famous in that movie. My getting involved with the International Federation of Body Building, the National Physique Committee, and the fitness industry started off as the dream of a kid who thumbed through the old bodybuilding and fitness magazines. Becoming an author, speaker, and TV and radio personality began as a thought that germinated into a dream and has now bloomed into the life I am living. Don't be held captive by your own mind; instead let God captivate and guide you into the life he intended for you!

Minding Your Own Mind

What you put in your mind is up to you! Put garbage in, you will get garbage out in your life. It is up to you what you think about, what you allow yourself to focus on, and what you let penetrate your mind. Your actions and your life will be greatly affected by what you are thinking about. If you are thinking about all the great things that God has in store for you or on the pure, the lovely, and the beautiful things in life, you will have a much different view of your life than if you are focusing on the negative things in this world. Take control of your thought life and you will take control of your life. What you think about is what you believe to be true.

The first step is to believe what God says: "Look at the birds of the air; they do not sow or reap or store away in barns, and yet your heavenly Father feeds them. Are you not much more valuable than they? Can any one of you by worrying add a single hour to your life."[2] We have enough on our plate today, so don't sweat tomorrow. You do the best you can and let God do the rest!

I have lived life both not following God and following him. I can tell you that the storms of life still come, but they just don't seem so bad when I focus on God and his righteousness. Let's face it: we live in uncertain times but most of the time today is okay and maybe even pretty good until we start worrying about tomorrow.

As I write this book, one of the businesses my wife and I own has died. It was tied to the housing and construction industry which is almost non-existent in our market at the moment. Most of our builders either went out of business or have no business, so our income from that business has dried up. I know that Jesus said that God would take care of us and he has! I believe what the Bible says: "God is not human, that he should lie, not a human being, that he should change his mind. Does he speak and then not act? Does he promise and not fulfill?"[3] It is really very simple. God said it and you can take that to the bank. I can't explain it other than the fact that my Father in heaven loves and takes care of me and my family, and he will do the same for you.

Think BIG

Hey, if you are going to think, you may as well think big! If you can achieve your dreams on your own, they aren't God-sized dreams. God will give you dreams so big you could never achieve them on your own. You will be way out of your comfort zone and the only way you could pull it off is with God's help. David may not have been as big as Goliath, but that didn't matter. David didn't kill the giant, Goliath, by looking at his own abilities. No. He knew his God was bigger than Goliath. Before David went after Goliath he grabbed five smooth stones from the river bed. I think he grabbed five in the event Goliath's brothers jumped in. David knew his God was not only bigger than Goliath but bigger than Goliath's whole family of giants.

Unfortunately, most people don't expect very much from themselves and, as a result, they are seldom disappointed. Is that you? Are you cheating yourself out of God's best for your life because you are afraid of disappointment? I have news for you. Deep down inside, you are disappointed anyway if you are not doing what you were created to do! The thought of, "What if?" sneaks in, followed by a myriad of possible outcomes. "If only I'd reached higher or did a different thing." The good news is, you can change this. Look at the world and see what it has to offer you and how you can serve it. Dig deep down inside yourself and try to remember those old childhood dreams you had. You know the ones. You had them long before anyone told you that achieving them was impossible. You used to think about them and the wonderful life you would have—back when nothing was impossible. Also your passions, abilities, and skills will usually be right in line with that big dream because God lays these foundations in you in advance for the work you are to do on this earth. Now, write those dreams down, start nurturing them, and then write a plan to achieve them. Bring them to God in prayer and let him reenergize you for the work he has prepared for you. Think big!

A Big Man—An Even Bigger Thinker

At 6 foot 2 inches Ronn Torossian is a big man. A *New York Times* feature story on Torossian referred to him as "The consummate hard-driving, scrappy NY publicist." CBS National News said, "Ronn Torossian knows spin"; the *New York Post* referred to him as a "Publicity Guru"; Fox News called him a "high-powered PR CEO"; Tyra Banks said he was a "Crisis Management Guru"; and CNN characterized him as "A leading PR expert." Regardless of how you slice it, Ronn Torossian, founder, president, and CEO of the New York-based 5W Public Relations stands out in the crowd and demands attention by his very presence.

In speaking to Ronn, you soon find out that he is also a very big thinker. Ronn grew up in the Bronx and worked as a pizza delivery boy. But Ronn had his sights on a much bigger world. You can just feel the energy when you are with him and you can't help but have your eyes opened to a larger world view when you are around him. Others feel the same way, which is why his conference room is over flowing with a who's who from every industry at his *invitation only* monthly networking meetings. These meetings are incredibly powerful and productive to all who attend and we all fight to be on the invitation list. I love those meetings because Ronn makes sure everyone benefits through the relationships he has nurtured over the years and everyone leaves with new friends and possible business relationships.

I met Ronn through mutual friend, Dr. Keith Ablow. Keith told me, "When you work with Ronn, you will get results. Ronn will not settle for anything less than his company's best effort when representing a client. He is honest, aggressive, and results-focused. He is simply the best!" Ronn is all that Keith told me and more. He is a big thinker with a big heart and is a man of unparalleled integrity. These are the traits I often see in high achievers. They work tirelessly and don't have time for games, so they say what they mean and honor their word.

A pizza delivery boy from the Bronx isn't what comes to mind when you ponder the attributes of the successful—unless you are Ronn Torossian. You see, Ronn didn't look at where he was coming from, only where he was going. His focus and energy have brought great success. At 5W Public Relations, Torossian's client experience has included PR programs for Coca-Cola, Microsoft, Anheuser-Busch, Barnes & Noble, Cantor Fitzgerald, IHOP, McDonald's, Evian, EDS, VeriSign, XM Radio, Seagram's, The Loews Regency, Bad Boy Worldwide Entertainment, Marriott Hotels, Vail Resorts, Pamela Anderson, Snoop Dogg, the Government of Israel, and others. In 2010, Torossian was named a semi-finalist for Ernst & Young's Entrepreneur of the Year, was named to PR Week's "40 Under 40" List, and Advertising Age's "40 Under 40" list. Not bad for a big thinking kid from the Bronx! He is doing what he set out to do and isn't looking back!

Don't Look Back—You Don't Want What's There!

When I was a runner training under Coach Fraley, he would always bellow at me, "Rowley, don't look back! You don't want what's back there! You want what's in front of you!" No truer words were ever spoken. Over the years I have watched various runners be passed at the finish line. While they were looking back, their opponent passed them on their blind side. They didn't want what was behind them, yet that is what they got. They were looking for the second place runner and *became* the second place runner. How many people lose what God has for their future because they are so busy looking back at their past?

Few things in life are more tragic than watching someone destroy their future because of a devastating past. Equally as destructive is focusing on your "glory days," which is like trying to drive looking in the rear-view mirror. Things happen, good and bad, but just realize that if you've been knocked down, you can't do anything about it now. Getting knocked down may be out of your control but staying down . . . now, that is something you can control. If your future is being controlled by your past, then give your past to God right now and start looking at what you are supposed to be doing with your life. You don't want what is back there anyway. I know people who were abused by a parent in a way that should never happen to a child. It could have broken them, but instead they went on to be, not only successful, but contributors to society. We have absolutely no way to change the past, but we don't have to give it power by looking back at it. You may want to bellow at yourself what coach Fraley often bellowed at me.

"(Inert your name here) don't look back! You don't want what's back there! You want what's in front of you!" This is how you go from victim to victor in life.

Many people use yesterday as an excuse for doing nothing today. They are victims of their past. No one wants to hear your sob story anyway and you are probably sick of it yourself. This doesn't mean people don't care; they just know they can't help you change what has already happened. Start talking to everyone about where you are going and you will see many people who want to help or at least to cheer you on.

Today is a new day. Stop holding yourself back by telling yourself and everyone else what happened yesterday and just start living successfully today with hope for a great tomorrow. Focusing on the past can stop you from the future that awaits you. I know you lost your job, your parents weren't nice enough to you, your teachers put you in the corner, and you weren't nursed as an infant. Okay! I get it! But by focusing on yesterday, you are missing out on all God has for you today. If yesterday knocked you down, get up, brush yourself off, and get on to tomorrow with a passion and a determination that will set you apart from the crowd. Then the world will stand up and take notice!

Why Power

Know your why and your what and how
will take care of itself. —John M. Rowley

Hellen Keller once said, "Many people have a wrong idea of what constitutes true happiness. It is not attained through self-gratification, but through fidelity to a worthy purpose."

Your worthy purpose is your "why." I believe we are all here for a reason and this reason, this "why," is the way we are to serve the world. Recognizing and honoring your "why" is one of the hallmarks of successful people. They take enough interest in their own lives to examine "why" they are here and what they are meant to do. Then they do it with passion, enthusiasm, and abandon. Once you know your why, you will figure out what you need to do and how you will do it.

Knowing *why* you are doing something is much more important than how you are going to do it. Your *why* will set you on fire for your purpose in life. If you have a big enough *why*, the *what* and *how* will take care of themselves. An inspiring *why* will have you run right over the very obstacles that may have stopped you in the past. Knowing and defining your *why* will also help you with your goal setting. I think traditional goal setting has failed many because they don't have a *why* tied to it. Goals without a clearly defined *why* are just words on a paper.

Going through the motions of life can be exhausting, but find your purpose, your *why*, and you will be living a delightful life.

❧ ❖ ☙

Marcus Aurelius said, "Everything—a horse, a vine—is created for some duty . . . . For what task, then, were you yourself created? A man's true delight is to do the things he was made for."

That Marcus sure had a way with words. "A delightful life." It is almost musical. He was right. We all want to live a delightful life and the way we do that is by doing the very things we were created for! When you are doing that, everything else seems to fall into place. Many years ago someone told me that if I took what I liked to do on vacation and made that my vocation that I would not only be successful but happy and fulfilled. The reason why it works like that is because the things we are good at, passionate about, and love doing are part of our makeup. It is part of who we are and why we are here. Not only will you be more fulfilled, but the world will benefit because you are serving through your life's work.

Knowing why you are here is probably the most energizing revelation you can have. You can be a bundle of energy, but if you don't know what you are supposed to do with your life, you can short circuit your life and in the process feel exhausted. Have you ever had a day when you knew exactly what to do and you felt great and the day flew by? The reverse is also true. We have all had days where we didn't have a clue what we were supposed to do, and we felt tired, frustrated and bored. Knowing your why in life keeps you energized and on target.

The Spirit Makes the Man

Sometimes your *why* sneaks up on you like a thief in the night. Personal tragedy is often the defining factor in one's life. Do you fight or go home? The ones who fight can inspire a generation! I know a man who embodied this, a man that took more hits than most but kept moving forward. He is my aunt Lu's brother, Dr. Joe Panzarella. I have known Dr. Joe, his wife Josephine, and his family my whole life and he was an incredible inspiration to all who knew him and a legend in the medical profession.

Dr. Joe went to medical school during the Korean War and while in medical school he found out that he had Multiple Sclerosis. Nearing the end of medical school, he decided to become an anesthesiologist even though that wasn't his first choice. He thought it would be best because of the MS. After medical school he started to lose the use of his legs. Eventually it progressed until he lost the use of his arms as well and he became a quadriplegic.

Dr. Joe could have given up right then, but decided to fight! He decided to specialize in rehabilitation and went on to great success. Just as things seemed to be moving along, status quo, suffered a heart attack and was rushed to the hospital. His son Jeffrey was Dr. Joe's driver and assistant. Twenty-four- year-old Jeffrey got into Dr. Joe's car and followed the ambulance to the hospital. Jeffrey never made it. There was an apparent brake malfunction and Jeffrey crashed and lost his life that night. No words can express the pain of losing a son. As you can see, Dr. Joe had more setbacks and hardship than most of us could ever expect to have. Yet he went on to be a legend in the medical profession. He received the outstanding American of the year award from President Carter and was very instrumental in fighting for the rights of the disabled. In fact, among other things, he played a part in pushing the bill through requiring access ramps for the disabled.

Dr. Joe had a long and distinguished career and impacted the world, but this never would have happened if he let life beat him. When I spoke to Mrs. Panzarella, I asked what it was that pushed Dr. Joe. In a loving and longing voice, she told me that her husband just loved people and was passionate about helping others, especially the disabled. *He knew why he was here.* She told me that God had him here for a reason and he did what he was supposed to do. Dr. Joe passed away in 1984, but while he lived he stood taller while sitting in his wheelchair than most men do on their feet. Dr. Joe was quoted as saying, "We may not be able to make the person whole again, but we in rehab medicine can help patients to live as dignified a life as possible." And, as he consistently stressed to his patients, "With disabilities, I've learned that the fighters live, while the quitters die."[4] Dr. Joe was a fighter who impacted the world because he was true to his *why*!

The MS Bodybuilding Challenge

Yes, you read that right. David Lyons, Executive Producer and President of Bishop-Lyons Entertainment, has won over thirty international awards for directing, producing, and writing, and has partnered with some of entertainment's top executives and producers. Included in his long list of partners are award winning producer Andrew Bishop, the CEO at Bishop-Lyons; Joel McGee, Executive Producer at Silly Monkey Media and former Animal Planet and Game Show Network director of development; Triage Entertainment, producers of the hit show *Iron Chef*; 3Ball Productions, producers of the major hit *The Biggest Loser*; Pink Sneakers Productions, producers of the hit show *Hogan Knows Best*; Emmy

Award winning director Lane Bishop; and many others. Oh . . . and David has MS. When MS entered the ring, David decided to fight and not run. His field of battle? A bodybuilding stage. His weapon? A desire to fight and an old gym bag!

This is a true David and Goliath story. David looked at the giant, Goliath, grabbed his sling shot out of his bag, and ran after the giant! Likewise, David Lyons faced his own personal giant in the form of MS. Much like King David, David Lyons reached into his bag as well, his well-worn gym bag. He chose to fight this giant with the tools that are familiar to him. David has been working out most of his life and knows the benefits of strengthening the body. But David is taking this one step further. He is taking this very personal battle and bringing it to a public bodybuilding stage. David wants to expose MS and bring awareness to this silent giant that claims countless lives. David wants to inspire others to action and to find a cure for MS. I am humbled to be part of David's team and I can't wait to see David run over to the giant of MS and cut its head off.

Like Dr. Joe, David has chosen to fight and not roll over and play dead. Would Dr. Joe and David be so noble as to take on MS if they had a choice? Of course not. They both loved their lives the way they were, but what started as a personal setback has now become a defining feature in both of their lives. Your *why* may not come in the form of a disabling disease but you still have a *why*. You are here for a reason. Take enough interest in your own life to discover your *why*, so you can touch the world with your unique talents, abilities, and skills that God has entrusted you with.

Chapter 6

Snap Out of It! This Is YOUR life!

Often I meet people who have tremendous regrets. Some have regrets because they did something wrong, but most regret what they didn't do—the business they didn't start, the education they didn't get, the challenge they shied away from. Sometimes you just need to have someone say, "Snap out of it, this is your life, make the best of it!" If it weren't for my friend Lou Buschi and a 48-hour trip cross country in a blizzard, I may not have snapped out of it in time, which would have left me with a heartbreaking regret today.

I was home in New York for Christmas break and my buddy Lou Buschi decided he would drive back to Kansas with us and stay a week or so until school started for him. Lou was an incredible athlete and one of the best high school quarterbacks in the Northeast. We loaded up the car and had a caravan of about five or six cars driving from New York to Kansas. I am pretty sure it was snowing when we left New York, but I know for sure by the time we hit Illinois we were in a full-blown blizzard. It was so bad that we couldn't see the hood of the car. It was about that point that our car went into an uncontrollable spin and we ended up in a ditch on the side of the highway. Amazingly, none of the other cars in our convoy hit us, but when they got to the point where they could see through the driving snow, they realized they were missing a football player, a runner, and a very bad driver. They were one car short and waited until we finally showed up. Somehow we pushed the car out of the ditch and got back on the road. We kept driving so we could catch up with the rest of our group.

When we got to Kansas, track practice started right away. I was just coming off an injury and I was holding back and the only one who knew was big Louie! He could just tell I was coasting. Lou pulled me aside and told me, "Snap out of it,

Johnny! If you keep holding back and fail, you will always regret not giving your all. But if you give it your all and fail, you will have no regrets!" Well, I did stop holding back and started to run better, but that isn't the important thing about this story. Unknown to both Lou and me at that time, I would have a car accident nine months later that almost cost me my life and completely altered the direction of it. The car accident brought an abrupt end to my running career. I thank God that Lou called me to task, standing there in three feet of snow, on my lack of inspiration on the track. I had no idea that it would be my last season. In fact, I had no idea that I would never be able to run again. But thanks to Lou, I snapped out of it right away, took control of my life, and today I am able to look back with no regrets.

※ ❖ ※

"Catch on fire with enthusiasm and people will
come for miles to watch you burn." —John Wesley

All great success follows the fire of enthusiasm and passion. A passion that burns so hot and so deep that if you let the fire dwindle, your life's light goes out. Let it burn and people will come from miles away to watch. Passion is the immeasurable factor. It cannot be tested in school or measured on a chart. It is the inspiration of God in your life that either motivates or frustrates! It burns hotter with every step or it frustrates and sucks the life from you if you deny it!

I would rather look back on my life and say, *"I burned hot but didn't succeed"* versus *"I didn't burn at all."* One thing I know for sure is that the people who get set ablaze for their purpose in life are seldom disappointed. They always find a way because they are living an inspired life. I want no regrets due to lack of action. Whether you come in first or not, it doesn't matter as long as you are in the race and give it your all. If you try something and it doesn't work, you learned what doesn't work. Try something else and if you don't give up, you will succeed. Ordinary people give up. Be EXTRAordinary!

I will never forget a chilly, Saturday morning when I was in tenth grade. I had a track meet, yet the night before I decided to go out with my buddies. My dad thought it best for me to stay home because of the meet but of course this tenth grader knew better. I got home too late, had a lousy night's sleep, dragged myself out of bed in the morning, and traveled into Harlem for the track meet at the armory. Although I went on to win all the events I was competing in, my times reflected much less than my best effort. My dad sat me down and told me that I had insulted the rest of the runners. "The other runners may not have your natural ability, but they stayed in last night and gave it their best shot. They gave

100% and if you can win by only giving 75%, you are insulting the other athletes. Worse than that, it seems you are willing to accept less than your best, which is very disappointing. John, I've seen you get a hand-off in dead last in a relay race where you didn't have a shot at winning. When you got the baton you were set on fire, ran the other runners down, and crossed the finish line in first place. You would not accept anything less than your best effort. If you had lost that race, no one would have thought a thing because you gave it your all. This has nothing to do with winning and losing and everything to do with you being willing to settle for less than you are capable of. You will have to decide what type of person you want to be and what you want to achieve." This was a good lesson and one that I never forgot. My dad has the best work ethic of any man I have ever known and he instilled that into me and my brothers whether we liked it or not.

❧ ❖ ☙

"Give me a stock clerk with a goal and I'll give you a man who will make history. Give me a man with no goals and I'll give you a stock clerk." —J. C. **Penney**

When you know where you are going and why you are going there, nothing will stand in your way! The difference between a janitor and a successful executive is not always what it appears to be. I was a janitor with a goal and a burning desire to succeed as an executive in Manhattan real estate. I interviewed with numerous companies and everyone gave me the same answer. Go back to college and get a degree, then go to Brooklyn, Queens, or the Bronx and get fifteen or twenty years of experience—then and only then will you be ready for Madison Avenue.

These people overlooked a couple of ingredients that turned this janitor into a rising star in Manhattan real estate. This janitor didn't hear no. He thought no was just another way of saying that they didn't have enough information to make an intelligent decision. They overlooked the fact that he would not stop until he was successful. They disregarded his driving desire and passion that would eventually affect all of those around him. Lastly, they never thought he was willing to pay the price it would take to get what he wanted. For the most part, I liked working in the New York City school system. I was not ashamed of where I came from, I knew where I was going, and I would not stop until I got there. These traits don't show up on a college transcript or a resume.

My friend, Barbara Corcoran, was a straight D student who didn't come from an affluent family and had twenty jobs by the time she was twenty three. Hardly a pedigree that leads to success in Manhattan real estate, but she had a burning desire and did whatever it took to succeed. She borrowed $1,000 from her boy-friend and turned that into a five-billion-dollar real estate empire, which she sold in 2001 for $70 million.[1] The Corcoran Group was and is one of the most visible and successful real estate companies in the world. Today, Barbara is an in-demand expert with many media outlets, a best-selling author, and an investor/shark on ABC's reality hit *Shark Tank*. Many would have pegged Barbara as a good candidate to be a stock clerk, but she had different goals. She had a dream that propelled her, along with a lot of hard work, to be incredibly successful. She is exactly what J.C. Penney was talking about. She is making history. If you have been settling for less than God's best for your life, then snap out of it! Be all you were created to be!

You Die before You Quit

Everyone who came from my neighborhood looked up to Al Oerter and I was blessed to have the opportunity to get to know him, train with him, and even go to competitions with him. I learned everything I could about him. How could I not? He was one of my heroes. Al won gold medals in four consecutive Olympics. One of those victories stands out clearly in my mind as an example of living your passions and not letting go of your destiny, no matter what the cost.

Al was seriously injured during the 1964 Olympic Games in Tokyo. Six days before he was to compete, he slipped on a wet concrete discus circle and tore his rib cartilage on his right side—his throwing side—causing internal bleeding and reeling pain. In addition, he had a cervical disc injury that required him to wear a neck harness. The team doctors told him to forget the Olympics and not to throw for several weeks. He refused. "These are the Olympics," he said. "You die before you quit." He competed and won his third Olympic gold medal that year and broke his own Olympic record!

Coach Fraley asked my team once, "How could Al do it, when he was injured so badly? He could barely move, yet he WON!" He then called on me, which he liked doing because I was always ready with a quick or interesting answer. Besides, he loved picking on me Fraley style! Ah! But this one I knew I could answer. Al Oerter was one of my heroes. I'd not only read up on him, I had spent a good bit of time with him during that summer's training sessions and at competitions. I said, with smug confidence, "Because he wanted it so bad that he could taste it and was willing to put up with the pain to win."

I got royally chewed out and publicly denigrated the way only Jim Fraley could do. He then gave us the answer: "It was because he was well trained, you bull pimple!" Bull pimple was a term of endearment from my tender coach—and this was one of his softer terms. He could curse like a sailor, lead like a general, and yet love and care for young men and women more than anyone I have ever known before or since. He was a tough taskmaster and an incredible mentor.

I'd always wondered what it was that drove Al. A few years ago, I contacted Al to ask him what the real answer was to this thirty-year-old question. I asked him, "Was it training, true grit . . . or both?" This was his response to the question I had been carrying with me for thirty years:

"I don't know if it was grit or training. All I can remember when walking out on the field in Tokyo was that I was determined not to cheat myself out of four years of training. I honestly felt there was some capability still inside, regardless of how much pain I was bombarded with. I had trained for 365 days a year, throwing as hard as I possibly could in every throwing session. I just flat out knew myself and could not bag it."

He could not bag it! Al expected more from himself than anyone else would have possibly expected, especially under the circumstances. History now shows that Al Oerter won the discus throw and broke his own Olympic record. All because he couldn't bag it! Al Oerter, a great man and champion.

Al became a highly acclaimed artist and traveled around the country with Art of the Olympians, which consists of fourteen Olympian artists from seven countries. Unfortunately, Al passed away at the age of 71 on October 1, 2007. He was an Olympic legend, a loving husband, father, and a hero to many. Al had a passion for his sport and country and would rather die than quit! What are you so passionate about that you would rather die than quit? That is the "it factor" that will define your life. Don't deny it . . . embrace it!

Coach Fraley was instrumental in guiding Al toward the champion he became and I want to take just one minute to honor a man who touched not only my life but the lives of many. Jim Fraley was not only a coach to many champions, but a champion of the human spirit. I remember seeing him one minute chewing someone out, calling him names, screaming at him, and even occasionally giving him a good swift kick in the butt. And then the next minute, slipping a kid some cash so he could go to the dentist and get his teeth fixed or enough money to go home and feed his family.

On one occasion, one of my teammates got into trouble for doing something illegal. I got called to Fraley's office and he asked me if I was involved. I told him I wasn't, but this wasn't good enough. He told me to bend over with my head facing the wall. He then started literally kicking my butt. My head would bang into the wall, all this while he interrogated me. He was finally satisfied with my answer and let me go back to class. He wasn't just a coach; he got involved with every area of your life so you would grow into the person you were meant to be.

Coach Fraley called Kansas, where he was raised, God's country. And he also had a name for whatever color or creed you were. By today's standards, he would not be allowed to teach. He would be considered rude, politically incorrect, and abusive. Today's educational system would never look at the heart behind the man, just the actions and take them out of context. If it wasn't for Jim Fraley, his strong will, and his ability to never give up on a young boy, I might not be here today. I certainly wouldn't be the man that I am. I know I am speaking for many men today who span several generations when I say, "Thank you, Coach Fraley, for not giving up on me and for taking the time to show me that I was valuable!" With the exception of my mother and father, Coach Fraley had the most dramatic impact on my life. More than anyone I have ever known.

Change Your Reality in an Instant

Many believe that your life is the sum total of how you feel. Too often, people use their emotions as the barometer of the quality of their life. So, if you think that how you feel is your reality, wouldn't you like to know how to change your emotional state in an instant? Imagine this scenario. You walk into a hospital room to visit a friend who was badly burned in an accident. Your emotions are running high and the sorrowful pain for your friend is consuming. You are thinking, What can I do for him to ease his pain? What do I say? What do I do?

Then, as you approach his bed you stub your toe. Not only did you stub it, you broke it. The pain is incredible and all you can do is hop around. The pain is unbearable, overwhelming. In that moment, your pain is more real to you than what your friend is going through. Your physical pain changed your emotional state in an instant, didn't it? This doesn't make you a bad person. It just means that the way we feel, in that moment, is our reality. Your physical body mirrors what you are feeling and what you are feeling mirrors how your physical body is moving.

Psychology and Physiology: The Dynamic Duo

I mentioned earlier that I had a near-fatal car accident. I was a mess. When my youngest brother came in my room and saw me he "lost his lunch." Everyone who visited me made me feel worse just by the look on their faces.

Then it happened. In an instant it all changed.

My friend, Brian McLaughlin, walks into my room, takes one look at me, looks around my room, and sums up the whole situation in an instant. He walks over to my desk and empties out my wallet saying, "You won't be needing any money for a while." Then he starts going through my closet taking my best clothes saying, "You won't be wearing this for a long time."

I started laughing so hard that I was crying from the pain of my broken ribs and breast bone. Brian was hysterical as well. In an instant, it changed. Even though I was in pain, my physiology changed. When you laugh, you breathe differently. You use your face differently and it changes your emotions for the better. In that instant, I knew I would be all right!

We have all experienced this in one way or another. You go to a ball game exhausted and then your favorite team scores. You jump up and cheer, and before you realize it, you are more energetic and upbeat. A couple of years ago, my oldest grandchild Jennifer was born. My son John called me when he and his wife Jocelyn were on their way to the hospital. Well, my wife and I jumped out of bed, got into the car and met them at the hospital along with my oldest son Jim, my daughters Jessica and Jacqueline, and Jocelyn's mom, Nancy. The whole family came out to support Jocelyn and John and to greet baby Jennifer on her first day.

It was very exciting. But the baby was not ready to be born for many more hours. We all waited, fell asleep, chatted with one another, and fell asleep again. It was the middle of the night and we were all tired. John came out to let us know that Jocelyn was getting ready to deliver and then a little while later he came out to tell us through tears of joy that his beautiful baby girl was born!

If anyone was looking at us, they could tell in an instant what we were feeling. We were all elated. Instead of slumping in our chairs or lying on a couch, we were walking around with a bounce in our steps, hugging each other, and no one was tired any more. Your physiology is tied to your emotions! The way you carry yourself, the way that you stand and move, it all has an impact on how you feel emotionally. This is very important. Are you listening? If you want to learn how to change your emotions, you must learn how to direct your physiology. When you learn how to do this, you can change the way you feel in an instant!

Master Your Physiology!

Often we don't feel fulfilled because we simply don't move enough. The more you move, the more you feel alive. In today's society, many people get out of bed and have a cup of coffee to wake themselves up. Then they get into their car to drive to work, go into their office, sit behind a desk all day, and don't move very much.

Being rigid and not moving at all is what happens when you are dead. This rigidity in death is called rigor mortis, and many people are just a step away from rigor mortis. If the quality of your life is dictated by the quality of your emotional state, and if your emotional state is directed by your physiology, can you see why so many people are sad, lethargic, depressed, unmotivated, and unhappy? You must master your physiology! You have to move in a powerful, deliberate way in order to feel alive.

Mr. Mopey

Let's face it . . . we all know a Mr. or Ms. Mopey and, to be honest, we all have our mopey days. We all have or have had a Mr. Mopey in us for a time and he surely knows how to master some part of your physiology already. If you want to get depressed or sad, you already know how to do it. You know how to move and think if you want to arouse the Mr. Mopey in you. In fact, some of us have mastered how to be a Mr. Mopey!

Have you ever had a day when you were totally exhausted? All you wanted to do was sit down and rest? Then all of a sudden you had to do something physically challenging and you woke up and even got energized? I try not to work out in the evenings for this very reason. If I go to the gym or work on creative business stuff too late at night, I can't get to sleep.

Just a few nights ago, my friend Doyle Yager came over to visit. At about 10:00 PM, my wife walked in while Doyle and I are pacing around the kitchen talking about future business opportunities. My wife just walked in, looked at the two of us, smiled, and said, "Okay, neither of you will be able to sleep tonight." She said good night and went to bed. A few hours later, I tried going to sleep but just lay there with my eyes wide open looking at the ceiling. My physiology got engaged as Doyle and I spoke, and that was all she wrote as far as me getting any sleep that night.

No One Is Looking!

If I asked you what a depressed person looked like, what would you say? Shoulders are rounded and maybe hunched, face is slack and looking down, eyes are empty or without spark. The person is breathing shallow and speaking slow. Yes, you know this because many people have mastered this part of their physiology. Remember, the way you move your body controls your attitude and emotions.

Now try this. No one is looking, and if they are, so what! Give it a try. After all, it is your life! Go for it and have some fun with me! Relax and clear your mind. Think about something funny that happened to you recently—repeat a joke to yourself, anything to get you in a great state of mind. Now, stand up and stretch your arms as high as you can into the air. Take several really deep breaths and hold the oxygen in for ten seconds, then exhale forcefully. Repeat a few times. Bounce around a little, pretending you're Muhammad Ali getting ready to face George Foreman. Get yourself physically vibrant and ready for anything. No one is looking so have some fun with this! Get your energy up.

While you're in this powerful state, try to think about something that would ordinarily make you feel down or depressed. Don't change your position—keep breathing deeply, keep bouncing around, hold your head high and shoulders back as if you're ready for anything. If you're speaking to yourself (internally), which we all do, make the volume louder and the tempo quicker.

What you'll find is that it's virtually impossible to get down once you are physiologically up. Your motions can and will direct your emotions. The physical and the mental are all part of the same process because it is all part of you. Therefore, the fastest way to stop feeling a certain way is to radically change your physiology. Move as if you are full of joy, exuberance, passion, and excitement for life . . .whatever works for you. That's the power of your physiology.

You can see this at a concert, at a sporting event, or even at church. If you are sitting there and just watching the event, you get a little bored and listless. But the moment you get up and start cheering, your physical energy begins to pick up. At my church, we do about a half hour of praise and worship music before the pastor begins to speak. When the songs are slow, you can see the energy of the congregation sag a little. But as soon as an up-beat song is playing and everyone begins to move a little, you can see the energy in the whole building begin to build. This is the physiology of success with the help of music. And by the way, music is a great accompaniment to getting yourself up out of a slump. Put some up-beat music on, move yourself in a powerful and energetic way, and before long you will feel powerful and energetic too.

If you're physically fit, using your physiology is even more powerful. Can't you see how this all fits together? We are body, mind, and spirit, and you can't neglect any one of those parts because they are all part of you. Once you know how to direct your physiology in a way that will support you, you'll find that vision, focus, and consistency will help you cross the finish line.

Chapter 7

The Fastest Way to Succeed

*"The way to succeed is to double your
failure rate."* —**Thomas Watson, founder of IBM**

Tom Watson, Jr. was the legendary president of IBM when it was considered one of America's most successful businesses. He encouraged what he called "wild ducks." These are people with unconventional, and sometimes disruptive, ideas. We often we see dead ducks running around corporations. I agree with Mr. Watson. We need more wild ducks running around, shaking things up and challenging the status quo! In stark contrast to Tom Watson, many corporate leaders today are so afraid of failure that they take the God-given creativity away from the people who work in their companies, in turn sucking the creativity right out of them. This turns the work place into a graveyard for *wanna be* successes.

Some people are so afraid of failure that they never try. This is tragic! I was recently involved with a business in the medical field. It was on the verge of failure. They brought me in to help turn the business around using my contacts and promotional skills to bring attention to their business. I did bring attention to the business, but unfortunately the principals were unwilling to change anything they were doing. They didn't want to try anything different or new. In fact, they were unwilling, really, to do anything. They were so afraid of failing that they refused to even try. They kept doing the same things that led them to failure but expected a different outcome. Well, that is the definition of insanity—doing the same things and expecting a different result. In fact, it almost drove me insane.

I was brought in by one of the investors who is a trusted friend and thought I could have a positive impact on this business. He even put his money where his mouth was by infusing more capital into the company in an effort to redirect the company's fate. Before I committed I met with the founders several times; I wanted to make sure they were willing to make some much needed changes. During one of these meetings, I was told by one of the founders, "Look at me as a tool in your toolbox. How will you use me? What will you do?" I was encouraged by this and gave him a detailed plan of action that we would act upon once I was on board. He and his partner agreed and appeared to be very excited about going in a new, positive direction. I was getting constant text messages, phone calls, and emails because they were so anxious to turn the company around. Until it was time to actually do something.

They needed media attention and I knew just who to call. With the help of Ronn Torossian, CEO of 5WPR, we were able to get an incredible start. We were working with everyone from the *Wall Street Journal* and Martha Stewart to Fox News and everything in between. They talked a great talk, but their walk didn't match their talk. They told me that they were looking to get to the next level, but all of their attention was on the failure, with every meeting being started by discussing how much money they were losing. After this downer pep talk, they expected people to come up with creative ideas or to act on the ideas that were given. That is like dowsing the coals with water and expecting the fire to burn hotter. Running a business like this is like trying to drive while looking in the rear-view mirror. You will get some distance but you will crash.

Then it happened! Nothing! No effort, no change, nothing. The travesty is that this business could have been a world class organization. The key point here is don't get frozen by failure. In fact . . . .

Embrace Failure

Ask any athlete about failure and they will give you a completely different answer than if you were asking the average person. Most people look at failure as the ultimate punishment for a bad decision. Athletes look at failure as one of the necessary steps to success and embrace it! It may be hard to believe but one of the best basketball players of all time was actually cut from his high school basketball team. Fortunately, Michael Jordan didn't let failure stop him, in fact he has a very healthy attitude towards failing and attributes his success to his failures. "I have missed more than 9,000 shots in my career. I have lost almost 300 games. On 26 occasions I have been entrusted to take the game winning shot, and I missed. I have failed over and over and over again in my life. And this is why I succeed."[1] In the weight room athletes know that when they bring their muscles to failure while lifting a weight their muscles will respond by growing. When runners fail, it is called hitting the wall. They know that as they hit the wall in training that each subsequent time they run, the wall gets further and further away. Yes, athletes not only know they must fail to get better, they actually deliberately fail, and love it.

In the weight room you have a spotter. A spotter is a training partner who is with you to make sure that when you fail you don't get hurt. An athlete lifting weights knows who his spotter is. What and/or who is your spotter when you fail in various activities in life? *Your attitude toward failure is your first line spotter in life!* When you do fail, keep your head up and keep on keeping on because it will turn around. If you are trying your best and you haven't succeeded yet, don't worry. You will succeed if you don't give up! If you learn, change, and adapt you will succeed.

When I was looking for an agent and publisher for my first book, I called Rick Frishman who is a legend in the publishing industry. He is one of the top publicists, so I figured I'd call him. He was polite enough to return my call and let me know he didn't have time to speak to me. I asked him if he could please just give me 90 seconds of his time and he told me no. I then asked for 60 and then 30 seconds of his time, still to no avail. I then asked for five minutes. "Wait a minute!" he said. "I just said no to 90, 60 and 30 seconds why are you asking for five minutes now?" I simply told him that going down wasn't working, so I was going to start working my way up. He laughed and said, "What do you want, kid?" That started not only the road to my first book, but also a lifelong friendship with one of the nicest men that I know.

The rest of the story is that I was turned down by a few hundred agents and publishers by the time I ever got to Rick. I had nothing to lose unless I quit. Rick introduced me to dozens of agents who all said no. They said I didn't have a large enough platform. Rick was starting to get annoyed because he liked the project and even more than that, I think he liked me. At one point he told me something that I want to sink deep down inside of you.

Rick told me, "You are going to be an incredible success and one of the top authors because you refuse to give up. You stay positive and upbeat in the face of incredible rejection and just keep pushing towards what you want. THAT is the key to legendary success!" Rick was affirming what Robert F. Kennedy once said: "Only those who dare to fail greatly, can ever achieve greatly."

I did get published. Once the publisher was lined up, I decided I wanted Mark Victor Hansen, one of the authors of *Chicken Soup for the Soul*, to write my foreword. I then told Rick I wanted Mark to do my foreword. Rick told me that Mark was so busy that he wouldn't do it. I called Mark's office and they told me that, quite frankly, unless I got face to face with him, he was so busy I may not get a response at all. In my determination I decided to meet Rick Frishman in New York at the Book Expo America. Rick told me that Mark was much too busy and would not do the foreword. As Rick and I were standing there talking, Mark came walking toward us. He looked at me and said, "It must take some discipline to look like that." I said, "Yes sir, it does, and wouldn't you agree that discipline, desire, and the willingness to never give up are the keys to success?" Mark smiled and agreed, and that is when I asked him to do my foreword. I told him I had been trying to get in contact with him for months and even sent him a request on a silver platter. Mark laughed his big, hearty laugh and agreed to do my foreword. I immediately walked over to Rick and told him that Mark would write the foreword to my book. In classic Rick Frishman style, he simply said, "I told ya he would do it, kid!"

❖

"Fail often to succeed sooner." —John M. Rowley

Many people experience the ultimate failure because they are afraid to fail. It sounds confusing but is very simple. Failure is the tuition you pay for success. Many are so afraid to fail that they never, ever really try. Honda Motor Company is a perfect example. Honda entered the U.S. market in 1959 with some low-powered motorcycles. Honda was schooled through massive failure and learned that the little motorcycles popular in Tokyo weren't embraced in the U.S. Honda eventually changed gears and introduced high-powered bikes that became very popular. Soichiro Honda, the founder of Honda, said: *"Many people dream of success. Success can only be achieved through repeated failure and introspection. Success represents the one percent of your work that results from the 99 percent that is called failure."*

I can attest to the 99 to one ratio Mr. Honda was talking about. The more things you try, the greater the odds of failure. When someone tells me they have never failed, I immediately know they also have never really tried. At this point in my life, I am always looking at or trying to create business opportunities of one type or another. In the past, I would hang onto every possible deal as if my life depended on it, but then I came to realize that although I may have 100 things swirling around me, only one will turn into anything. I have learned to give everything my best but try not to get emotionally attached to any one business proposition. I have also learned not to talk to many people about all I am doing because they don't realize that, even though I am putting energy into these things, most will never see the light of day.

Failure is really just a mindset. Successful people look at failure as being part of the success process and others look at failure as a devastating event. Failure is neither an event nor a person. It is just an opportunity which is ending that signals you to put your energies and focus elsewhere. Getting upset just gives the so-called failure more energy than it needs or deserves.

A Valuable Lesson in the Big Easy NOLA Style

Not long ago, I was in New Orleans as a guest at the *Great American Seafood Cook-Off*. What a place! Incredible food! Jazz musicians on every corner, and where I stayed on Bourbon Street every night is Mardi Gras. My friend Ewell Smith runs the event and graciously invited me down and treated me like royalty. We had a motorcade of police to lead us around the city so we could sample the food and atmosphere of some of the best seafood restaurants in the world. The chefs took out all the stops.

Left to right: John Rowley, Dean Max, and Ewell Smith

At the cook-off competition, sixteen incredible chefs from around the country were competing for the coveted crown presented to the king of *The Great American Cook Off*. As the chefs started to cook, it was hectic and very serious. TV crews were swirling around as they cooked their meals. It was very high energy. One thing that stood out was the number of things that got tossed in the trash.

The chefs would be cooking five or six items, but only one of them would go to the judges table. The rest didn't measure up and got tossed. The chefs kept their complete focus directed toward the food that was going to be judged and easily discarded the other food. The rejected food was just part of the process, not a failure to be bemoaned but one of the steps toward winning the crown. This is a great picture of success in any area of your life. Focus on where you are going and what you want to achieve and give little attention to the things that don't work out. Just say, "It didn't work out—NEXT." It is simply part of the process and part of your education.

Education in Failing

Jack Matson is a prize-winning innovator who developed courses in innovative design based on "intelligent fast failure." He was on the faculty at the University of Houston where he created the course Failure 101 for which he won national recognition.[2] This course should be in every university. The first question I ask someone who seems to be afraid to try something in business is "What were your grades in school?" Most of the time they were very good students, but when faced with the real world they became frozen. In school $1 + 2 = 3$ but in the real world it isn't always that simple. The fact is that most of these people are achievers, but school taught them that failure (F) is bad and you must avoid an "F" at all cost. When you avoid failure you avoid the very route that brings you success.

The fact is, many great successes start out as great failures. 3M invented glue that was a failure—it didn't stick. Well, what is the main job of glue? It is to stick, so this would be considered a complete flop . . . wouldn't it? This unstick-able glue is now the basis for the Post-it Note—which has been a huge success. If the glue had been sticky, then they would have had a new glue; but by trying and failing they came up with a whole new product.

Pfizer tested a new drug to relieve high blood pressure. Men in the test group reported that it was a failure with regards to high blood pressure—but it had one beneficial side effect. This failure is called Viagra and became one of the most successful failures in history.

Even if your failure does not lead directly to a success, it is certainly a rung in your ladder of success. Edison's attitude to failure was very healthy. When asked why so many of his experiments failed, he explained that they were not failures. Each time he had discovered a method that did not work.

❦

Think, Believe, Dream, Dare. —**Walt Disney**

For decades I had Walt Disney's quote hanging on my office wall as a reminder to take up his challenge to "Think, Believe, Dream and Dare." Early on, life tried to impress upon me that I wasn't smart enough, educated enough, or good enough to do the things I wanted to achieve. Life can discourage you if you let it. No one is a mistake. Everyone is God's personal handiwork and if he planted a dream in your heart, he will also give you the means to achieve it.

Most people are not being malicious when they try to discourage you from striving for outstanding success. They are just voicing their own fears. To them, failure is the worst thing that can happen. But we know that failure is simply a part of the success process and that not trying is true failure.

Walt Disney certainly marched to his own drummer. I heard that he wouldn't take on a project unless everyone on his board of directors told him *not* to do it! You heard right—*not to do it!* He believed that if everyone agreed with him he wasn't thinking big enough. He also said, *"We did it [referring to Disneyland], in the knowledge that most of the people I talked to thought it would be a financial disaster—closed and forgotten within the first year."* What great dream have you had that others told you was impossible or that you were nuts to even consider? If Walt Disney is any example, the very things you *"aren't"* doing may be your road to greatness. *Think, Believe, Dream and then Dare* to go for it!

Chapter 8

Vision Is More Than Just Opening Your Eyes

Vision

"When one door closes, another opens, but we so often look upon the closed door that we do not see the one that has opened for us." —Alexander Graham Bell

Vision is one of the traits that I see most often in successful people. They focus on where they are going and not on the inevitable road blocks that jump up in front of them. From my observation, the people who are not fulfilling their potential spend too much time and energy focusing on the closed doors or the road blocks in life and end up receiving or creating more of the same.

I don't care if you look at the life of world-class athletes, top business people, or outstanding parents. They have a vision that allows them to overlook the closed doors in life. I think most people look at life as if looking through a pair of ordinary binoculars. They see everything that is in front of them and give equal energy and attention to the entire landscape. High achievers turn the binoculars around and look through the other side. The whole picture changes then. Looking through the other side gives you a much smaller picture but a laser focus and when you have a laser focus, the obstacles don't have the same impact.

I think obstacles are good; in fact, I welcome them. Many times they cause you to re-evaluate your position and come up with a better idea. Recently I was consulting with a business that wanted to hang onto the way things used to be even if it meant going out of business. While working with the website developer, I tried to get everyone to get on board with new ideas. They gave no insight and were quick to shoot down anything we presented. Instead of getting frustrated, I decided to ponder their concerns. I glanced at the roadblocks and looked for a different route. Then something exciting happened! I came up with a few ideas that were 100 times better and much more useful for the company. What was meant to close the door to progress actually accelerated our success. The key is not to let obstacles blind your vision, but to open your eyes to the possibilities!

<hr />

"Good business leaders create a vision, articulate the vision, passionately own the vision and relentlessly drive it to completion."
—Jack Welch, legendary chairman and CEO of General Electric

At a meeting with this same company, I asked one of the founders to describe, in thirty seconds or less, the vision of his business and to explain what made it different from the rest of their competitors. He couldn't do it, so I gave him three minutes to do it, with no luck. I finally told him to take his time and explain the vision and purpose of this company. Thirty minutes later, after much rambling and no specific answer, I finally stopped him and told him that if he doesn't know, how could we possibly expect any of our clients or potential clients to know. This man was a very smart doctor, and yet he couldn't describe the vision for his company which was the culmination of his life's work. Before you judge this doctor, I want you to close this book and write down what the vision for your life is in three sentences or less. This is called an *elevator pitch* and isn't as easy as it seems.

Vision has a very interesting dynamic in life. When I was a kid back in New York, my friend's family owned a junkyard. It was by far the most successful in the area. One day we were over at his junkyard and one of the other kids said, "Man, look at all this junk!" The boy whose family owned the junkyard shot back, "What looks like junk to you, looks like CASH to my Dad!" We all chuckled, but he made a point that day that I never forgot. Everything is relative. One man's garbage is another man's fortune. And the man with vision can turn garbage into cash!

The Power of Focus

What we focus on, is our reality. Focus on whatever is true, whatever is noble, whatever is right, whatever is pure, whatever is lovely, whatever is admirable—if anything is excellent or praiseworthy—think about such things. [1] If we want true, noble, pure, lovely, admirable, excellent, or praiseworthy things in our lives, this is what we must focus on. If you want despair, fear, depression, sorrow, hate, violence, perversion, and poverty, that is what you must focus on. Since we are made in the image of God we have the power to direct our thoughts and, in turn, direct our reality.

Too often people direct their focus on the exact thing they don't want. They are struggling financially, yet constantly talk about their lack. They are overweight and all they think about is food and why they can't lose weight. A big part of success is focusing on what you want, focusing on things that are uplifting and staying away from anything that distracts you from what you want to do. Often I see people in business focusing on their weakness. If you do that, you just have a stronger weakness. Focusing on your weakness will frustrate you and not get you where you want to go.

A Lesson from NASCAR

Now that I live in the South, I have lots of friends who take driving lessons at the Lowe's Motor Speedway in Charlotte, North Carolina. I even have a friend who owns a race car company. My world greatly changed when I moved to the South. When I lived in New York and someone called you a Yankee, they were describing your alliance to the great baseball team. In the South, when they call you a Yankee, it has a totally different meaning. But that is a story for another book. For now, let's get back to my NASCAR lesson.

When you go to race car driving school, one of the first things they teach new drivers is what to focus on when they go into a spin. Most drivers will naturally focus on the very wall they are trying to avoid hitting. If you focus on the wall, you will drive right into it. Our natural inclination is to look at the wall because you want to avoid it. Instead, drivers are trained to focus on something other than the wall because you'll more likely go towards what you are focusing on. They are taught to focus on where they want to go instead of what they are trying to avoid. Isn't that just like life? Focus on the obstacles in life and you end up running into them. Instead, focus on your vision, on your passion, on the fire that God has put in your belly! Focus on your purpose and you will not only get there faster but you will avoid the wall along the way.

Focus on Your Strengths

By focusing on your strengths and not your areas of weakness you not only will excel, but you will love what you are doing. There are only a few things I do well and I focus all my energy on them. I communicate, create, lead, and network. That's it, so this is where I invest my energy. All the successful people I know have an uncanny ability to discover their strengths and to organize their life so that these strengths shine. Greatness lies in focusing on and strengthening your strengths because that is where your God-given gift lies. For many years I thought I had to focus on my weaknesses so I could get better at them and be more well-rounded. What happened, though, is that I just got mediocre in those areas and neglected my areas of strength and so lost out on both ends. I am not saying that you shouldn't try to get better in things you are no good at, but you should spend the majority of your time operating in your gifting. You will enjoy your life much more. When I am operating in the areas I am strong in, the day seems to fly by and I get a lot accomplished. When I am operating outside these areas, I flounder and the day drags.

Desperation Not Inspiration!

When I first entered Manhattan real estate, I couldn't read a financial statement to save my life and I thought that taking corporate minutes meant timing how long the meeting was. My very first day at work, I had a board of directors meeting at 7 Park Avenue and Mr. Harris asked me to take the minutes. The next morning Mark Harris asked me publicly if I did the minutes for 7 Park Avenue and I exuberantly shouted across our Madison Avenue office, "Yes sir, Mr. Harris! It took exactly 128 minutes!" He just laughed and told everyone in the office that I was such a card and asked that I have the minutes on his desk within an hour.

My secretary, Linda, came blasting into my office and slammed the door. "You don't even know what minutes are, do you!" she exclaimed.

"Calm down," I said. "Based on your rosy attitude, I am assuming it isn't timing the meeting, is it?"

"Well no," she said in a huff. "Okay, well let me know what they are and we will get them done." I was trying hard to stay cool, but I was sweating! Just the day before I was in a janitor's closet and today I had my own office on Madison Avenue. I thought I was on the fast track back to Brooklyn and my broom. She explained that the minutes were the corporate records of the meeting and then she threw in that she wasn't going to lose her job because of me. I told her that if she helped me keep my job for the first year she wouldn't regret it. "If I get fired, you would have to work with one of the boring guys in this office who knows how to do everything. I can guarantee working with me will not be boring or dull," I said with an impish smile. Linda was incredible and I wouldn't have made it through my first year without her!

After this experience I realized that I wasn't going to excel on Madison Avenue based on my vast knowledge of the corporate world, so I did what I knew how to do. All of my co-workers were older than me and had many years of corporate experience. Yesterday . . . I was . . . well . . . a janitor. No one thought I would make it through my first week--except me! I was excited and up to the challenge. I knew if I was going to stay on Madison Avenue that I had to be different so I focused on my strengths. My main strength was buildings. I understood the physical, structural, and cosmetic aspect of buildings. I also had a knack with people of all walks. I could speak to my maintenance staff in the building as easily as I could speak to a board member and I was very ambitious. I also expected success—and failure wasn't an option. I focused on my strengths and what tools I had and put no mental energy into what I didn't have. You need to read that again until it sinks in because it is very important.

And boy could I network! I immediately set out to get to know anyone and everyone in the real estate industry who was powerful and influential. I went after the best of the best and many of them are still friends of mine today. I focused on the physical aspect of the buildings which quickly set me apart from the other managers. Sure, they could read a financial statement, but I could make noticeable improvements in a building overnight. Changes that everyone could see!

I decided to go into each of my buildings every Friday at midnight and train my staff. I also put on my work clothes and worked alongside them, which blew their minds. The only time the staff ever saw the managers before this was when the managers were walking around in their $2,000 suits and wearing their Rolex watches, not dressed in work cloths and working hand in hand with them. The unexpected happened after that very first Friday training session. The residents got up Saturday morning to shining brass, glowing marble, and to the sound of the staff buzzing about this new "crazy but cool" manager. I didn't stop there. I also got to know every superintendent in Manhattan and won over all of the board members of the buildings under my control. Within a few short months I was very well known, highly respected, and offered a huge raise to go to another company, which I took. I certainly wasn't the best manager, but I was different, stood out, and excelled because I focused on my strengths. I also knew where I was going . . . and it wasn't back to Brooklyn! Please don't get me wrong. If your job requires a certain skill that you must have, then learn it while continuing to strengthen your unique skills.

Don't Try This at Home

Even though my main focus was always on my areas of strength, I had to be competent in reading financials and doing the minutes for each of my buildings. First thing I did was befriend everyone in the accounting department so they could show me how to interpret the financials. I had to be a little more creative when learning how to do minutes because no one would show me. I was able to get copies of minutes from some of our better Park Avenue and Sutton Place buildings and I used them as a template. A few years later I was running a company and Mr. Harris from my first company asked me if I would hire him part-time. He had retired and was driving his wife nuts sitting at home. I agreed to let him help out and in preparation for a meeting I handed him some minutes to review. While looking at the minutes, he blurted out, "John, these minutes are absolutely superb!" I just chuckled, and pulled out my template file for him to look at. A bit puzzled, he asked why his old minutes were in my file. I told him how I copied them and had been using them as a template for years. He just laughed and continued to prepare. Mr. Harris was always very supportive and was the one who gave me my first shot and he never regretted it.

Many times in life we get exactly what we are expecting to get, don't we? If you are expecting failure and defeat, your subconscious mind will work with you to make sure you aren't disappointed. But if you are expecting success and victory, your subconscious mind will work with you there as well. It will support you and have you doing the things that will bring these positive things into your life. You will get what you focus on. You make the decision where you direct your mind. If you don't someone else will.

Train Wreck

Focus isn't one of those areas I am naturally gifted in. I am a train wreck waiting to happen when it comes to focus. ADD, ADHD, Dyslexia, AIMP! I have been told that I have them all. I really like the ADHD which is ADD for overachievers. My dad never bought into that stuff, he just said I have AIMP, "Ants In My Pants"! My parents did not let me make any excuses and expected me to try my best. I was never tested for dyslexia but my brother has it and I had a very hard time learning to read, so the odds are good I have it as well. Reading was always a huge stumbling block for me, but I stumbled right into the solution after my car accident. I was working as a janitor and sweeping floors while using my walker. In the garbage I saw a broken music stand and a light bulb went off. I was moving so slowly that I decided to attach the music stand to my walker so I could try to read a little. I started off by reading motivational and bodybuilding books. A few days into this, I realized that I was not only starting to read better but I also was retaining much more than I ever had in the past. Maybe moving while I was reading was the key!

As the years went on, I did most things standing up. When I was in New York real estate I attached a very long cord to my phone so I could stand up and talk on the phone. When I had to review financial statements I would often read them while I walked around the office and said hello to everyone. Sometimes I would take what I had to read and walk down Park Avenue reading. At one point, one of the executives in a company I was working for came over to me and said, "Can't you ever sit still? You read walking around. You walk all over the place when you are on the phone. John, you need to learn how to relax a little."

I told him, "I am relaxed." Then I asked him a question, "Have you ever seen the movie *Butch Cassidy and the Sundance Kid* with Paul Newman and Robert Redford?"

He said, "Of course I have, but what does that have to do with this."

I asked him yet another question: "Do you remember when Robert Redford's character was trying to get a job as a payroll guard and the man doing the hiring asked him if he could shoot and then threw a can into the street to test him? He then proceeded to shoot at the can and every shot missed—until Redford asked the man if he could move. Once moving he shot the can all over the place. The boss says, 'What was that?' Robert Redford simply said, 'I shoot better when I am moving.'"

This executive was getting a little annoyed now so I just cut to the chase. "It's simple. I work better when I am moving!" He just laughed and was on his way.

I set up a chest high filing cabinet as my desk and only sat at my "real" desk when someone came into my office for a meeting. Many years later I heard that Michael Dell, the founder of Dell Computers, works at a stand-up desk as well, so I am in pretty good company. If you are distracted easily or have a hard time focusing, experiment with different things until you find out what works for you. Try to design your life so your strengths are emphasized and your areas of weakness are minimized.

Consistency

"In baseball, my theory is to strive for consistency, not to worry about the numbers. If you dwell on statistics, you get

shortsighted; if you aim for consistency, the numbers will be there at the end." —**Tom Seaver, legendary N.Y. Mets pitcher**

We live in a world where quick results are expected and rewarded. Patience is something your dad had. Consistency is "old school" and not relevant in today's fast-paced world. Well, if you haven't noticed, you will see that the quick results we are after have backfired on us. Corporations focus on stock prices instead of quality products. In the old days that would have been called a get-rich-quick scheme that everyone knew would send you back to square one very fast. Just the same, this seems to be what our universities are teaching our up-and-coming business leaders. Today you can't turn on your TV without an infomercial showing you how you can get rich with minimal work. You can make millions of dollars in real estate with no money down, and become financially independent investing in stocks even if you have no money in the bank. Over the years, we have seen the collapse of financial institutions that were tied to poor real estate deals. We have watched the real estate industry crumble and people lose their life savings on Wall Street. Get-rich-quick schemes lead to poverty. You have to focus and work consistently in order to achieve. King Solomon, who was the richest man in history, said, "Those who work their land will have abundant food, but those who chase fantasies will have their fill of poverty."[2] Even though the world is changing at the speed of light, consistency is still essential to fulfilling your vision.

Lasting and meaningful success requires sustained and consistent effort. Period. Anyone can cold-call, market, do the books, exercise, or diet for a day. Anyone can work hard for brief periods of time and most people do. But the key is doing it over a long enough period of time so that you reap lasting results. Sometimes the results will come fast and that is fantastic. But mostly they come over time, from hanging in there and consistently doing the things that produce results.

The same is true for negative results. We don't become obese by eating one candy bar. One drink probably won't turn you into an alcoholic and one lapse in judgment will rarely destroy your life. But consistently eat the wrong things, drink too much alcohol, and make poor choices, and you will most certainly produce catastrophic results. Consistency is a trait we admire in others. You want your accountant, doctor, employees, and business partners to be consistent. We cheer for the sports star who produces consistent results on the field of competition. So why should you expect any less from yourself? Consistency is doing the right things on a regular basis.

One Step at a Time

As a kid, I started reading stories about real people who had to overcome incredible odds in order to be successful. One of these stories still stands out in my mind all these years later as an example of what we can achieve when we consistently apply the principles we've been talking about. This is a story about a six year old boy who had the job of heating his tiny country schoolhouse with his older brother, Floyd. They would come in early so the building would be nice and warm when everybody arrived. One February morning in 1916 the kerosene container was accidentally filled with gasoline. The stove exploded killing Floyd. This little boy was dragged out of the flaming building barely alive and with horrific burns over the lower half of his body.

From his hospital bed, the painfully burned, semi-conscious little boy faintly overheard the doctor telling his mother that her son "would certainly die, which was for the best because the poor little boy would absolutely be a cripple." But this boy wasn't quitting! He made up his mind then and there that he would survive.

Every day his mother would massage his little lifeless legs, but there was no feeling, no control, no nothing. Yet his determination to walk was as strong as ever. When he wasn't in bed, he was in a wheelchair. One sunny day, his mother wheeled him out into the yard to get some fresh air, but this day was different. Instead of sitting there, he threw himself from the chair. He pulled himself across the grass, dragging his lifeless legs behind him. He worked his way to the white picket fence and with incredible pain pulled himself up holding onto the fence. Then he dragged himself along the fence, determined that he would walk again. Through his mother's daily massaging of his legs, his unwavering persistence, and his iron will, he did develop the ability to stand up, then to walk with assistance, then to walk by himself—and then to run. And man, did he run. This little boy, who was told he would never walk again, made the track team at Kansas State. Then one day in Madison Square Garden this young man—who was not expected to survive, who would absolutely never walk, who could never ever dream of running—this determined young man, Glenn Cunningham, ran the world's fastest mile!

One of the other runners of his day, Dr. Jack A. Lovelock, later said this about Cunningham: "Consistency in running, consistency in rearing his children, consistency in discipline, consistency in values, these were all Cunningham's hallmark." This story exemplifies exactly what we are talking about. Consistently take deliberate action toward a desired goal and the world will not deny you! In fact, the world will somehow help!

Consistency Just Plain Works

Consistency is one of the most overlooked attributes of successful people and the easiest to acquire. Not long ago Lou and Carla Ferrigno showed up at one of the seminars that I was doing for the Yagers' Amway group in Los Angeles. At the end of my talk, I asked Lou to come on stage and share some of his secrets to success. What he said was simple but powerful. He said, "Consistency and discipline are the key." I know Lou and he is one of the most consistent people I know in every area of his life, which is why he can have it all: an incredible wife and family, thriving career and business interest, and one of the best bodybuilders ever to walk on this earth. I am proud to call him a good and trusted friend.

Consistency works on all fronts. Want to get in shape? Plan your workouts and meals and you will get in shape. Want to succeed in business? Find out the traits you need to succeed and apply them daily and you will succeed. Want to write a book? Consistency is what works here too. Many authors would panic if they got the accelerated deadline that was attached to the contract of this book, but the advice I got from Barbara Corcoran really helped. She told me to schedule how much I would need to get done each day and stick to it. Well for this book, 90,000 words divided by eight weeks is 11,250 words a week. If I work six days a week, that is 1,875 words a day. At 1,875 words a day I was half finished by the time we signed the contract because it took thirty days to go through the process. Once we signed, we still had sixty days, but I stuck to my schedule so I would be done thirty days early. I wanted to still have thirty days for editing, review, and final changes. I made a plan and stuck to it—it's as simple as that.

Raw Knuckles

In 1996, I was out walking my dog and noticed a young man rapidly approaching me. To say he walked with a purpose was an understatement. He was here for a reason and you could see it with every stride he took and in his eyes when he finally got to me. Whatever he was going after he would get, you could just tell. His name was Gary Gruber and he had just graduated from the New York Chiropractic School. Dr. Gruber was on my block to knock on doors so he could introduce himself to the community. A doctor knocking on doors? Now that got my attention! We quickly engaged in a conversation and found out we were both recent transplants from New York to North Carolina. He and his wife Kristin decided they would move to North Carolina to grow their practice. This was not unusual. What was unusual was his attitude. Dr. Gruber, it seemed, would do whatever it took to fulfill his dream. He didn't have an "I'll hang up my license and open the doors and they will come" mentality.

When Dr. Gruber was not with patients or doing the paperwork necessary for growing practice, you could find him going door to door, knocking with a big smile on his face as he let everyone know there was a new doctor in town. He knew that if he did the right things consistently he would get the desired outcome, which was to grow his practice. Knowing and expecting that *all* businesses take time to get off the ground, he added a second job working in a grocery store to ease the financial burden. While he was doing this, Kristin, also a chiropractor, worked in their practice during the day and worked the front desk of a local hotel by night. They had a plan, knuckled down while executing it, and are reaping the rewards today.

Today, Dr. Gruber not only has an incredible thriving practice, he sets his hours to benefit his life and Kristin is able to stay home with their two beautiful daughters. They are active members of their church and community.

One More Round!

As you saw with Glenn Cunningham, a vision is fueled by energy, kept alive through focus, and given life through consistency. In order to be successful in any endeavor, you need to overcome much discouragement, frustration, and failure. These traits can turn someone who is ordinary into someone who is EXTRAordinary. In Glenn's case they made a cripple into a world record holder.

In the movie *Cinderella Man*, Russell Crowe plays a down-and-out boxer who makes a dramatic comeback. The backdrop to this movie is the Great Depression and all the hardship and travesty that came with it. Previous to the Great Depression, Crowe's character, Jimmy Braddock, was a champion boxer who had lost his way. Once the Great Depression hit, Braddock was only offered a few fights and didn't do well in them. He made what little income he had from working on the loading docks. Braddock never gave up and was offered a one fight deal that led to his comeback. After his comeback, a reporter asked him, "You have lost before. What's the difference this time, Jimmy?" Jimmy Braddock answered, "I know what I'm fighting for." The reporter followed up with, "And what's that?" Jimmy came back with what I feel is the most memorable and inspiring line in the whole movie. He simply said, "Milk." That says it all.

He now knew why he was fighting; he had a vision. Fighting to feed his kids gave him the will to be consistent. He was able to look defeat straight in the face and say, "Okay, one more round . . . I'm not done yet!" He was able to overcome failure because he had the passion to fulfill his vision of putting milk on the table. This is the story of America! A passion for a worthy vision that will let nothing stand in the way. "Okay, let's go one more round" was the unspoken mantra for generations of Americans and has made America the greatest country in the world. Live your passions so you can live your dreams. Live an EXTRAordinary life and let God's vision for your life shine through and burn white hot! That will give you the determination to say, "One more round, I'm not done yet." Then you get up, dust yourself off, and become the person you are destined to be!

Chapter 9

The Lifestyle Restoration Cycle

Your Why

Know your why and the what and how
will take care of itself. —John M. Rowley

Your "why" in life is your purpose in life. This is the time to put in a little work and define why you want to do what you are setting out to do. Once you know your why, it will be so much more powerful as you go about implementing the principles in this section. This section is on "Unleashing the MINDset of Success!" Knowing why you want to achieve certain goals will give your goals life and set your life ablaze.

Step 1

Write down "why" you are passionate about where you are going. Next to each "why" on your list, write a brief paragraph defining why you are committed to achieving the result you are after. "Why" is very powerful. (E.g., I want to start a new business and in order to do that I must put together a business plan.)

1 _____

_____

2 _____

_____

3 _____

4 _____

5 _____

Step 2:
This is where we put the plan together.

Take the above list and put together an action list of things you would need to do to achieve them in your life. This is where you formulate your plan. It is easier to put a plan together once you know why you are doing it.

1 _____

2 _____

3 _____

4 _____

5 _____

Step 3.
Master your habits or they WILL master you!
—John M. Rowley

For each step in your plan, write down one or more habits you will need to develop and the disempowering habits you will need to get rid of in order to support your ultimate outcome. Imagine if you exchanged six limiting habits for six empowering habits every year. In five years, that would be 30 empowering habits that you do without effort and 30 disempowering habits that don't hinder you any longer. Do you think your life would be different?

List of Disempowering Habits

1 _____

2 _____

3 _____

4 _____

5 _____

List of New Empowering Habits

1 _____

2 _____

3 _____

4 _____

5 _____

List Which New Empowering Habit Will Replace The Old Disempowering Habit

(For example: replace bringing work home with spending more time with my family)

1 _____

2 _____

3 _____

4 _____

5 _____

Congratulations! You just defined your first lifestyle restoration cycle! You found your why. Then you put a plan together. You identified disempowering habits that you are going to replace with empowering habits on a regular basis so they become part of your lifestyle, hence closing the loop on The Lifestyle Restoration Cycle.

Now go to http://habitfoundry.com to supercharge your habits. We will check in with you daily by email to see how you did the day before. You can either "Go solo" or "Join a Group" of people who are working on a similar goal as you.

Part III

FLEX
YOUR SPIRITUAL
MUSCLES

Chapter 10

Do You Know Who You Are?

Yeah, you! I'm talkin' to you! Do you really know who you are? Not what you were told growing up, not what your job description describes you as, and certainly not the way your driver's license picture portrays you. The real you!!

No. You're not that guy who couldn't get an A in class if you paid for it. You're not that girl that couldn't get a date if you stood on your head all day long. You are certainly not the drug addict, alcoholic, pervert, thief, unfit mom, abusive dad, failure in business, college dropout, ineffective business executive, or social retard you have been told you are all your life. Oh, and for the narcissist in you, you aren't as great as you think you are, either! No, those are all lies from the pit of hell that have kept you from receiving what is rightfully yours and from being who God destined you to be.

Who Do You Think You Are?

When I got into trouble growing up, which happened more times than either my mom or I would like to recall, my mom would get me alone and start the lecture off with, "John Rowley! Who do you think you are?!?!" I would ordinarily come back with something snappy which I thought would be funny and, depending on my mom's mood, she would either laugh or get madder. That was normally dependent on the kind of trouble I was in. Mom had a great question because we will usually act in alignment with "who we think we are."

I was told by teachers from first through eighth grade that I was dumb, couldn't learn, would never be able to read, and was not high school material. What the heck is *that*? "Not high school material." My parents were at home trying to get me to do better in school, but I was tragically defeated before I ever got home. Why try when the authorities, the experts in the field, are telling you that you are damaged goods? I felt frustrated, stupid, and angry that the world would never be mine. After all, what kind of success could I achieve if I could never even master high school?

Then there was high school. I became an accomplished athlete and it was there that the teachers, realizing that I just learned a little different from the other kids, encouraged me. It didn't happen right away, but every year I got better. By eleventh grade, my grades were good enough for me to know that I could get into a good college. I felt more confident and a little part of me wanted to shove my high school diploma, along with my college acceptance letters, in the face of the teacher who said I wasn't high school material.

It was funny, in a not-so-funny way. When I was in college, I was taking a calculus course and wasn't doing well. The teacher liked me and offered to tutor me. During the very first tutoring lesson, she told me, "Your problem isn't with calculus—you have that down. Your issue is with the basic math skills that you should have learned in grammar school." As a college student, I had to go back and learn what I should have been taught as a young child. I see now, looking back, that the teachers projected defeat onto me because they were inept at helping me learn the material they were supposed to teach me, bringing my head down so theirs felt a little higher. I'd been putting in more effort so I could learn not only the elementary math but calculus as well; I could see that effort brought success which would lead me places. I was no longer defeated. My point is that we will always act in accordance with who we think we are. In grammar school I was told I could never learn and I began to believe it. I thought, "Why bother?" But then in high school my outlook and my mind changed. At first I didn't know who I was, and then I learned.

You were created to be the child of a king! Not just a king that has one of the kingdoms here on earth, but the King of kings. The king that created every kingdom on earth. The king that created every king. The king that created the very air you breathe and the ground you walk on. The creator of the universe is your dad and you are his kid. Yes, that is right, you are royalty. NOW START ACTING LIKE IT!

Maybe You Need Princess or Prince Lessons!

Have you ever seen the movie *The Princess Diaries*? It's about Mia, a socially awkward fifteen-year-old girl (played by Anne Hathaway) who suddenly discovers that she is the princess of a small European country. She is put in the position where she must choose between continuing the life of a San Francisco teen or stepping up to the throne that is rightfully hers. While Mia contemplates her future, her grandmother (played by Julie Andrews) insists on turning her from a social misfit to a lady fit for the throne, by making her take "princess lessons."

Is this you? Yes, it is and it is me as well. We have to realize that we are the rightful heirs to the throne. We too need princess and prince lessons and often must be forced into it just like Mia. Mia had to unlearn some of the things that teenagers come to do naturally and learn the proper behaviors of a princess. We have to unlearn what we were told about ourselves and learn the truth about who we are as heirs to the throne. The world tells us one thing and God tells us quite another.

Who Are You? Really?

Who do you want to believe? The choice is yours! Do you want to believe a loving God, the God who created you and everything around you and who wants the best for you? Or do you prefer to listen to the lies that are sent to destroy you? Jesus said that "The thief [Satan] comes only to steal and kill and destroy; I have come that they may have life, and have it to the full."[1] Even without looking at this from a spiritual or religious perspective, which viewpoint is better for you? Which is going to empower you more? Let's face it. Some things are going to push you higher and higher, but others will stop you way short of your life's purpose!

You are here for a purpose.

Like Mia, you are here for a purpose and God wants to help you fulfill that purpose. No one is here by mistake. We all have our unique way of serving the world. Even princesses and princes serve. Each of us has our own unique talents, abilities, and skills, and there is no one else like any one of us. There is no one like *you*! It is God himself who has made us what we are and given us new lives through Christ Jesus; and long ages ago He planned that we should spend these lives in helping others.[2] I know this is in stark contrast to self-help books that show you how to "get" all you can out of life. When you live a life focused on getting, often you live a life that leaves you feeling empty because you were created to add value to this world, not just use up its resources. You were created to serve and God has prepared your service in advance. God told Jeremiah, *"Before I made you in your mother's womb, I chose you. Before you were born, I set you apart for a special work . . . ."*[3]

But I don't know what my purpose is or how to serve.

The answer is actually very simple. Anytime you use your God-given talents, abilities, or skills to help someone, you are fulfilling your calling. You want to find your area of service? Then take a good accounting not only of your talents, abilities, and skills but also of your passions. I believe that your passions (as long as they are godly) are the key that unlocks the door to your service. Seldom are we passionate about an area in which we are ungifted. Your area of service doesn't need to be something gigantic like moving to a foreign country or taking on worldwide poverty. Many times it is just things that seem simple to you—but gigantic to others.

Then where do I serve?

Your service is in high demand. Just ask any local church if it has any unmet needs. What you take for granted, others will see as a gift from God. In fact, your area of service is a gift from God and you are the gift wrapping. Don't negate some of your giftings. If you are good with cars, people in church need your help. If you enjoy entertaining, you may host a small group in your home or assist with various events going on in your church. If you have a burden for children, serve in the children's church the way my wife Cathy and my daughters Jessica and Jacqueline do.

Now don't serve just for the sake of serving because it may backfire on you. I've worked in the children's church, but that wasn't my calling. I have worked with various men's and businessmen's groups, loved it, and felt I brought value to the groups. I served on the Mission's Council at one time because I am passionate about Christ impacting the lives of others the way he has impacted mine, but—and this is a big but—I was not called to sit on a board of directors and that became clear right away. I hated going to the meetings and everything that came with serving in this capacity. I felt I brought very little value. I've learned the hard way that it is just as godly to say "no" to an area of service as "yes," and the people who sat on that Mission's Council board with me would gladly give this a big amen.

Some people have church service backwards. I seldom hear someone say, "I am looking for a church in which I can best serve." Most of the time I hear, "I am looking for a church that will meet the needs of my family and me. A place where we will be blessed." You were created to serve and there is no area of service that is too small or insignificant. Be a blessing to others in the ways God designed you to be and you will be fulfilled. I challenge you to find an area of service in your local church that you are passionate about, regardless of how big or how small, and start serving. Then watch how your life is enhanced by serving others with your God-given gifts—how you all of a sudden come alive!

Where Do You Get Your Identity?

Growing up on 10th Avenue was the combination of a Norman Rockwell picture and a Little Rascals adventure. Mostly mischievous adventure, followed by a trip to the ice-cream parlor with our parents, where we all acted like little angels, and then back to terrorize the neighborhood again.

Growing up, I was a lousy student, lousy athlete—well, basically just plain lousy at everything—with a steady stream of reminders of this fact. I was the last to get picked for teams in most sports, unless it involved running or being fearless. In school, I was the first one the teachers picked on because, as they so lovingly put it, I wasn't as bright as the other children. I came to hate the outside world. A world that took no prisoners and would hurt anything that was weak. I especially hated it when it was cloaked in religion. This distaste is with me to this very day.

Fortunately, on 10th Avenue it was different. We split up sides when we played sports and tried to make it as fair as possible. 10th Avenue was my safe haven, where I was protected from the outside world. If anyone outside of 10th Avenue started with any one of us, for any reason, they had to deal with the whole block. We protected our own with the fearlessness of a mama lion protecting her cubs. Still, 10th Avenue lived by rules—jungle rules. In jungle rules, the strong thrived and the weak got eaten alive. But it was our jungle, our rules, and our friends.

Now I wasn't free from being "the kid with two left hands," even on the block. One day, we were playing stickball. I couldn't have been more than five or six at the time. We determined the playing field based on what cars were in the street. On this particular day, the older kids decided we would run the bases in reverse to accommodate the cars that were in our way. The tension was mounting as I was waiting for my turn at bat. If I could just catch a piece of that ball, I had a shot because I was so fast that I could get to first base—but that was a big *if*. My hand-eye coordination was awful and I was very nervous stepping up to bat on that warm, sunny day. I would much rather have sat on the curb, pop the tar blisters on the street, and simply watch the game instead of being in it; but on "the block" that was not an option. Everyone was a player. Everyone was a contender.

Up to bat I stepped with all the confidence of a blind marksman. The pitcher wound up and that was all I saw before they said, "Strike one, Johnny!" The pitcher quickly wound up again, but this time I caught a piece of it and off running I went until I came to a sudden, painful stop. "What the heck are you doing running the bases backwards? You just ruined the whole game for us!" Joey yells at me. He decided to redirect my base running by punching me square in the stomach while I was running. I couldn't breathe or catch my breath at all. I thought I was going to die. If this ever was to happen off the block and someone else hit me like that, Joey not only would have beaten them up, but he would have made me beat them up once he was finished with them. Sounds odd, but it worked. Like I said, it was our jungle!

Being on the block was my sanctuary from the torment of the outside world. I could easily deal with the occasional punch in the stomach because I knew we all cared for and protected one another. Most of the time, if you messed up there was a guiding hand there to teach you the right way to do things and the teaching wasn't accompanied by condemnation or insults. It didn't matter if it was learning how to tie your shoes, sitting on the curb, or learning to ride your bike. The whole block was there to cheer you on and encourage you!

One year, I got a brand new bicycle for Christmas and I wanted my dad to teach me how to ride. When we went out to practice, my dad ran behind me holding onto the seat to make sure I didn't fall and the whole block emptied out to watch. Then my dad gave me a good lesson in sharing. He went on to teach a lot of the kids how to ride on my new bike. I didn't want the bike getting scratched since I had just gotten it. I even told my dad that and he just leaned over and whispered a simple question in my ear: "If it was one of their bikes would you want them to share?" My answer was a begrudging, "Yes, Dad." Dad just smiled and said, "Let's have some fun with all the kids learning how to ride today."

Looking back as an adult, the one who gave the most that day was my dad. He was working three jobs and going to college at night, and this was one of his very few days off; but yet he was willing to sacrifice so all the kids could learn how to ride that day. That is a good picture of our Father in heaven. He runs behind you making sure you don't fall over and gives much while asking for little, if anything, in return.

For a good part of my life, the block was a plumb line in my life. I could always go back and be reminded who I was. Who I *am*. In fact, on a recent trip to New York to do a radio and TV appearance, my wife and I went back to the block to look around. The houses were smaller and much closer together than I remembered.

But my vivid childhood memories came rushing back. I could hear the block parties where we used to see who could hold their hand in the ice water longer. I could see Joey outrunning everyone and Beverly throwing a football better than Joe Namath. Anthony poised, looking like Pistol Pete with a basketball and, of course, Billy's legendary fights. There were stories and jokes, going down to the "yard" with Chrissy and Nicky. I remember sneaking over the fence to get into trouble with Paul. And who could ever forget the sump fence? The police would close it up and before the patrol car ever left the block someone was out there with the bolt cutters re-opening our shortcut to the park again. Oh, memories are great—though sometimes a bit faulty. I am not 100% sure Bev was as good as Namath, but I bet she was. Joey was fast and Anthony could out dribble anyone in the NBA. I would bet money on it. Well, maybe a small amount of money.

As a kid, I got my identity from the block. As a young man, I got it from my athletic ability and then from my business accomplishments. Now, as a man, I get my identity from God and his word. I find this to be much more reliable than all the rest. Plus, God has an uncanny way of taking your past mistakes and turning your life into a restored work of art.

The Power to Restore Your Life

Once you come to the realization of not only who you are but *whose* you are, you will become keenly aware that the seed of greatness is planted inside you. Sometimes very deep inside, but it is there. The cares of this world, our upbringing, and our experiences all have a tendency to push that seed down so far that you forget it is even there.

For many people dreams, ambitions, and life's destiny or calling are things from their childhood—things kids think about but which now as adults they don't have time for. After all, you have to grow up sometime. These things are buried so deep that one would have an easier time finding that old, water-stained Polaroid from that wonderful vacation taken the summer between eighth and ninth grade. It is there somewhere, but is it really worth the effort to go find it? And even if you did find it, it might be so faded that you wouldn't even recognize it.

Several years ago my wife Cathy gave me a framed photograph of Arnold Schwarzenegger. Arnold was probably twenty years old. It was pristine and in a beautiful frame. As I unwrapped it my eyes filled with tears. "Wait, this is it! This is the picture we found in the basement of the gym, isn't it?" Cathy, knowing she found the perfect gift, gave me a resounding, "Yes!" I found this picture in an old box in the boiler room of the gym I had bought in Brooklyn. I kept it and some of the other pictures, but this was my favorite. I remembered that the picture was torn right through Arnold's face and in many other areas. It was wrinkled to the point that the photo was unusable and water stains had destroyed what was left. Cathy enlisted the help of a photo restoration company that was able to bring it back to its original splendor. She had two copies made, one for me and one we gave to Arnold. Somehow, I think this restored photo of a great champion means more to me than it does to him. Arnold has thousands of old photos; but this one is my treasure found in a musty old Brooklyn boiler room, brought back to life.

If you are looking at your dreams and even your life's calling as a musty old photo that is destroyed beyond recognition, think again. Just like that photo of Arnold, God can take your life and completely restore it. In fact, God specializes in taking the water stains, cracks, rips, and tears of our lives and transforming them into a majestic masterpiece, useable by and for the master. *"And I will restore to you the years that the swarming locust has eaten."*[4]

We serve a God of restoration! You may have had some disappointments or some terrible things that have happened in your life. Much like the picture of Arnold, the water stains and tears are so visible that it is hard to see what is really there. Focusing on this is the fastest way to living a defeated life. Instead, choose to focus on God's promises. He wants to restore your health, joy, peace, and finances. You have to see God's vision for your life. Be bold, be different, get excited about what lies ahead, and start thinking and speaking faith-filled words over your life. Start today! Decide to focus on a bright future instead of a dim past. Today is the day that you draw a line in the sand and say, "I am a child of the most high God, and I refuse to live a negative and defeated life. This is a new day. This is the day that the Lord has made and I'm taking back what belongs to me!" This "restoration mentality" will not only transform your life, it will restore it to the original splendor that God intended. Isn't that great news!

The Good News

The meaning of the word "gospel" is "good news," therefore the gospel of Christ is the good news of Christ. The good news is that God, who created the universe, sent his son, Jesus, to live as a man, die as a man, and be raised from the dead by the power of God so that you and I could be set free from the power of sin.

Jesus is 100% man and 100% God. As a man, he knows what it means to be tired, tempted, beaten down, discouraged, and separated from God the Father.

As a loving God, he came to earth so we could be set free from sin and have His power, authority, and resources working in our lives. Sounds cool so far, doesn't it?

Or maybe it doesn't. Maybe like me, you had years of religion blocking you from God's truth. I was searching in all the wrong places because I wanted nothing to do with man's religion. I didn't want what I saw, didn't want what they had, and I certainly didn't want to be like anyone I knew who was religious! Religion was the very thing blocking me from the unmerited favor of God. Kind of ironic, isn't it? Something meant to lead me to God actually pushed me away.

Maybe you are the same way. Or maybe it is something else. Either way this section is not going to be a religious rant. No. It is just going to cover a few things that have helped completely transform my life and the lives of many people whom I know. This is a section on a relationship, not a religion. In fact, I started my search with a polar bear in Central Park.

The Central Park Polar Bear

When I was in Manhattan real estate, I was searching for something. I couldn't even put my finger on it. Just a few short years earlier I was a janitor in a high school in Brooklyn. While the other guys leafed through girly magazines, I read self-help books. As I worked, I listened to self-help tapes. This was long before CDs. I used the tools that I gained—the thousands of hours of study and implementation of these skills—to open businesses and to propel myself into the world of Manhattan real estate. To everyone's surprise and to my delight, I not only survived but excelled.

Yes, many of the concepts I learned worked, but once I started to succeed at a very high level, I was left feeling empty. As I started to look around me, I noticed that my role models didn't really have what I wanted. Yes, they held esteemed positions in the real estate community and a great many of them were Manhattan socialites traveling in high society circles, but many were miserable. Broken marriages, destroyed relationships, alcoholism, drug addiction, and criminal activity. I found out very quickly that people have the same challenges regardless of their bank balance.

At the high school in Brooklyn where I worked, I saw kids from broken homes who got addicted to drugs; a great many were destined to live defeated lives if they didn't change something. Later, on Madison Avenue I saw men and women whose kids lived in broken homes. Some of these kids, along with their parents, also got addicted, but to even more expensive and sophisticated drugs;

they too lived defeated lives. The only difference between the two groups was that one walked to their troubles and the other took limousines.

For the longest time I couldn't understand why these people who seemed to have everything lived less than glorious lives. So I entered on a mission to find what was missing. Yes, I was becoming successful in business, but I was not fulfilled. What was missing? One day I was sitting in my Madison Avenue office, pondering true success and was reminded of something my dad told me years earlier. I came home from a track meet, arms overflowing with medals I won that day. I walked into the kitchen, plopped my medals on the kitchen counter, grabbed something to drink, and started heading for the back door, running shoes and stop watch in hand. My dad, with a knowing look on his face, asked me where I was going. I told him I was heading over to the track to train for a while, that I had some big meets coming up. He just smiled and said something to me that has stayed with me my whole life—something profound but also something I struggle to implement to this very day. He simply said, "You will never be happy. Every time you reach a goal you are immediately going after tomorrow's goal and forgetting today's victory!"

With this in mind, I went to the office next to mine to glean some wisdom from an older man who seemed peaceful in the midst of the craziness of Manhattan real estate. I asked him how he handled it all. He told me that he goes down to the Central Park Zoo and sits with the big white polar bear for a while and that helps center him. When I left his office, his secretary, who overheard our conversation, whispered to me with a slight chuckle that he also stops by the bar on the way to and from the polar bear for a couple of cocktails. I was interested in trying the polar bear technique, but wanted to stay away from the cocktails.

Up to this point, I tried everything in the self-help world. For months I went to Saint Patrick's Cathedral on Fifth Avenue which was just a few blocks from my office. I went to some other churches in the area as well. Also, back then, L. Ron Hubbard's book *Dianetics* was very popular and I would wander over to a Scientology office not far from where I worked. I never went in but would peer through the window. As you can see, the search was on and the polar bear seemed like the most logical solution, based on what I had seen.

Every day for quite a while, I would go to the gym, eat lunch, and then on the way back to my office I would sit with the polar bear. Did the bear bring any significance to my life or provide me with answers? Sadly, no. But we did have a kindred spirit of sorts. He was in his prison against his will and I was in my own self-imposed prison—and neither one of us knew how to get out. The very success I was seeking was just amplifying my uneasy spirit. I couldn't help but think that there should be more in life. Dad was right—I needed to enjoy the victories, but how? I thank God that I had the gym in my life. That has been one constant my whole life and it gave me a healthy focus. But it didn't fill this void in me. I once heard someone say that we are all created with a void, a donut with a hole in the middle, so to speak, and the only way to fill that void or hole is with Jesus. That is exactly what my experience has born.

Maybe, just maybe you can relate to my struggle for life's significance. The biggest struggle that I had was getting past my head and letting God first work on my heart. This is an ongoing struggle for me even to this day. So keep in mind as you read that I am just sharing part of my journey with you, and that I am nowhere near finished. There are still races to be won, mountains to be conquered, and people to get to know and serve.

Forget What You Have Heard

For just a few minutes forget what you have heard about Jesus, church, the Bible, religion, and anything else pertaining to faith. Human beings have a wonderful way of perverting and muddying the waters with regards to faith in Christ. Somehow we can take the free gift that God gave us and distort it so no one wants to listen to it. Jesus is not a religion, a building, a denomination, a not-for-profit, a slot machine, or anything else man has made him out to be. He will not conform to what we want him to be, but he will help us be transformed by the power of the Holy Spirit into what he created us to be. Now isn't that exciting? The creator stepping in to help the creation, who just happens to be the apple of his eye.

Does God Really Care about Me?

It is easy for us to think that the creator of the universe doesn't really know us or even care about us, much less love us. I love my wife, kids, and grandkids, but I have never taken the time to count the number of hairs on their heads, yet the Bible tells us that God even numbers the hairs on our heads.[5] No detail in your life is too small or unimportant for God. He takes the time and effort to know you . . . yes, you! So yes, you are important to the creator of the universe. He knows exactly who you are and loves and accepts you, warts and all. When this starts to sink in, it will change your life.

When it comes to your hopes, desires, and dreams, no detail is too small for God to take an interest in. If it is important to you, it is important to him. If you go to him in prayer about a small decision you need to make, he isn't going to say,

"Are you kidding me! Here I am running the universe and you come to me with that!! Handle this one on your own and come back to me with something worthy of my efforts." No, he isn't like some of your fair-weather friends who can't wait to poke fun at you and pull you down. No, he wants to be there for you to help you climb higher and higher and to achieve all he has put in you. On our own, the best we can do is what the self-help industry strives for, which is behavior modification. Only with God can you experience true restoration, which results in a life of victory.

The unmerited, unearned favor of God in your life will help you overcome every weakness, shortcoming, and imperfection in your life. If you are struggling in any area, such as financial lack, addiction, fear, sickness, or broken relationships, God's favor will prosper, free, protect, heal, and restore you to wholeness all by the goodness of God. This isn't something you can earn, buy, or strive for. It certainly isn't something you deserve. This isn't about self-effort but about God's goodness.

Chapter 11

The Secret to Lasting Success

I don't know about you, but I have been searching my whole life for the key that unlocks the door to success. I was like Sherlock Holmes searching every book I could get my hands on for the clues to success. I went to every seminar and I interviewed and modeled myself after some of the most successful people in the world. And yes, I got results, but not lasting results and never found what I was looking for.

I was and am a master goal setter. For over thirty years I have been taking the week between Christmas and New Years to clearly define my goals. I separated them into long-term, mid-term, and short-term goals. I wrote them in the first person, reviewed them on a regular basis, and achieved the goals I set out to achieve. Year after year I was more "successful" and year after year, I was more miserable. I was chasing what I thought was success, but I was actually very empty. Part of my problem was that I could never successfully define success. The reason I did this whole goal-setting process was because, though less than 3% of Americans actually set goals, they are among the wealthiest people in the nation—and that is what I wanted! But is that true success?

Then I read about Joseph and how he became a success in Egypt.[1] Now this made absolutely no sense at all to me. It was completely contrary to everything I had ever learned. This guy had nothing going for him, so how was he a success? Joseph was beaten up by his brothers, thrown into a pit, and then sold into a lifetime of slavery. He had no bank account, no holdings, no influence. In fact, his brothers even ripped the clothes from his back. He had nothing, yet Joseph's master, Potiphar, just knew something was different about this kid. Couldn't explain it, just kind of knew, you know? And he was right. Everything he gave Joseph to do was successful.

You need to understand. Potiphar didn't believe in God. He worshiped idols. Potiphar wasn't looking at Joseph's spiritual blessings. No, he was witnessing something tangible, something that would make sense to a businessman. The Bible says, "Now his master saw that the LORD was with him and how the LORD caused all that he did to prosper in his hand."[2] The things Joseph did must have been so spectacular that there was no way a man could do it on his own. Maybe the cattle that Joseph tended to were healthier, bigger, and sold for more money. Maybe he dug wells that produced much more water than anyone else's. Whatever it was, it was enough to catch the attention of those around him. Joseph was not just successful but significant.

From Success to Significance

In our day, success and significance seem to be two different things because they are often measured by different standards. Too often we measure our success using the yardstick of wealth, fame, power, and status. Then you get to a certain point in life and realize you were running after an elusive goal. You may achieve short-term "success" but find little significance. In fact, I think it is impossible to be successful without significance. Okay, John, so what does significance look like?

Let me put this in real estate terms. In real estate a term often used when looking at a piece of property or a building is "highest and best use." This means that the value of a property is a direct reflection of the use of that property. Often a property is undervalued because it is not being put to its best use. This is very pertinent to what we are speaking about. I often meet people who are very successful in their chosen field but miserable. These are really good, hard working people but they are in the wrong field. They are not living life with a "highest and best use" mentality.

I know an attorney who really wanted to be a missionary. Early on he took a short stint as a youth pastor at a church but it just didn't work out and at that point decided to go to law school. He went on to be a very accomplished but unsatisfied corporate attorney. He had the money, the influence, and the power but didn't feel significant and was very frustrated. Looking back at his time as a youth pastor, he realized that it didn't work out because he wasn't called to the youth but to the nations. So one year he takes his vacation time and goes to Kazakhstan on a mission trip, which is where I entered the scene.

On our trip Dale saw how poor all the medical conditions were. This man who was on the brink of corporate burnout was set on fire. By the time he came back from the trip, a plan had started to form in his mind. In fact, he and I sat in his car one night for hours while he batted ideas around. He was a corporate attorney with a large international healthcare company. He formed a plan to use the humanitarian resources of this company to bring aid to third-world countries. Dale still works as a successful corporate attorney and has gained new significance through the way he is serving the world.

> *"Significance is when your God-given talents, abilities and skills collide with your passions!"* —John M. Rowley

As you can see from Dale's experience, you don't have to throw your whole life away to find significance. You just need to be open to different opportunities. When I worked in Manhattan, I saw this all the time. I knew a very influential businessman who really wanted to be a jazz musician. His family had convinced him to conquer the business world, which he did in a huge way. This man knew the difference between success and significance, so he formulated a plan. Monday through the close of business Friday, he worked very hard in the business world. But Friday and Saturday nights, however, don't look for him in the office. He was too busy touring the jazz clubs in New York City and feeling very significant using his God-given talents, abilities, and skills. He would light up every time he told me about how the crowd reacted to his new bebop. I knew an actor who played a very successful real estate agent by day and on an off-broadway stage by night. He had found significance in his life.

The key is to incorporate your *why* with your *what* and *how*. Our *what* and *how* is normally our career path. What are you going to do and how are you going to do it? Our *why* is "why" we are here and this is usually where our talents, abilities, skills, and passion lie. Unfortunately, well meaning parents and teachers guide us away from our *why* because they don't see the practicality in it. This is how an incredibly gifted and passionate musician ends up becoming a frustrated dentist, or an outstanding athlete becomes a bitter gym teacher. I am convinced that our talents, abilities, skills, and passions are put in us by God so we can serve the world with our unique gifts. As I said earlier, we serve a God who loves to restore our lives. Look for ways to serve with your giftings. Your local church is a wonderful place to start because wherever there are people there are needs. If you are the musician living in a dentist's body, join the praise and worship team at your church. If you are the bitter gym teacher, start a men's softball league and get those other misplaced athletes working on their *why*. If you and your buddies are a little out of shape, go back and review Part One of this book. If you are willing, God will open a door for you and before you know it not only will you feel significant because you are using your giftings but you will feel super significant and blessed because you are helping others to do the same.

The Rocky Syndrome

Many of us have been taught that we must conquer this world on our own. Enter the ring of life like Rocky Balboa—scared, yes, but not backing down. You may get knocked down, but you won't stay there. You are going the distance! You will take all life has to dish out, but you will keep coming. You are in there on your own, taking on the toughest opponent there is. In fact, he is the heavyweight champion of the world. The crowd roars every time you get up again. In the end, you just know you will be left standing to get a hug from the love of your life! Yo! Adrian, I did it!

As I write this chapter, I am going through a period of self-discovery much like many of you. The Lord tells us to live by faith, but what does that mean? We are so used to being in the ring alone that we don't know how to take the gloves off and let God fight our battles. It is easy to be faithful and believe that God will provide for you when you have money in the bank, a secure job, and are secure financially. But when you are having your brains pounded in, it is hard to take off the gloves, stand center ring, and know that God will be your defender. But that is exactly what God wants. In fact, it is what gives God glory. God doesn't want you to do it alone; he wants to hold the ropes open for you as you enter the ring and then he steps in the ring with you. He wants to fight your battles with you and enjoy success with you.

Remember in the movie *Rocky*, Rocky was given the opportunity to fight Apollo Creed for the championship of the world and Rocky said no. All Rocky wanted to do that day was to get a job sparring with the champ. He didn't want to fight for the title. Have you ever had a time when you knew God had given you a job to do, a destiny to fulfill, but it seemed too big and you just don't see how you can get in the ring? You know what God wants you to do, and you even start doing it; but then you hit a wall. You are ready to throw in the towel. You are lying on the floor not able to get up on your own. Right then you hear Mickey . . . Oh, I mean God, echoing in your ears, "Get up, you son of a gun! 'Cause God loves you!" You get up to go just one more round, but this time God gets in the ring with you! You can't go another round, but God can. This is where your faith meets the pavement. You stay in the ring and tell the ref, just one more round. Please ref, I know I am a bloody mess . . . just one more round!

As I write this, I am on my own faith walk. In fact, if you are going after God's best for your life, you are as well. If you have something burning inside of you so big that you can't possibly see how you can pull it off . . . Welcome to God's will for your life. If you can do it on your own, the dream is simply too small. If you can do it on your own, you don't need God and what kind of glory does God get out of that? God is glorified by your faith, by believing what he says and stepping into the ring even though it looks like certain defeat! This is called dependency and it is where God wants all of us to live.

All the cards are stacked against you, yet God wants you to do it anyway. My friend Dexter Yager says, "If the dream is big enough, the facts don't matter!" Dexter also says, "Don't let anyone steal your dream!" I love this quote because of the passion in it. "Steal your dream." When someone tries to steal something, we will fight to defend it. Someone may come over and say hello to my wife while I am standing there and that is alright; but if he tries to steal my beautiful bride, my best friend, and the love of my life, he has taken his life into his own hands because I will fight for her! When you are going for your dreams you will meet "dream thieves" at every turn. It may be a friend telling you that you could never do it. It may be your education whispering in your ear that it has never been done this way before. It may even be your bank account telling you not to take the chance. You are the one who has to fight for your dream. But never forget—God is the dream maker and, "If God is for us, who can be against us?"[3]

Believing God

My parents brought us all to an exquisite resort in Virginia for their fiftieth anniversary. One day my whole family went to King's Dominion. The very first thing everyone did was head to the huge roller coaster. I am not a big fan of some of these roller coasters. I used to love them as a kid but since my car accident I have been a little leery of things out of my control, especially things that could hurt me. Well, my kids, nephews and nieces—everyone—was up for this roller coaster, so I gulped, not wanting to be the sissy of the group, and went on it. We had a blast.

The rest of the day we went from ride to ride and even from roller coaster to roller coaster. I faced my fears and had a victorious time at the theme park—until we turned this corner. It was the mother of all roller coasters. I stopped dead cold in my tracks and said to my wife, "No way!" She just laughed and said, "Okay, Big John is too scared to go on. Who is with me?" Well, everyone was in but me and my sister-in-law Holly! I didn't care a bit; I was happy to sit and watch. I knew thousands of people had been on that ride that day. You are strapped in and the ride is safe but scary. My mind kept running through my checklist of what ifs.

What if the car comes loose? What if I slip out? What if the tracks break? What if I'm too heavy? Boy, oh boy! My mind was terrifying me and I wasn't even getting in the line.

Sometimes our walk with God is the same way. We know God's word is true . . . but what if? We know God has the best of intentions for us . . . but what if? We know God has a plan for our life and we just need to let him open the doors no man can open and close the doors no man can close . . . but what if? We can "what if" ourselves right out of the blessings of God! God wants us to believe him!

How would you feel if you had one of your young children standing on the edge of the pool and you were in the water telling him to jump in and he just started crying. "I don't want to drown so I am not jumping in. No way!" he says. "I'm afraid you are going to let me sink right to the bottom and let me die!" Then the little tot turns around and runs right into the arms of a man that you know is no good and before you can get out of the pool your child is playing in the wading pool with this very bad person. How would that make you feel? After all, you are the loving father with only the best intentions and this other person is a proven scoundrel.

What if you believed everything God is telling you in his word. What an adventure it is to walk with God! He seldom shows you where you are going up front. He may show you the big map. You may know your ultimate destination, but walking with God is often a one-step-at-a-time journey.

Several years ago, I was standing on top of a mountain over looking Hong Kong. It was very beautiful, but right where we were there were no lights. You couldn't see two feet in front of yourself. I was discussing walking with God with my friend and mentor Ross Paterson.

I told Ross that it is so hard because God doesn't seem to want to show me much of what I am to do. Ross, in his thick English accent, tells me very bluntly, "That's because he knows you will mess it up and that goes for me as well, mate," he said laughing. Then he goes on to tell me that the word says God is a light unto our path. Ross asked me, "How far could you walk in this darkness, with the light we have, safely."

"One or two steps at most," I told him.

He added, "But once you took that step or two, you would then have enough light to see the next step or two, wouldn't you?"

"Well, yes," I said.

"That is precisely what walking with God is like. He will show you your next step or two and once you take them in faith, he will then reveal your next steps. It's bloody exciting to walk with the Lord!" he said with the exuberance of a school boy.

The Power of Belief

I was immersed in the self-help world for years, where I was told to believe in myself and to think and speak positive thoughts. This is all good, but limp in comparison to believing God. Now listen closely: I didn't say believing *in* God, I said *believing* God. This is where the power is. This is not a play on words. Many of us believe that there is a God. But it is one thing to believe *in* God and quite another to *believe* God.

"You believe that there is one God. Good! Even the demons believe that—and shudder."[4] I believe James was saying, "Great, you believe that there is one God. Big deal, so do the demons; in fact, they believe so much that they shudder, which means they believe in him more than you." Now listen to what the Apostle Paul says, "I pray that the eyes of your heart may be enlightened in order that you may know the hope to which he has called you, the riches of his glorious inheritance in his holy people, and his incomparably great power for us who believe. That power is the same as the mighty strength he exerted when he raised Christ from the dead and seated him at his right hand in the heavenly realms."[5]

Okay, John, this is very nice, but what is your point? Walking with God begins as an act of faith that leads you into a beautiful relationship with his son Jesus. But it shouldn't end there. Once you believe in Jesus you are called to continue believing everything he came to do and everything he said. Unfortunately for many, belief stops after accepting Christ as their savior. They start off believing *in* Christ, but never really *believe* him. We need to believe in what he came to do and what he said. This is why the Christian faith, for many, doesn't jump off the pages of Scripture and into the streets, boardrooms, and schools with them. They believe *in* God, but don't really *believe* God!

Paul likened this faith to the power that raised Christ from the dead! Do you have anything in your life that this incredible resurrection power couldn't overcome. No? Me either. God can raise careers from the dead and marriages from the rubble. He can restore passion and vision to those who have given up. He can make pure the filthiest, most vile sinner. God specializes in bringing things back from the dead and making impossible things possible—and in fact delights in it.

Walking in faith is the most exhilarating way to live. I know some people like jumping out of planes and skiing down slopes never before conquered. They search for the killer wave and find ways to make the impossible possible. I am here to tell you that walking in faith with God makes all those other things look like kids stuff.

In 1999, my son Jim and I were invited to go on a trip to China to serve the struggling Christians. I didn't have the money for such a trip and getting away from my business seemed impossible. Jim was 100% in and knew God would supply. Dad wasn't as sure. I told God that, if he wanted me to go, he'd have to raise the funds, I wasn't even going to try. What a man of faith! Just a few days after I told God I would go, I got a phone call from my church saying that someone donated a large sum of money for my son and me if we wanted to go on the trip to China. Along the way some friends and family were nice enough to support our efforts. But on the morning we were leaving, we were still $500 short for our home bills and didn't have much money to buy food in China. I decided to believe God and step out in faith, so we got up and headed to the house where everyone was meeting. Once we got there I learned that someone was looking for us. Well, that person was looking for us because God told him to give us $500.00, which he did. Once in China, even though I didn't have enough money to eat, I never missed a meal. People would invite me to dinner and pick up the tab.

I always jokingly say I want to have shirts made up that say, "Give your life to God and see the world." When you walk with God you will see and do things you never would have dreamed of—if you believe him! Nothing is more powerful than the resurrection power that God exerts in the life of a person who dares to believe him! Hear me on this. The creator of the universe wants to show up and do amazing things in your life simply because you believe him.

I can believe God, BUT . . . . Big buts are keeping many people from living in the true glory that God has for them.

But I drink too much . . . .

But I fight with my spouse . . . .

But I committed adultery . . . .

But I stole . . . .

But I was in jail . . . .

But I hurt my kids . . . .

I am not minimizing any of these things, BUT the price for all of these things and more was paid in full by Jesus. Jesus was beaten and then hung on a cross to die a terrible death by suffocation, but before he died he was separated from his

Father in heaven for the first time. Then after being dead for three days, he rose from the dead to conquer even the power of death. Jesus paid the price so we don't have to! If you think your sin is unforgivable then you are saying your sin is more powerful than God sacrificing his own son for you. Don't be so pompous and arrogant to think you can "out sin" the blood of Jesus. You can't, and neither can I!

When you look at the life of Jesus, you see that he never turned his back on sinners or was harsh with them. No, he embraced them and set them free. How about the woman caught in adultery? The Pharisees brought her to Jesus and wanted to stone her, but Jesus simply started writing in the dirt and said, "Let any one of you who is without sin be the first to throw a stone at her" and continued writing in the dirt. [6] These men were badgering Jesus so he stood and suggested that the innocent among them start her "just" punishment. With this they all started to walk away, one person at a time. I am not sure what Jesus wrote in the dirt because Scripture doesn't say. I think he was writing down the names of the women the Pharisees themselves had committed adultery with or maybe other sins they committed. The fact is everyone left and then Jesus said, "Woman, where are they? Has no one condemned you?" "No one, sir," she said. "Then neither do I condemn you," Jesus declared. "Go now and leave your life of sin."[7] Jesus doesn't condemn you, he sets you free!

Let me circle back to where I started. The power to change your life is simply in believing God!

Believing God That You *Are* Who He Says You Are

I walked into my Madison Avenue office, scanned my new domain, and promptly went into my office. The next thing I know Linda, my new secretary, is at my door with a notepad in hand. She asked, "Mr. Rowley, what do you have for me today?" Mr. Rowley. Oh man, I am Mr. Rowley. Yesterday, Mr. Rowley was my dad and I was a janitor in Brooklyn. But today, I have an office on Madison Ave and a window office to boot! After Linda went back to her desk, I got up, closed my office door, and threw open the drapes so I could see the wonderful view of Manhattan. I hadn't yet looked, so I was curious to see what it would be. Do you want to know what that glorious view was? A wall. A brick wall! That was my view! I just laughed, opened my door, and went for a little walk around the office introducing myself to people.

At first, I was excited to finally be working for such a prestigious real estate company. Then after a few days it hit me. I was an impostor! I was way in over my head. Who was I fooling? You can take the kid out of the janitor's closet but could you take the janitors closet out of the kid? Everyone knew my background. I was being given a shot because I was tenacious, ambitious, hardworking, and wouldn't take no for an answer. I didn't let them down. I succeeded. I put in more hours and out worked everyone, but deep down inside I felt like a real faker. I was so insecure about myself that I pushed harder and harder, sacrificing my family in the process. Even after I knew what I was doing, I constantly felt as if I had to prove myself. No one else expected this of me; if fact, I was encouraged to take time and enjoy life. But I felt as if I couldn't. Inside I felt like Tom Hanks in the movie *Big*. Hanks plays a boy who wishes to be big at a magic wish machine. He wakes up the next morning to find himself in an adult body. But he is still the same twelve-year-old kid on the inside. Now he has to deal with the unfamiliar world of grownups—including getting a job and having his first romantic encounter with a woman. The only one who knew was his best friend and so he constantly sought refuge in this knowing friend.

That is exactly how I felt. I was a janitor stuck in a real estate executive's body. I would go to the buildings I managed on a regular basis. This helped me excel at my job, but the main reason I went was that I felt more comfortable with my superintendents, porters, and doormen than I did with the executives in my company. I was going back to my familiar friends for refuge. Being with the workers in the building was the same comfort for me as Hanks' friend in the movie was to him.

Then it hit me. I was in a boardroom with my friend Barbara Corcoran. Barbara and I were negotiating to buy a property management company. Barbara founded the Corcoran Group which was and is an elite real estate sales company. The Corcoran Group was the major player in New York real estate sales, but they didn't have a property management division. Barbara and I became friends and this friendship was to turn into a partnership, if we could find the right opportunity. We never did find that opportunity, but during one of the negotiations I found myself. Barbara helped me see who I really was. After the meeting Barbara and I were talking. She looked me straight in the eyes and said, "You are the new lion on the prowl in Manhattan. The rest of the guys are old dinosaurs and you are going to eat them alive." This was a long time ago and the quote may be a bit off, but it is very close. I left that meeting actually believing that I was the person my business cards said I was. The fact that Barbara Corcoran believed in me made me believe in myself. Barbara knew who I was and where I came from and she still believed in me.

We all go through this, not only in our daily lives if we try enough things, but also in our walk with God. We know God is our Father, wants the best for us, and loves us. He even knows the number of hairs on your head. In my case that isn't very impressive or comforting—but he also knew how many hairs I had on my head when I had hair! We know all these things. But knowing and believing are two different things. The longest distance that God ever has to travel in your life is from your head to your heart. Of all the challenges I have walking in faith, this one is the hardest for me.

Maybe you are like me. You can believe that your pastor or even the person sitting next to you in church is who God says they are. But me? You don't know what I've done, what I think, what I want to do. Focusing on our faults, as opposed to who we are in Christ, is like shooting off a flare for the enemy. This is where I am weak—hit me right here. This is where I know I stumble—so put some of that right in my path. In order to walk in victory, you will have to make a conscious choice to believe who God says you are and not what your head is telling you. If you're like me, this is a daily challenge.

Chapter 12

Super-Sized Success

Okay, now I am getting into some shaky territory. We just talked about believing God, and now you are talking about success. John, don't tell me you are one of those "prosperity gospel" guys. I am not one who believes God is beholden to give us a new Cadillac or a Rolex if we know the right formula. I am also not one of those "poverty gospel" guys! There is only one gospel and it is the good news of Jesus Christ. I don't think God wants us reaching in our pocket only to find a leg. God does not get any glory when his children walk around broke and discouraged.

How would you feel if your kids were walking around in rags and complaining that their parents couldn't afford clothes for them? You would feel like a lousy parent, wouldn't you? Not long ago, I was having a conversation with my good friend Dov Baron. Dov is an expert in quantum physics. He is one of my dearest friends and would walk through fire for me and I for him. He is always there for me to offer encouragement or valuable business guidance because he wants to see me succeed. Although we differ in our faith, he holds me to a higher standard in my faith and will not accept anything less than me walking my talk. Recently we were talking about how to expand a certain area of my business that was going to take a substantial investment and I simply didn't have it. In response to my situation, I told Dov, "I am broke, I can't afford to do that!" Immediately Dov shot back at me: "Never talk like that again. That is a complete disgrace to the higher power that you call God! How insulting is that? Instead, say that you are having a temporary cash flow problem and the timing isn't right. This is more accurate and honors God, mate!" Dov is 100% right. In order to have integrity in your life, consistency is key. If you believe God's word, you need to take that to the streets Monday through Saturday, not just on Sunday.

❧ ❖ ☙

Poverty often deprives a man of all spirit and virtue; it is
hard for an empty bag to stand upright. —Benjamin Franklin

God told Abraham, "I will make you into a great nation and I will bless you; I will make your name great, and you will be a blessing."[1] God blesses us so we can be a blessing to others. You cannot be a blessing to those around you, your family, your church, your community, or the poor if you are not first blessed by God. Many people like to say that "money is the root of all evil." The Bible does not say that anywhere. It says, "For the *love* of money is a root of all kinds of evil. Some people, eager for money, have wandered from the faith and pierced themselves with many griefs."[2] God has no problem with you having money. He just doesn't want money having you! I know many poor people who are controlled by money. Their main focus is money and how to get it. Benjamin Franklin was right. Poverty often deprives a man of all spirit and virtue. God doesn't want to deprive you. He just wants your priorities in order. Money can be an idol consuming every thought whether you have little or much. God wants you to be consumed by him, not by anything else. God is jealous for your attention. God doesn't want anything standing between you and him.

God wants your focus on him and in return he wants to care for you. Even in Jesus' day they had worries about lack, but this is how Jesus explained it: "So do not worry, saying, 'What shall we eat?' or 'What shall we drink?' or 'What shall we wear?' For the pagans run after all these things, and your heavenly Father knows that you need them. But seek first his kingdom and his righteousness, and all these things will be given to you as well."[3]

When we focus on God, everything else gets taken care of and we're not just talking about our basic needs because he is the God of "more than enough." We talked about Joseph earlier. He was a prisoner in a foreign land. He had nothing; but, since the Lord was with him, he was successful in the eyes of God and man. This isn't what we are taught in business school. I can't explain it. All I know is that God honors his word.

Let's Eat and Drink

When Jesus was around there was always plenty to eat and drink. The first miracle Jesus ever performed was turning water into wine. Jesus' mother Mary told him they were out of wine and told the servants to simply do as Jesus instructed. The servants were told to fill up the jars with water and to give those jars to the master of the banquet. The master was thrilled because what he poured was wine. Really good wine. Normally you bring out the good wine first and then bring out the cheap stuff once the guests have had enough not to know the difference. When Jesus gets involved, the good stuff comes out! Mary told the servants to do as Jesus said. Remember what we said earlier, "But seek first his kingdom and his righteousness, and all these things will be given to you as well."[4] The servants didn't have to do any sleight of hand; all they had to do was do what Jesus said and he would do the rest!

Now, let's look at eating with Jesus. There are two accounts in the Bible of Jesus feeding large groups with very little. Jesus feeds four thousand people with seven loaves and a few small fish[5] and then five thousand people with five loaves and two small fish.[6] Jesus didn't use this opportunity to teach everyone a lesson in poverty. He didn't say, "I am doing it for your own good and one day you will appreciate it." No, just the opposite: Jesus had compassion for them. The Bible says that Jesus is the same yesterday, today, and forever.[7] If Jesus is consistent, then he has compassion for us when we have a need and he wants to give us more than enough. Both of these accounts say that there was a lot left over, so he blessed them with more than they needed. This is important because we are supposed to bless others out of our abundance.

Jesus fed four thousand with seven loaves and a few small fish and five thousand with five loaves and two small fish. He fed the larger group with less bread and less fish. I think God did this to show us that no problem is too big for him. He can take even fewer resources and do more with them. Maybe you are at a point in your life where you feel as if you have nothing left. Your money is gone, you are not educated enough, and you just simply feel defeated. Take heart! God can take the loaves and fish of your life and turn them into a feast. He can even take the water of your life and turn it into choice wine fit for a king! God simply wants to be a part of your life. He isn't a religion. In fact, Jesus didn't get along so well with the religious people of his day. Religion is created for and by man. Religion will tell you that God wants you sick and broke so you can be humble. It all sounds so self-sacrificial, doesn't it? It isn't God who wants you sick and poor, it's the devil. Jesus put it this way, "The thief comes only to steal and kill and destroy; I came that they may have life, and have it abundantly."[8] Jesus wants you living a full and abundant life and he wants you to put your life in his hands. That is why he said, "But seek first his kingdom and his righteousness, and all these things will be given to you as well."[9] God wants the best for your life. Jesus wants to be your savior and have a relationship with you.

It is ironic. Some of the leaders of religions who reject that God blesses his children with material blessings are not opposed to doing their best to get a nice home and provide the best education money can buy for their own children. They just don't want to give God the credit for it. They want all the accolades for themselves.

Eisenhower Park

Every summer when I was growing up, we had a picnic at Eisenhower Park on Long Island. My dad and the rest of the men from my father's chapter of the Knights of Columbus would get together and go shopping. They would get hamburgers, hot dogs, chicken, sausage, corn, chips, soda, beer—basically anything that was good for a picnic. The men would play softball while the women spent some quality time together watching the younger kids play. It was always a great day for all and a day we all looked forward to. And there was always tons to eat.

I used to love hanging out with my dad and his buddies while they made the food. They functioned as a team and made sure everyone was having a great time and ate all they wanted. When anyone asked if there was enough hot dogs or hamburgers so they could have another one, the men would always say, "No problem, we have more than enough!" I did, however, begin to notice that they would say this even when we were running low. The men would wink to one another when they said that and then have an informal strategy session. "Okay, we have plenty of dogs, burgers are low, buns are low, and get some more beer. We may not be low now but we will be." All the men would laugh at this. A couple of them would leave for a while and, by the time they came back, we had more than enough. These men made this look effortless and fun and it was because they loved serving everyone and seeing everyone have a terrific and memorable day. I think this is how it was when Jesus fed all those people. I don't think he made a big production of it; he just simply thanked his Father for providing more than enough and then joyfully served. Just like my dad and his buddies, God gives to us out of a joyful heart. He wants us to have more than enough so we can not only enjoy ourselves but also serve others out of a fun-loving and grateful heart.

Very Rich

The word of God is very rich! You need to get into it and look up the promises that God has for your life. A few years ago, I was having some very challenging times in my business and personal life. I knew what my life's purpose was but it was getting very difficult to see how I could make it happen. One Friday morning

I was with Chris Mangum, my prayer partner. As we chatted he looked at me with tears in his eyes, which was very unusual, and told me that he felt the Lord told him to give me a certain scripture. To this day this scripture is one of my favorites and one I personally declare over my family's life. It is from Psalm 1. I am just quoting what Chris gave me, so you should go read the whole thing. It is short and very rich: "That person is like a tree planted by streams of water, which yields its fruit in season and whose leaf does not wither—whatever they do prospers."[10]

God does use other people in your life because, if you are anything like me, you may have a hard time getting out of your own way. Also notice above how I said that it was getting very difficult to see how "I" could make it happen. God used this time in my life to let me know that I can't make it happen because he put too large a dream in my heart. The only way it will happen is with his help. Looking back I can see that I would be diligently working on a certain area, project, or relationship that I thought would supersize "my" success. The things I was working on did okay, but nothing to write home about. But during those same times, I had incredible things come out of nowhere that were huge. In fact, they are still huge in my work and life. God was showing me that, while I was striving, he could hit a grand slam home run for me and all I had to do was run the bases. God doesn't want us doing nothing, he simply wants us looking to him for guidance and then working on what he puts in front of us. Someone once told me that God can't bless your steps if you're not walking. God wants us to walk but he wants us to use our GPS for guidance.

Are You Using Your GPS?

Your GPS is God's Priority System. God has given us his word, which is meant to guide us through life. It is the GPS for our lives. Some of us are here to be models and some of us look like my brothers, Mark and James. Some of us are here to bring beautiful music to life, like my wife Cathy, and some sing like me. Whatever road you may be on, God has given you a GPS to make sure you don't get lost. Get into his word and see what he has in store for you. Having clear direction brings peace into your life. It will help you skip and sing through life, even through the hard times.

This week my wife and I had the good pleasure to have our grandchildren spend a few nights with us. As we were eating lunch in the kitchen, my granddaughter Jennifer went skipping by singing a very sweet song while checking on her younger brother Jacob. My wife looked at me and said, "Jennifer is just so happy!" I was glad, but I wondered why Cathy said that. Sometimes I am dense, but I didn't want to miss out on learning something, so I asked Cathy what she meant. My wife explained that it is impossible to skip and sing and not be happy! Now, whenever I hear my kids, grandkids, or Cathy singing around the house, it just makes me smile knowing that it is impossible to sing and not be happy. Using your GPS will have you skipping and singing because you will have good directions for your life. But isn't the opposite true as well? When you go on a trip without good directions, that trip becomes very frustrating after a while and you lose all your joy. Buckle up, plug in your GPS, and enjoy the ride—it will be one you will never forget!

Karela (bitter melon) or Dates

My dad always told me that if I don't have anything nice to say, not to say anything at all. I have had times in my life when, if I went by this guidance, I would never have uttered a word. We should all be uplifting and positive to others when we speak to or about them as well as about ourselves. Words are very powerful! In fact, the Bible says, "The tongue has the power of life and death, and those who love it will eat its fruit."[11] I think many of us would prefer to eat a sweet date instead of a karela, which is a bitter melon. Dates are considered to be the sweetest fruit and karela the most bitter. Even though our taste buds would prefer a sweet date, we often speak words of karela and the Bible says we will be eating the fruit of our mouths. When I was a young child I used to bite my nails a lot, so my mother got something from the drug store that she put on my nails; it was similar to nail polish but it tasted nasty. Needless to say, I didn't want to taste that so I didn't bite my nails anymore. I think if we truly ate a karela every time we spoke sour words we would be very careful with how we used our tongues.

James compares your tongue to the bit in a horse's mouth or the rudder of a ship. A bit and a rudder are both small but direct the course of the much larger and much more powerful horse and ship. Likewise, our tongue sets the course for our lives. If we are speaking life and prosperity over our lives as stated in the word of God, we are speaking God's very blessings intended for our lives. If we are speaking curses over our lives, our tongues will set our course in a negative direction.

Let's face it. We have all put our foot in our mouth—and in my case I have had both feet in my mouth at the same time. Words have power. Have you ever had someone in authority, a parent, a teacher, or maybe even a spouse say something very nasty or degrading to you? We all have to one degree or another. Those words can ring in your ears for years. How many times have you said something and wished you could take it back? You get into a disagreement with your spouse and something comes blurting out of your mouth and you feel like eating your own head. Words have the power of life and death over every area of our lives including relationships, and if we use the wrong words, we can kill a relationship. The reverse is also true: start speaking life to your spouse and to others and watch them perk up.

Talking to Yourself

The most important conversation you ever have is the one you have with yourself. The way you speak is the way you are thinking, so you must guide your tongue and your thoughts. Paul tells the Philippines, "Finally, brothers and sisters, whatever is true, whatever is noble, whatever is right, whatever is pure, whatever is lovely, whatever is admirable—if anything is excellent or praiseworthy—think about such things."[12] Paul was saying to focus on the positive. Let me ask you this. If you are focusing on what's true, noble, right, pure, lovely, admirable, excellent, and praiseworthy, will you feel, act, and speak differently? Will your life be better or worse?

Let's take a quick break. Look around the room you are in and look for everything that is navy blue. Be careful not to miss anything. Really scan the room for everything that is navy blue. Now close your eyes and tell me what in the room is red? The odds are that you can't do it. I do this exercise with live audiences and they all laugh and know everything that is navy blue but didn't notice anything red. The reason is that our brain picks up on what we are focusing on. This is why Paul thought it was so important to focus on the good in life. If you are looking for good you will find more good. If you are looking for bad you will find more bad. Have you ever bought a certain model of car and as soon as you got it noticed that everyone is now driving that same car. They were there all the time, but when we are aware of it in our own lives, our minds and eyes start to gravitate in that direction.

What's in Your Heart

"You brood of vipers, how can you who are evil say anything good? For the mouth speaks what the heart is full of."[13] Have you ever heard a song first thing in the morning and it keeps ringing in your head all day long? Then as you are alone you may even sing it out loud a little. What goes in your head will stay there and eventually come out your mouth. The same is true with everything, not just music. If you are feeding your mind good music and thoughts, good music and thoughts will come out. It is very important to guard what you look at or listen to because

that enters your mind, affects your heart, and comes out your mouth. When my kids were younger they would listen to music like most teenagers. One day my son John was listening to music that just sounded like it would put you in a bad mood and affect your attitude in a bad way. My wife went over to him to tell him to turn it off and he says, "Mom, this is my angry music. I listen to it when I'm angry." From then on "angry music" was a term we used in our home and we didn't allow any of them to listen to it.

The same is true with movies, books, radio, and friends. My daughter Jessica is a terrific girl, but she had one friend her freshman year of high school with whom she broke our rules. My wife and I would not let her hang around with this girl any longer. Jessica asked her mom why she didn't like her new friend. Cathy just said, "I don't know your new friend, but I don't like the way you are when you are with her!" My father always told me you become like those you hang around with, so make good choices or I will choose your friends for you! I know Cathy's mom and dad had a similar viewpoint so it was easy for us to implement this rule in our own home. As a side note, Jessica has some incredible friends. The old saying, "Birds of a feather flock together," is true and Jessica attracts incredible people because she is spectacular!

You are responsible to protect what goes into your life. You don't have to watch certain TV shows just because they are on, and the same is true with music, movies, newspapers, and the internet. One evening Cathy and I went out for a date. We were going to see a movie and get dinner afterward. The first three minutes of the movie was nothing but nudity and foul language. We just looked at each other, got up, went to the ticket counter, and got our money back. Zig Ziglar has said that "hypocrites are those that complain about all the sex, drugs, and violence on their VCRs." Cathy is my queen and she should never be exposed to such filth, plus neither of us want to be hypocrites.

Talk the Talk

Back in my New York neighborhood, people on the block would say, "Okay, you can talk the talk, but can you walk the walk?" This was a way of saying, "Okay, you have a big mouth, but it is one thing to say it and another to do it." When it comes to walking in faith, you have to do both—walk the walk and talk the talk. In fact, when you talk the talk in faith, it makes the walk much easier because God is in it. Earlier I said you have to take it one step at a time and then God will show you the next step, and this is true. But now it is time not just to walk the walk, but to talk the talk. God gives us promises in the Bible and we need to use those promises as positive self-talk or affirmations. I know that a lot of self-proclaimed self-help gurus tell you to speak positively to yourself. I agree 100% and have been doing this for years—until I found a way to blow this practice out of the water. I found that using what God is saying about me and then repeating that out loud is like throwing gasoline on a fire.

You have to realize that the tongue really *does* have the power of life or death. This is true when you speak things to others, but also when you are talking to yourself. You are always having a conversation with yourself whether you know it or not. And no, you are not nuts—everyone does this. These mini conversations are the most important conversations you will ever have and it is critical that you direct them. In fact, many times they turn into endless loop conversations where you keep repeating the same thing over and over, which can drive you nuts if it is the wrong conversation. Which of the following do you think will have a more positive impact on your life? "How can I be so stupid?" or "Wow! That didn't work out, but I know that God is working out all things for my good!" Of course, the second one is best.

Decide in advance how you are going to speak to yourself. I like to see what the word of God says about me, and then repeat those things to myself, with gratitude.

Thank you that I am the head and not the tail.

Thank you that I am to be a lender and not a borrower.

Thank you that I am to owe no man anything but to love him.

Thank you that I can do all things through Christ who strengthens me!

Thank you that this is the day that you made. I will rejoice and be glad in it.

Notice that I always start the sentence with "thank you." Being grateful puts you in a powerful mindset and opens your heart up to the wonders that God has for you. I suggest starting your day like this, then let these truths repeat in your head all day long. Just like that song that plays in your head all day just because you heard it when your alarm clock went off, these words will echo back to you. Get God's promises into your head and let them play all day long—and watch your life change.

Walking the Walk

Walking in faith can be one of the hardest things to do. It just isn't natural for many of us. Like many of you, I have relied on myself a good part of my life with mixed results. Even though the results were mixed, I still took great pride in being self-reliant. Walking in faith is also one step at a time. Take a step in faith, find

God is already there and you will have more faith for the next step, and when you do God shows up again so your faith keeps growing.

The word faith was used twice in the Old Testament. I find this very interesting and revealing. In the Old Testament the Jews, God's chosen people, were to obey the law. In the New Testament we are to follow Jesus. Following Jesus requires faith, but God also says it is faith that pleases him. Paul told the Hebrews, "Without faith it is impossible to please God, because anyone who comes to Him must believe that He exists and that He rewards those who earnestly seek Him."[14] When you believe God it not only pleases him but it pleases him to the point that he wants to reward you for your faith. People get so confused over faith and God, but it is really very simple. A relationship is a two-way street with both people contributing. God wants you to believe what he says in his word just like you would want one of your kids to believe everything you wrote to them in a letter. If you came home after a long trip and you overheard your son or daughter saying, "My dad told me he was going to take me out to dinner when he gets home, but I doubt he will." I bet your feelings would be hurt, wouldn't they. God tells us in His word that "God will meet all your needs according to the riches of His glory in Christ Jesus."[15] And then God hears you telling everyone that you are broke and don't know how you will pay your bills. That isn't faith. That is calling God a liar.

Just as I was writing this—literally as I was writing this—my wife called to tell me that our friend Tom, who cuts Cathy's hair, refused to take any money for her haircut. The hair cut, I would guess, would be in the $50 range. He simply said he wanted to bless her with this haircut, and Cathy said she wanted to bless him by paying. When all the dust settled, Cathy got a free haircut. This is significant to me because last night I knew I would be writing on faith today. I wanted to execute my faith in a way I haven't in a long time. With my own thoughts guiding me, I started believing someone would give me a cup of coffee in the next 24 hours. I felt God nudge me and tell me to up the ante. So I said, okay, I will believe for $10 but I still felt his holy nudge. I then upped it to $50 in the next 24 hours and that seemed to be okay. Well, less than 24 hours later, Tom blessed us with a free haircut. You see, God loves us so much that he wants to reveal his goodness to us. He loves it when we believe his word. A very important note! I am not saying that God is our own personal ATM card or a free pass to the house of your dreams and a Mercedes or even a free haircut. I am just using this story because it is recent and relevant.

So if faith is so important, how do you get faith? I came across this years ago, but it took many years to actually travel the twelve inches from my brain to my heart. Paul says, "So faith comes from hearing, and hearing by the word of Christ."[16] I find that the more I read the Bible or listen to it on my iPhone, the more I listen to Christian teachings, the more my faith grows. Joshua said, "Do not let this Book of the Law depart from your mouth; meditate on it day and night, so that you may be careful to do everything written in it. Then you will be prosperous and successful."[17]

The whole key is to let this sink deep down into your heart. "God is not human, that he should lie, not a human being, that he should change his mind. Does he speak and then not act? Does he promise and not fulfill?"[18] If God says it, you can bank on it!

Well, if God does not lie, and if the way to have more faith is by hearing the word of God, then we need to fill ourselves with his word and to meditate on it day and night. When we do this we will believe all he is telling us in his word and we will grow and prosper in every way!

Chapter 13

I Want It NOW!

We want everything now. It starts when we are kids and never stops. In fact, in this day and age I think it is even worse than ever before. We have restaurants with instant food, the internet with instant information, cell phones, email, and chat for instant communication, social networking for instant recognition. We want instant gratification. We don't just want it, we demand and expect it. We are the same way with God—we want it *now*.

Good thing we serve a *now* God! King David knew he served a God of the now. God calls himself the great I AM, not the great I *was* or the great I *will be* He is the Great I AM because he is present and with us *now*! King David asked to be blessed with prosperity *now*. "This is the day the LORD has made; we will rejoice and be glad in it. Save now, I pray, O LORD; O LORD, I pray, send now prosperity."[1] David had a *now* faith and the Bible says that David was a man after God's own heart.

When in Rome . . .

Want to develop faith? Then do as the Romans did. Paul told the church in Rome that you develop faith by hearing the word of God.[2] Want more faith? Get more of God's word into you! You can do this in several ways. You can read the Bible. You can use some of the many study guides available. You can even read the Bible online with organized readings for each day. You can listen to it on CD or MP3, in your car, while you are exercising, or even when you are walking your dog. You'll get fed God's word at any good Bible-believing church, and you can read books that teach about God's word. I think it is a good idea to do all of the above at various times, but the key is to do it.

How to Go from Self-help to God's Help

Having Barbara Corcoran believe in me was the nudge I needed to push me over the edge in believing I was who my business cards said I was. How much more powerful is it to have the creator of the universe not only believing in who you are, but actually creating you to be who he says you are! Let that sink in and it will change your life. That is the secret to living a victorious life!

Just as getting in good physical shape takes daily disciplines, shaping your spiritual life does as well. Oh, I can hear you now saying, "This is the boring part; I think I'll skip it." Don't! I spent my whole life searching and reading every self-help book I could get my hands on, and what I was really searching for was my God. We are all created with a void by our creator so we would search after him. At some level do you feel that? Throughout the rest of this chapter I am going to lay out some disciplines that will help you walk closer with God. Spiritual disciplines are to the believer what exercise is to the athlete.

Paul told Timothy: "But have nothing to do with worldly fables fit only for old women. On the other hand, discipline yourself for the purpose of godliness; for bodily discipline is only of little profit, but godliness is profitable for all things, since it holds promise for the present life and also for the life to come."[3] Our life is comprised of daily disciplines, which are simply daily habits that help you live well. The most successful people are typically the most disciplined people. Discipline is not a dirty word the way some people would like to have you think. It's passion that puts us on a certain path and commitment to that passion that moves us to action, but it is discipline that gets us to follow through on a daily basis. Eating well is a discipline (habit), but so is eating poorly. Being on time is a discipline, but so is being late. If you don't deliberately design your daily disciplines you will end up developing weak disciplines that will dis-empower your life. The key is to implement effective disciplines into your life in order to live an effective life.

Your spiritual life will flourish if you have certain disciplines in place. Just like your body needs to be exercised and fed on a regular basis, your spirit needs to be exercised and fed on a regular basis as well. I am going to lay these out the way I laid out the workouts in Appendix 2. I am giving you a beginner, intermediate, and advanced training routine. I do this only to simplify it and to make it a little more fun. Feel free to incorporate any of these at any time you want to. Please realize that this is not an exhaustive list, but it will get you started. If you want to learn more about any of the subjects below, there is no shortage of resources on these various subjects, with the best resource being the Bible.

The Power of Positive Fitness Top 10!

Beginner Training Routine

1. Read the All-Time Best-Selling Book in History

This is the bestselling book in history for a reason! Man, this book has it all! Violence, sex, alcohol, murder, war, double-crossing scoundrels, deceit, miracles, and much more. If this book had a different title it would be a bestseller year in and year out and a block buster movie would certainly be in the works. Oh wait, it is! It is the bestselling book in history! It is the Bible and it is the cornerstone of Christian life. No spiritual discipline is more important and nothing can take its place.

Paul told the Romans: "So faith comes from hearing, and hearing by the word of Christ."[4] People often ask me, "How do I go about strengthening my faith?" and I have asked the same from others. I want to have the faith Paul had after the road to Damascus or what Thomas had after seeing Jesus risen from the dead. I want the faith that transformed a raggedy group of cowardly apostles into men who were willing to die for their faith and who transformed the world. I want a life-changing faith. I have looked under every rock for this answer because I want my life to be all it can be. The answer is faith. "And without faith it is impossible to please him, for he who comes to God must believe that he is and that he is a rewarder of those who seek him."[5]

So in order to please God, you must have faith and faith comes from hearing the word of God so it just makes sense that Bible intake is very important. I find that reading the Bible first thing in the morning is critical for me. It sets my barometer for the day and helps me keep my priorities in order.

Pastor Danny Collins once told me that you can substitute certain things in your life. If your car breaks down, you can walk or ride a horse; but there is no substitute for the word of God. He then went on to say that we all know certain people who are always driving their car on empty and are constantly putting two or three dollars worth of gas in the tank. Then there are others who also put two or three dollars of gas in the tank, but they started off full so the gas gauge is always on full. The same, he says, is true of Christians. Some are constantly on empty adding just enough of God's word to get by, while others are always on full and top it off every day. Staying on full is the key to a victorious life.

There are many ways to read, study, and implement the principles of the Bible into your life. You can most certainly find an organized Bible study in your town. You can do in-depth topical studies, book studies, use a yearly plan, play Bible roulette (just opening it up with your eyes closed and pointing at a page where you start reading), memorize scripture, meditate on God's word, and listen to it on DVD or your iPhone. In my opinion, you need to find a way of reading the Bible that you enjoy. Much like exercising. If you don't like it, you won't do it consistently.

The Sword

A lot of people, especially guys, want to be like Arnold Schwarzenegger in *Conan the Barbarian*—wielding a huge sword effortlessly to fight off the enemy. I remember reading an interview with Arnold after he filmed the first Conan movie. He said he had to work many hours, day and night, in order to be able to use that sword and make it look like a natural extension of his body. Learning to use the sword of the spirit takes time and effort as well, but it is more powerful than any sword made of metal.

When Jesus was tempted in the wilderness by Satan, Jesus used the word of God. Jesus was fasting in the wilderness for forty days. He was exhausted physically when Satan came to tempt him will all the things of the world. To everything Satan said, Jesus had the word of God on the tip of his tongue. Keep in mind, Jesus was and is God and he still used Scripture to combat the enemy. You and I should do the same, which is why it is critical that we know the word of God.

Real Power Talk

Sharpen the Sword with 3 x 5 Cards

Get some 3 x 5 cards and write down scriptures that mean something to you and are encouraging to your life. Put them on your bathroom mirror, in your car, on your refrigerator or on your desk. Whatever is the best way for you to personally put these verses to memory is the way you should do it. Memorize them and use them as your positive self-talk, given to you personally by the creator of the universe. Also use these scriptures when you are being tempted by an old habit, feeling weak or discouraged. Let's take Jesus' lead and use the living word of God in our own lives.

I've read his books for years. I have studied his message, listened to tapes and CD's so much that I could recite them verbatim. Yes sir, I am a dyed in the wool fan and student of Zig Ziglar. I know everything he says, word for word. But that doesn't mean I know Zig, it just means I know what he writes. Well, one day Laurie

Magers, Mr. Ziglar's assistant and my friend, arranged for me to see Mr. Ziglar at an event he was speaking at and afterward I had the opportunity to speak with him. He wanted to know what I did and how I did it. We got to know each other a little bit and I would have loved to have spent even more time with him if I could. He is a wonderful man and has helped millions change their lives. You see, I could read Mr. Ziglar's books all I want and would learn a lot about him, but that is different than knowing him . . . Isn't it? That is like when we read the word of God. It is critical to read the word and let it change and affect our lives but prayer is the backstage pass at the seminar to actually speak to the author. Take a minute right now and look out your window. Go ahead and do it; no one is watching, and if they are, ask them if they want to go with you. Everything that you can see and so much that you can't was created by God, yet he still wants to get to know you and for you to get to know him. The creator of the universe is madly in love with you and wants to have a relationship with you. That is why we pray.

2. Prayer

"Do not pray for easy lives. Pray to be stronger men. Do not pray for tasks equal to your powers. Pray for powers equal to your tasks. Then the doing of your work shall be no miracle, but you shall be the miracle." —**Phillips Brooks, U.S. Episcopal bishop (1835–1893)**

God wants to change us! We were created in his image so we should be powerful, creative beings. The Bible is full of men and women who took on incredible tasks that could only be completed with the help of God. I believe that God gives us all a dream so big that the only way for it to happen is with his help.

Prayer a Waste of Time?

There. I said what many are thinking. Prayer is a major waste of time; I have so little time as it is, I can't afford to waste more of it. I think a lot of people don't pray because they have this very view of prayer. Let's face it, we are goal-oriented people and prayer seems to just take time and give nothing back in return which gives it a very poor ROI (Return on Investment). Come on, you business people out there. You can relate to that, can't you?? We are used to putting in effort in order to achieve a desired outcome. In fact, as a speaker, one of the things I try to do is inspire people into action. "Want results? Take action." I say, "Want massive results? Take massive action!" I still believe that is true—especially if your actions are prayerfully considered.

Martin Luther once said, "Tomorrow I plan to work, work, from early until late. In fact I have so much to do that I shall spend the first three hours in prayer."[6]

Prayer puts God's "super" on our "natural." Pastor Jim Sink tells about how he and his wife Myra went to the airport and they were very late and in a hurry. Myra stepped onto the moving walkway, but Jim saw how slow it was moving so he decided to walk along the outside so they wouldn't miss their plane. Jim, almost at a run, looked over at Myra, who was leisurely walking but still "beating" him, and gave him a nice cheery wave. Jim, not to be outdone, picks up the pace and is out of breath when they finally meet at the end. They both got there, but Jim was huffing and puffing and Myra was as fresh as a daisy. Jim then said, "That is what God can do in our lives. He puts his super on our natural and we can go places we never dreamed of, much faster than we ever thought."

The reason we work so hard is because we want to be achievers. Some of us want to be high achievers, much like Pastor Jim running alongside Myra. Let's take a step back for a second. I believe that our dreams and ambitions are often God's will for our life. If this is true, then God knows the best things for us to do. I know money can be tight and you need to strive but God said he would meet ALL our needs according to his glorious riches in glory! He didn't say *some* of them. He didn't say only the most pressing or important needs; he said ALL of our needs. And Jesus also tells us not to worry about what we are going to eat, drink, or wear, but put God first and knock off the worrying. He's got your back on the rest. This isn't an exact quote; it is from the NYV Bible (New York Version of the Bible). I am not saying just pray all day long and do nothing. That is ridiculous. Pray and work. Work and pray. Do what you can do and let God do what you can't.

How to Pray

I have always found prayer a very confusing issue. I was taught to pray to Mary, the saints, a statue, and even a grandmother. And then when you prayed you had some memorized speech that you chanted in the hopes that someone was listening. Prayer is simply talking to God. You don't need to speak in thee's and thou's. God doesn't speak in the King James dialect. He not only understands the words you say, he knows what you really need. He will come and meet you right where you are and speak to you in a way you can understand. You don't need a cell phone, internet connection, blue tooth, 3G, 4G or any other G. All you need to do is to speak to him.

Jesus expected us to pray, he said, "*When you pray*"[7]; "*But you, when you pray*"[8]; "*And when you are praying*"[9]; "*Pray, then, in this way.*"[10] Jesus didn't say *if* you pray, he said when. All through Scripture you see Jesus retreating to pray. If Jesus found it so necessary to pray in order to live a victorious life, then so should we.

Several years ago, I was at a Promise Keeper's rally. These rallies were designed to help teach men to be keepers of their promises. Wellington Boone was speaking and he got into the subject of prayer. One thing that he said was funny, but also changed my prayer life. He said, *"When you are praying SHUT UP!!! You aren't the one with something important to say!"* He makes an incredible point here. Prayer is a two-way conversation, not a monologue.

Learn to Listen

God seldom talks to us audibly, although he can if he chooses. He will not scream at us to get our attention, even though he can. He will not fuss at us and nag us until he gets his way. No. God is a gentleman. He is very patient and long suffering. His intent is to point out to us areas that we need to work on so we can move forward and he can bless us. He will usually get our attention through our circumstances and speak to us in a small, still voice. It is important that we learn to listen to the promptings of God so we can learn to take action on those promptings.

Are there things in your life that you know you should be dealing with but are avoiding? Should you be getting your finances in order, making your home more harmonious, dealing with an addiction, or maybe even restoring a damaged relationship at work? God doesn't want you dealing with these issues to make life more painful. He wants you to deal with them so you can go to a higher level. Many times these un-dealt-with issues are the weight that is anchoring you to the place in life you want to leave.

Do you want to increase? Do you want to rise to a higher place? Do you want to see more of God's blessings and favor in your life? If so, you need not only to listen to that small still voice of God but to respond to it. The quicker you act on God's prompting, the sooner you will get to the other side of the issues you are dealing with.

In my own life, I got involved with a business in the medical field. I thought it was a perfect fit. I was referred to this business by a very trusted friend and he knew the two men involved to be very honest men. My message was right in line with the mission of the business. It looked to be ordained by God and I was excited to move forward. Before entering into this business, I laid out all the things I knew needed to be done in order to make this business prosper, because I knew it would be an uphill battle and need all parties on board. I laid out not only a plan of action for the business but also the terms in which I would be involved with this business. I got a verbal agreement on everything and we moved forward.

To make a long, painful story short, it didn't work out. These men were unable to honor anything that we agreed upon. The problem here was not the other men but with me. I did not listen! Yes, outwardly, everything looked fantastic. But, and this is a big but, I had a check in my spirit from the beginning. I knew deep down inside that these men were not what they were presenting to be. I knew they were just saying the right words but lacked character and integrity. I went into this business and it was one of the most painful times in my life. God did honor everything I put my hands to even though I had zero cooperation from anyone else in the business. The more I learned about the integrity of this business, the more I knew I had to leave. Did I listen to the guidance God was giving me? Of course not; *I* was going to make this work! Famous last words. The point of this story is not a lesson in business but to learn to listen to that small, still voice deep on the inside and to trust it. All the things I felt on the inside were 100% true and all the things I saw with my eyes and heard with my ears were 100% false.

Walking with God is much like a pilot learning to fly with the instruments in a plane. The pilot doesn't learn while flying in a deep fog. No, the pilot practices and trains with the instruments in a very controlled environment and gradually goes to flying 100% with the instruments. Then, when an emergency arises and the pilot gets stuck in a thick, pea-soup fog, it is second nature to fly by the instruments. Learn to listen to that small, still voice in your spirit on a daily basis and when you need to hear it you will know it to be true and accurate.

Answered Prayer

Jesus said that God will answer a prayer if you believe God will answer it. "Have faith in God. Truly I tell you, if anyone says to this mountain, 'Go, throw yourself into the sea,' and does not doubt in their heart but believes that what they say will happen, it will be done for them. Therefore I tell you, whatever you ask for in prayer, believe that you have received it, and it will be yours"[11]

I love it when my kids come to ask me for something knowing that I will give it to them. They don't have to beg or bargain. All they have to do is come to Dad and he will give it to them. That makes me feel so good because they trust that I will provide for them. But if one of my kids came to me with an attitude, saying, "I know you won't give this to me because you never come through anyway!" I wouldn't be so excited about responding to that request, would I? Cathy and I are at the point in our lives where grandchildren are entering the scene and I love giving to those beautiful kids. Many times they don't even need to ask—I can tell by the glint in their eye what they want. Often when I am eating something and look down I see Jacob, not quite two years old, looking up at me with his mouth wide open. He just knows that Papop will give him some and that it will taste delicious. It gives me true pleasure to give the little guy some of what I am eating. I believe that is how God sees us. Matthew said, "If you then, being evil, know how to give good gifts to your children, how much more will your Father who is in heaven give what is good to those who ask Him!"[12]

The Prayer of Thomas

For years I have prayed the prayer of Thomas. Many over the centuries have called him doubting Thomas, yet Jesus found no fault in his request. You see, some of the others had been telling of seeing Jesus risen from the dead. Thomas would not just go along with what he'd heard. He wanted proof. He wanted to see it for himself and it seems Jesus didn't condemn Thomas but delighted in revealing himself to him. We all go through times of doubt; much like Thomas, we just want to see for ourselves. This is a prayer of revelation, a prayer to ask Jesus to reveal himself to you. I have never known him not to answer this prayer one way or another.

A Couple of Pointers

Start your day in prayer. Make God your first priority. Many of us have a tendency to go out charging after something and then pray that it works. It is much better to pray first and then act. Many times God will open unexpected doors and save you years of work in the process. And sometimes God will close some doors that looked great—doors through which we would have ordinarily charged but which eventually turn into just a huge waste of time and money.

A quiet time. I think one of the best habits is to carve out some time first thing in the morning for time in God's word and for prayer. This time is "just you and God" time. Consistency is very important and many times if you put it off until later in the day, you never get to it. One of the things I like to do is go for a prayer walk first thing in the morning. This gives me time in prayer, a quiet time, and exercise at the same time. I got this idea from Ross Paterson. I was embarrassed to tell him that when I prayed in the morning, I would often fall asleep. He told me he does as well, so he goes for a prayer walk. It's hard to fall asleep when you're walking.

Format

You don't have to have a set format but you may find it helpful. I find it very helpful to pray God's words back to him. A great way of starting is by praying the way
Jesus taught those closest to him how to pray: "Our Father in heaven, hallowed
be your name, your kingdom come, your will be done, on earth as it is in heaven.
Give us today our daily bread. And forgive us our debts, as we also have forgiven
our debtors. And lead us not into temptation, but deliver us from the evil one."[13]

Pray Always

All this means is letting God enjoy the day with you. Have a victory? Thank God.
Have a struggle? Ask God for guidance. Annoyed? Ask God to help you with
patience. Just include God and have him walk through the day with you. Many
of us have a tendency to only include God in our challenges, but I find the more
I include God in my whole day, the fewer challenges I have.

Pray with your Spouse

If you are married this is one of the most important things you can do. This will
join the two of you together and invite God into your relationship. Plus, God's
word says when two or three are gathered his name, he is there with you. How
powerful to have Jesus with you as you pray in his name to your father in heaven.

3. Be Part of the Pack

A few years ago, I was in the gym working out with my wife and we got a call
from my daughter Jessica telling us that our family dog Laney died. It was bit-
tersweet. Laney had experienced seizures for years and we were surprised she
lasted so long. In fact, we thought she was going to pass away years sooner than
she did, but the pack brought her back to life. When Laney was getting old, my
adult children started getting their own dogs for their homes; but one at a time,
for various reasons, we ended up with three of these dogs. They were all either in
the puppy stage or slightly past it, but they were fun, energetic, and loved Laney.
They would nip at her to get her moving, lie with her at nap time, and of course
try to steal her food at meal time. Through all of this, Laney came back to life.
She started feeling better, the seizures lessened by a lot, and she was very happy
and content being the leader of the pack.

When we arrived home Jessica told us that the other dogs were all curled
around her as she passed away. It was so sweet and so wonderful to hear this!
We wept, we laughed, and we talked about all the good times Laney brought our

family and how the puppies really enhanced Laney's final years. Much like Laney, we are all meant to be around others. We are meant to be a part of the pack. It is very important to be around others with the same faith because we are to help each other grow. I am lumping community, fellowship, and being part of a local church under one pack.

Intermediate Training Routine

4. Worship

When I first got married, I brought everything that was important to me. This included many boxes of muscle magazines. We moved to Brooklyn and the first thing that came to mind was "R & J Health Studio is in Brooklyn." That is the gym where the movie *Pumping Iron* was filmed, so I looked it up in the yellow pages and got directions. It was on the other side of Brooklyn, but that was no obstacle for me—I wanted to be around bodybuilding. Years later, I bought R & J. I didn't own the gym ten minutes before I called Jim Mannion, who ran the NPC, which is the amateur arm of bodybuilding. I told him I wanted to promote a show. Jim was thrilled and told me to call Steve Weinberger to help me out. Steve not only helped me promote a show, he did it with me so I wouldn't get hurt doing my first show alone. Steve also got me involved with the IFBB, the professional division of bodybuilding, at a pretty high level. My relationship with Steve put me on the fast track. So at home I was reading bodybuilding magazines, I was going to the gym, and I was working with the athletes and promoters of the shows. I was 100% immersed into bodybuilding. Nothing could detract my focus. I was engaged. I don't think I ever let this get to an unhealthy level, but it was certainly a form of worship.

What Is Worship?

The worship of God is to absorb yourself with God the way I did with bodybuilding. Nothing can distract you. Nothing will stand in your way. You are 100% engaged with your Father in heaven. This kind of worship isn't a song or an event; it is living your life to glorify God in all that you do. You can worship God in song at work, on the athletic field, at home, and even in a boardroom. When you are praying and asking God for strength, you are worshiping. When you are singing and giving thanks to him, you are worshiping. Certainly when you use the talents, abilities, and skills that he has entrusted you with, you aren't just going to work, you are going to worship. It is just a matter of what you are focusing on.

As I write these words, I am worshiping. I am so blessed that God allows me to do something I love so much. Worship isn't an event, it is a way of life.

A friend of mine from high school became a doctor. He has always been a very hard working guy. He told me that he started his search for God when he met an orderly in the hospital where he worked. She would be singing and praising God with all her heart, all the time. He told me, "She couldn't have been making much money, but she was happy and glowing all the time. I wanted what she had!" Living your life in a way that is glorifying to God is worship.

5. Be a Good Sharer (Witnessing)

I am not sure if this is a discipline, a spiritual gift, or a command. Regardless of how you interpret this, telling our story has a place in our lives. Jesus said, "But you will receive power when the Holy Spirit comes on you; and you will be my witnesses in Jerusalem, and in all Judea and Samaria, and to the ends of the earth."[14] Clearly Jesus wants us to share the good news of the gospel with others.

If you truly believe that Jesus died for your sins and was God's gift to you, wouldn't you want to tell people so they could receive their gift too? People don't feel funny telling others about the new and greatest self-help book out there, yet they shy away from telling people about the truths in the Bible and what Jesus did for them on the cross. Tell them your story!

How much do you have to hate someone not to tell them? Penn Gillette has a video on YouTube about a businessman who came to one of his shows to proselytize him or evangelize to him.[15] The first thing Penn said that stood out in my mind is that the man looked him straight in the eye and wasn't defensive; Penn said it was really wonderful and the man gave him a Bible. He said that he didn't respect "believers" who don't proselytize. He said that if you believe there is a heaven and hell and you believe people can go to hell, how much do you have to hate someone not to proselytize. He said that if he saw a truck bearing down on you that there is a certain point where he would tackle you to save your life— and this (salvation) is more important than that. Penn said that even though he knows there is no God, this guy was a really, really good man. He cared enough to speak to me about God.

How much do you have to hate someone not to tell them about Jesus? If you truly believe, why would you avoid telling them about Jesus? I know it can be socially awkward but this is important. You don't need to have the three step system to sharing your faith. You just need to be yourself and people will talk to you. Then you share your testimony. There is power in your testimony because no one can debate your testimony.

I avoid getting into theological debates because it's just a way to deflect from thinking and speaking about the truth. The truth is, Jesus was born of a virgin, lived a sinless life, was beaten, crucified, died, was buried, and on the third day rose from the dead. For you! You gave Jesus lordship of your life and your life has changed forever. Period! End of story! Nothing to debate! Nothing to argue about! Get over yourself and go out and tell people the good news of the gospel when God opens a door for you!

The last sentence is important—when God opens the door for you. Nothing is more annoying than someone trying to push something on you that you are not interested in. I don't care if it is insurance, a business idea, or faith. Someone once told me that you need to earn the right to sow into someone else's life. This leads right into our next subject which is serving. Serve people's needs and then you earn the right to contribute to their lives.

6. Service

We all have a slanted view of service today. You elect someone to government who will serve your needs as a person, family, community, and country. For many the service stops as soon as the election is over. Of course, this isn't true in all cases, but it is true enough to taint our view of service.

The high-rise residential buildings in New York have to hire a property management company to manage the affairs of their buildings. Unfortunately, many of the property managers hired to look out for the buildings' interests got indicted for extorting money from the companies that serviced the buildings. Some of the board members who were voted onto the board to represent the owners were also taking kickbacks. I have seen this with elected officials I have known over the years as well. The Bible says we all are sinners and have fallen short of the glory of God.

Serving has been given a bad rap. There was a day when you would help your neighbor, when your word was your bond and a handshake meant something. Today, not as much. The previous point in this spiritual fitness plan was the importance of witnessing. I think the biggest problem with witnessing is that people look at it as little more than a sales call, so to speak. In contrast, witnessing is *the natural fruit of a relationship and a relationship often is the fruit of selfless service to others*. Please read that last sentence again because it is very important.

Don't worry, I don't get poignant very often, but when I do I will be the first one to point it out to you!

One day in track practice, Coach Fraley told us all to get on our knees and start crawling around the track to look for one of our team member's contact lens. I blurted out, "Are you kidding me, we need to train!" Coach Fraley bellowed back, "Rowley, you are going to get on your knees and look for that contact whether you like it or not because it is the right thing to do!" First, Coach Fraley was right, and second, he could make my life a living hell and I didn't want that, so I crawled with the rest of them. Crawling on the track was painful. It was an old cinder block track with no cinder block, so we were crawling on dirt and pebbles. It was inconvenient, we were preparing for a meet and we needed to train. All these things are running through my mind and then I look over at the kid who lost his contact lens and saw the deep concern on his face. He couldn't see, probably didn't have the money to get another pair, and on top of it, his teammates were giving him a hard time. His face changed my attitude. I started encouraging the others to look harder and some of my other teammates were doing the same thing. We started to function as a team looking for the contact. Then someone found it. We cheered and the look on the kid's face made it all worthwhile.

Serving for the most part will not be convenient. It will not be fun and may very likely be a bit painful. But God has given me a great example of selfless service in our friends Brad and Lorrie Owen. I have never met anyone with a servant's heart like theirs. One day we are getting ready to move from our rental house to the home that we just purchased. My whole family is out loading things into trucks and cars. Then I heard someone shout at me, "Hey boy, how come I have to hear that you are moving from someone else?" I turn to look and there is Brad, a couple of his sons, and a huge trailer. The only thing that was missing was the superhero music in the background and capes waving in the wind! Was I ever glad to see them! The move that I thought would take three days was done in less than one and the Owens outworked everyone.

On another occasion, I got a call from Brad that he and his family were going to paint the house of a sick neighbor who didn't know the Lord. I told Brad I would help and we brought over some tools and went to work. I asked Brad, "Are you going to witness to him?" He said, "What do you think we are doing? We are witnessing, with our actions, by serving him. Besides, you have to earn the trust and the right to share your faith with someone! Remember boy," Brad said, "you may be the only Bible that some people are ever going to read. Be a good read."

When you live a life of service to others, you are a book that people are going to want to know more about.

When I was in the gym business, I bought a gym that didn't have any cardio-vascular equipment. My friend Steve Weinberger who, along with his wife Bev Francis, owns Bev Francis' Power House Gym in Syossott, Long Island, came into my gym one day and shouted at me: "You have no cardio! What the heck were you thinking!" Steve was right. I needed cardio, but didn't have the money to get any at that point. He promptly went to his gym, loaded up a truck, delivered several pieces of cardiovascular equipment to my gym, and told me to pay him later. Steve had no reason to do that other than he wanted to see me succeed. He was serving! Serving doesn't have to have violins and cymbals playing in the background. You do what you can with what you have.

Advanced Training Routine

Don't Try This at Home

It was the middle of the night. The alarm was blaring, the cars were whizzing down the street, and the guys in the bar across the street were looking at us. The people looking out their tenement windows were only interested to see if there was going to be a good show. Will these two white guys get shot, beat up, or both? In that frantic moment, my dad just looked at me and said, "Lock yourself in the car."

I said, "But Dad, you always told me never to go in the building when there is a break in, to wait for the police."

He snapped back at me, "That's right, YOU never do it! This is my building, my responsibility and I am going in!" That was it. He was in the door, walking with the determination of a pit bull protecting its master. It was like a scene from *Walking Tall*. Yes, my dad was and is a tough guy from Brooklyn. The strongest, most honorable man I have ever met. He taught me that you treat people the way you want to be treated. Your word is your bond. Your handshake should be firm and as binding as a contract written in blood. You look people in the eye, hold your head high, and never, ever back down from your responsibilities. A man of few words, his actions said it all.

A few years later, I was working at a High School in Brooklyn. This time, it wasn't my dad's building. I was working for someone else and it was a stark contrast to working with my dad. The blaring of the alarm was only background music to the scavengers I saw that night. As I walked up to the building, I saw brand new electric typewriters, office equipment, brass door knobs, and many other new and valuable things being loaded into cars. The thieves were long gone—this was my boss and his son doing this. "Say a word and you're fired," my boss tells me. "I don't like your father and I like you even less, so give me an excuse to fire you." He knew I needed the job, as I was married only a few months and I needed less than a year in that building to have enough time working on high pressure boilers to get my stationary engineer's license. You need five years working on high pressure boilers and my boss was sure I wasn't going to throw away all those years. He was wrong—I did! I couldn't continue to work for a man like that.

My old boss has long since died and I am sure his son is paying a price for his father's sins. The son had great dreams, but my guess is he never did more than ride on his dad's coat tails into a life of mediocrity. Not because he lacked talent. He lacked the backbone to stand on his own two feet. In stark contrast, my dad has always been a good steward of everything God has entrusted to him and in return has reaped the rewards in every area of his life.

7. Stewardship

Webster's Dictionary explains stewardship like this: "the conducting, supervising, or managing of something; especially: the careful and responsible management of something entrusted to one's care."[16] My dad was and is an honorable steward. My other boss was what the Bible would call "a wicked and slothful, servant." My heart bleeds for his son because he was being mentored by a wicked man. He was taught to rape, pillage, and plunder what was under his care. I, on the other hand, was blessed to be mentored by a man of great integrity. My dad always told me to own your job. If you work for someone else, be the best you can be and work as if you owned the company or your position.

When many people think of stewardship they think of money. Stewardship is so much more than money. God has entrusted you with many resources. Time, talents, abilities, skills, family, and money—in fact, everything in your life is given to you by God. The things God entrusts you with are God's gift to you; what you do with them is God's gift to the world.

For many years, I would contact the most successful and prominent people in Manhattan so I could get to know them and see what made them successful. How did they think? What was important to them? What did they focus on? Regardless of the other questions, my last question was always the same: How do you schedule your time? They would inevitably ask why I was asking that question. I would always say, "If you show me how you schedule your time, then I will know what you do and what is important to you. You may exaggerate the answers to the other questions, but how you schedule your time tells the whole story." They would always laugh and pull out their schedules. Often they would learn something by looking at their schedules under a different light and through the inquisitive eyes of a young, ambitious guy.

8. Fasting

This is one that I personally have a struggle with, unless I have a specific reason to fast. When I have a reason, I don't have much of a struggle with fasting, probably because I am not focusing on myself or my stomach. Someone once told me that fasting is not the same thing as a hunger strike. A hunger strike is when you stop eating until God responds. Fasting is the voluntary absence of food for spiritual purposes. You have to have a purpose when fasting. In our gluttonous society, fasting is harder and probably more important than ever before in history. Let's face it, we have everything, especially food, at our disposal. Most of us never have to give it a second thought.

The Bible mentions different types of fasts. The most common type of Christian fast would be abstaining from all food and drink, taking only water and maybe some fruit juice. You can fast from everything but vegetables which I have heard called the "Daniel fast." You can fast from an activity that you enjoy. The whole point here is to give something up that you enjoy and use that time to focus on God.

9. Silence and Solitude

This one isn't much easier for me than fasting. I love to eat, keep busy, and talk. But you can't listen when you are talking. Silence and solitude is so important to hearing the voice of God, but in our hustle-bustle world it is very hard to get. People and companies are always clamoring for our attention. Depending on which estimate you believe, the average American is bombarded with anywhere from 150 to 3,000 commercials a day! I have no idea which number is right, but either way it is a lot. If you are awake 16 hours a day and are exposed to the lower number of 150 a day, that is still over nine commercials an hour.

The importance of silence and solitude became very evident to me on a trip to China. No email, no cell phones, no car, no television. We had our Bibles, our God, and each other. As the first few days passed, I started to notice that I was hearing God more clearly than ever before and I know it was because of the lack of external stimulation. I like to have my time alone with my Father in heaven first thing in the morning. Since I haven't checked email or voicemail yet, my brain is uncluttered from all the demands in life, so I find it easier to hear God. I also use a journal to write things down that I feel God is telling me.

10. Journaling

Your life is a journey with many turns. Keeping a journal is a way for you to record the trip. It is also a great reminder of how God has intervened in your life. Going back and reading through part of your journey and how God brought you through certain challenges to incredible victory is sure to ignite your strength. If your life is worth living, it is worth recording for you to look back over—and also for those who come after you, like your children. It is a legacy of your life.

From Manhattan to the Hamptons in Style

It's Friday afternoon in Manhattan and horns are blaring; you loosen your tie or open your blouse a bit as you walk down the blistering asphalt. It's time to escape to the Hamptons. Getting out of Manhattan on a hot Friday afternoon is very stressful—all you want to do is arrive at your destination and enjoy the beach. And if by some unfortunate mishap you are not heading to the Hamptons, you can't help but see droves of people lined up for their luxury ride to the summer time capital of the East Coast.

"All aboard the Jitney" are the words you are waiting to hear as you anxiously stand in line. The Hampton Jitney is a fleet of luxury buses with on-board rest rooms and snacks. These buses leave almost hourly from the Eastside of Manhattan from 86th to 40th Street. In line you notice people in top physical condition, highly motivated movers and shakers and the best of the best in all walks of life. Once you step onto the Jitney, the driver glances at your pass, not at you. It doesn't matter if you are a high-powered business person, show business executive, homeless person, highly conditioned athlete, or Billy Joel. All that matters is that you have the proper pass. Once aboard the Hampton Jitney all are equal!

This is a good picture of what we see in Scripture and sums up the basis of the Christian faith. If you have the pass it doesn't matter who you are. During the first Passover, as long as there was the blood of the lamb over your door, the angel of death passed over your house and you and your family were safe. It didn't matter who you were or what you did; all that mattered was that you had the right pass. The blood.

Today, Jesus is the sacrificial lamb who has provided his blood as your free pass. It doesn't matter who you are or what you did; all that matters is that you have the right pass. The blood of Jesus.

Roosevelt Field, Garden City, New York 1991

It was a beautiful Saturday afternoon so Cathy and I decided to bring our three young children to Roosevelt Field for an outing. We had a great time stopping at every store that caught someone's interest. Somewhere along the way we got distracted and realized that we had Jimmy and Johnny but Jessica was nowhere to be seen. You see, the boys were a handful so they took all of our attention when we were out, but Jessica was so easy you could just hold her hand and she would be fine. Well, Cathy thought I had Jessica's hand and I thought Cathy did. As we realized that neither of us had Jessica's hand, the panic struck quickly.

Our beautiful, sweet daughter was gone. As Cathy frantically looked for her, I sprinted to security and told them to shut down the mall. Within 45 seconds this mall was closed tight as a drum. No one could get in or out! The security team was great and they called and made announcements looking for Jessica. Within just a couple of minutes, the security team got a call from a shoe store that she was sitting in there waiting for her mommy and daddy and would not go with anyone else.

We ran to the store. When we walked in, Jessica just calmly smiled and said, "That is my mommy and daddy." The saleswoman brought her over to us, we picked her up, and hugged her. We were whole again.

This is a picture of what Jesus does for us. He came to earth, searches near and far, and tells security to shut all the doors as he looks high and low for the Father's children. Then he brings them back one at a time and puts them in the Father's arms safe and sound, if they choose to go. He came so none would perish. He has permanently barred the doors to hell for those who simply receive his free gift.

Chapter 14

The Lifestyle Restoration Cycle

Your Why

Know your why and the what and how
will take care of itself. —**John M. Rowley**

Your "why" in life is your purpose in life. This is the time to put in a little work and define why you want to do what you are setting out to do. Once you know your why, it will be so much more powerful as you go about implementing the principles in this section. This section is on "Flexing Your SPIRITual Muscles." Knowing why you want to be more physically fit, vibrant and healthy is probably the most energizing revelation you can have.

Step 1

Write down "why" you are passionate about getting into physical shape. Next to each "why" on your list, write a brief paragraph defining why you are committed to achieving the result you are after. "Why" is very powerful. (E.g., I want to serve my local community through the talents God has blessed me with.)

1 _____

_____

_____

2 _____

_____

3 _____

_____

_____

4 _____

_____

_____

5 _____

_____

_____

Step 2: This is where we put the plan together.

Take the above list and put together an action list of things you would need to do to achieve them in your life. This is where you formulate your plan. It is easier to put a plan together once you know why you are doing it.

1 _____

2 _____

3 _____

4 _____

5 _____

Step 3. Master your habits or they WILL master you!
—John M. Rowley

For each step in your plan, write down one or more habits you will need to develop and the disempowering habits you will need to get rid of in order to support your ultimate outcome. Imagine if you exchanged six limiting habits for six empowering habits every year. In five years, that would be 30 empowering habits that you do without effort and 30 disempowering habits that don't hinder you any longer. Do you think your life would be different?

List of Disempowering Habits

1 _____

2 _____

3 _____

4 _____

5 _____

List of New Empowering Habits

1 _____

2 _____

3 _____

4 _____

5 _____

List Which New Empowering Habit Will Replace The Old Disempowering Habit

(For Example: Replace sleeping in with having quiet time with God.)

1 _____

2 _____

3 _____

4 _____

5 _____

Congratulations! You just defined your first lifestyle restoration cycle! You found your why. Then you put a plan together. You identified disempowering habits that you are going to replace with empowering habits on a regular basis so they become part of your lifestyle, hence closing the loop on The Lifestyle Restoration Cycle.

Now go to http://habitfoundry.com to supercharge your habits. We will check in with you daily by email to see how you did the day before. You can either "Go solo" or "Join a Group" of people who are working on a similar goal as you.

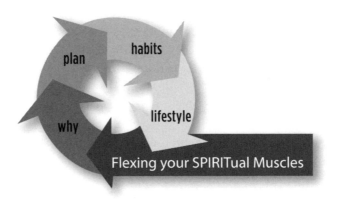

Part IV

LIVING
THE POWER OF
POSITIVE FITNESS

Chapter 15

The 90% Rule

What ultimately differentiates highly successful people from the rest of the pack? From what I see, the one common denominator of all successful people is a lifestyle designed around empowering habits. The most successful people in any field, be it athletes, lawyers, politicians, physicians, business leaders, musicians, parents, pastors, or sales people—those who are the best at what they do—all have successful habits.

Up to 90 percent of your everyday behavior is based on habit. Nearly all of what you do each day, every day, is simply habit. More than anything else this book is about lifestyle restoration by developing new empowering habits. The difference between those who are successful and everyone else is not more intelligence, talent, or harder work; it is rather that they have a lifestyle designed to help them succeed. This is very important! Although we have touched on this throughout the book, I am going to elaborate so it is fresh in your mind as you do your final Lifestyle Restoration Cycle.

Lifestyle is just another word for daily habits. An empowering lifestyle is the key to unleashing the power in our lives to reach our God-given potential and obtain a higher degree of success, happiness, and fulfillment. Do I have your attention now? If I don't, pinch yourself, get a cup of coffee, or go for a run around the block to wake yourself up. You don't want to miss this because this is the key that will open up the door to the greatness that God has placed in you!

The Power of Habits

"Motivation is what gets you fired up and moving,
but your daily habits are what catapult you to success
long after the motivation is gone!" —**John Rowley**

Every year diligent people sit down and define their goals for the coming year, and with good reason. Goals work! But in order to achieve goals you must have empowering habits to support your desired outcome. You become what you do all the time. We all have habits, some good and some bad. We get up on the same side of the bed, dress ourselves, and brush our teeth the same way every day. If you have empowering habits, you will be more successful in life. If you have habits that limit you, you can replace them with habits that support your goals—and you will watch your life transform before your eyes.

What Do Your Current Habits Look Like?

Are your habits helping you to be the person you want to be or are they having the opposite effect? Are your habits well thought out or are they ones that just developed over time and you're really not sure why you even have them? Now we are going to get into a little more detail on how to develop new empowering habits. Throughout this book we have been identifying our bad habits and replacing them with good ones as we finished each section. At the end of this chapter we will do that again so you can continue designing an empowering lifestyle.

How to Develop New and Empowering Habits

Benjamin Franklin once said, "Many people die at twenty five and aren't buried until they are seventy five." These are the same people who just let life happen to them. They develop habits as time goes by and become a slave to habits that don't support them. Developing new habits requires effort and takes time. The rule of thumb is that it takes 21 days to develop a new habit. This is probably true for small habits but large lifestyle changes take a little more time.

The best way to eliminate or break a bad habit is by replacing it with something else. The bad habit is serving a purpose in your life. When you eliminate the bad habit you are creating a void which needs to be filled by something else or the bad habit will simply creep back into your life. If you overeat to relieve stress, you need to find a more productive way to relax, such as going for a walk or going to the gym.

Imagine if you exchanged two limiting habits for two empowering habits every year. In five years, that would be ten empowering habits that you do without effort. That is with only two a year. What if you did six a year? In five years, you would have thirty empowering habits. Do you think your life would be different with thirty empowering habits? All your successes will pile up on top of each other and you will have an extraordinary quality of life by making these small daily changes.

In order to change your habits:

1. You must define them so write down all the habits that limit you.
2. Define your new successful habits in detail. Write down what new habit you will do in place of your old, limiting habits.
3. Develop an action plan for this new habit. This may be as simple as scheduling time to exercise, read your bible, prospect or return calls.
4. Keep it as simple as possible. Make it easy to be successful in all areas of your life.

Set up your environment to help you succeed. If you're trying to eat healthy, clean out your kitchen and get rid of all the junk food. Simply refuse to have junk food in the house. If you want to start doing cardio at home but you find yourself watching television instead, put your exercise bike in front of the television. If you want to exercise first thing in the morning, set the alarm, preset the coffee pot, and lay out your gym clothes the night before so they're the first thing you see when you wake up in the morning.

This is why we developed Habit Foundry, which is a free online tool. You will input your goals, and we'll send you a customized daily email following up with you. Succeed for 30 days, and the new action will be easier than ever. Skip a day and the clock starts over at day one. This is a great way to have automation help you make habits part of your daily lifestyle.

Don't underestimate the power of positive peer pressure. With Habit Foundry you can join a team. Also have your spouse or friend join you in some of your new habits. Get a training partner for the gym. Join a group at your church or an online group that will support you. Positive peer pressure is terrific because everyone is trying to accomplish the same thing and a group will provide accountability and support to help you on your journey.

Picture it. Review your list of why you want to create a new habit. Do you want to get into shape? Find pictures of someone with the body you want and place them where you can see them. I like the refrigerator for this so you see it right as you go to eat. For other habits, find images that represent the benefits of the new habit and put them somewhere you can see them, maybe on a bulletin board or even take them and make them the wallpaper on your computer screen. If you select one or two habits to work on each month, a year from now your life will be completely different from what it is today. Master your habits or they WILL master you!

Build a Stone Wall

So often, we look at success as being a gigantic event. Walking with God, having a harmonious household, incredible relationship with your spouse, getting into tip top physical condition and having outstanding business and financial success, all require the same thing. Empowering daily disciplines. Success is seldom the result of one monstrous event. It is the natural outcome of doing the right things on a consistent basis.

Nehemiah built the stone wall in record time because everyone paid attention to the wall directly in front of their own home.[2] I can only imagine how daunting it would have been to look at the whole wall and say, no way Jose or rather, no way Nehemiah, but looking at the wall in front of their own home with a narrow focus they could see victory. I can hear them now, "Hey Isaac, I can definitely get the wall built from my house to your house. How about you can get the wall done from yours to Abraham's house."

Then Isaac feeling challenged shouts back, "Not only will I get it done but I will be munching on some homemade Matza long before you are even thinking about being finished!" I took some creative liberty with this scenario but the point is, success comes one stone at a time. By implementing the building blocks of successful habits you will reap consistent results in your life with much less effort.

This may be one of the most simplistic explanations on how to be successful in every area of your life. Often simplicity is the key that opens the door to success and because it's so simple, it is over looked. I was looking for the common thread that knits together the successes in every area of your life. First we should have our priorities in the correct order. God, family, health and work seems to be a healthy order of things. Then what is the solution to living a successful, un-compromised life? It was so simple, I almost missed it. Although I have been teaching around it for years, I never clearly defined it.

❖

The Lifestyle Restoration Cycle—
Why ⇨ Plan ⇨ Habits ⇨ Lifestyle

Let's go over this together. When you look at overcoming the obstacles to living victoriously with God, being in good physical shape, and having an empowering mindset, we see that the solution is the same for all. Lifestyle restoration is the key. Taken individually this can become overwhelming. You are already very busy with work, home, kids, friends, church, etc. You couldn't possibly do one more thing without exploding. I get it, but that is why this is so powerful. Start by defining your why, which is your life's purpose. Then formulate the lifestyle solution driven by your why. This is very simple. Just list the things you need to do in order to achieve the outcome you desire. Then review your plan and identify the habits you need to have in order to fulfill your plan. Finally, commit to replacing your disempowering habits with the empowering habits you identified on your list. These new habits now become your new lifestyle. This is very powerful. Please, don't let the simplicity minimize its effectiveness.

The Power of Lifestyle

The key to achieving the peak performance
lifestyle is simply to make it part of your life.

"The more prepared you are the more confident you become." —John Rowley

I see this in every area of life. When people are not prepared for the task at hand they procrastinate doing what they know they should do because they feel they are not confident in that area. It's not confidence that is the underlying issue; it is competence. In the gym I can always tell the people who don't know how to use the equipment. They walk around a little, maybe even try one exercise . . . and then off to the treadmill for them. Since they didn't know how to use the equipment, they give up and go to what they know.

I see this often with sales people. The average salesperson will avoid prospecting because they don't know what to say when prospecting or they may not be comfortable with the paperwork they need to complete the sale, so they avoid contact with potential customers. This avoidance eventually leads to a different career, and is completely avoidable by taking time to gain training in necessary job skills. People will spend countless hours at the driving range practicing golf but those same people expect to waltz right into the business world with no practice or preparation at all and expect to succeed. As ridiculous as it sounds, you know this is true.

It is no secret that most people will spend more time preparing for and planning their vacation than they do their daily lives. The key to being prepared for all areas of your life is to look at what you want to achieve and then plan simple steps to achieve it.

Let's look at a simple plan for eating healthy. People are always telling me that they can't eat healthy at work or when on-the-go, but that is only because they are not prepared to do so.

> Plan out your meals for each day
> Make a grocery list for those meals
> Take one day to make the meals for the rest of the week
> Separate cooked food into individual meals
> Store individual meals in a zip lock bag or airtight container
> Put Monday through Wednesday meals into the refrigerator
> Put Thursday through Saturday meals in the freezer
> On Wednesday take the food out of the freezer for the rest of the week
> Bring your meals with you to work or when you go out

Put a plan like this together for every area of your life, implement them a little at a time, and you will be thrilled with the new direction your life has taken.

WOW Is MOM Upside Down

Cathy has always told me that WOW is just MOM upside down, and that is just what I thought the first time we saw Missy Currin leading an exercise class of moms with strollers. Missy is one of many moms who have become part of the Stroller Strides franchise. Cathy is an incredible mom and when our kids were young they would never stay too long in the house. They would be off in the stroller, maybe with some bikes in tow, to meet Carol, Berta, and other young moms. The moms got some exercise and much needed adult interaction while their kids were getting fresh air and exercise. You don't see that very often these days. Imagine our delight when we saw Missy leading an exercise class for moms. They were powerwalking with the strollers and then stopped, pulled elastic exercise bands out of the stroller for a few sets of well-thought-out exercises, and continued with more powerwalking.

Lisa Druxman founded Stroller Strides after the birth of her son in 2001. She knew there must be a way to blend her passion for fitness with motherhood. Apparently, she was not alone in the quest to become a fit mom because Stroller Strides has since become one of the fastest-growing fitness franchises in the country. The classes offer a workout while pushing a stroller. For 60 minutes, mom achieves a total body workout and baby has fun! Stroller Strides is an example of what we have been talking about—a wonderful way to make fitness part of your lifestyle. Missy helps the moms put a plan in place, the moms implement that plan on a regular basis, and they have a great time getting into shape. If these moms can do it, please don't tell me you don't have enough time.

It doesn't matter whether you are a student, businessperson, stay at home mom, entrepreneur, or employee, time is a rare commodity. Many people simply don't accomplish all they need to, but I don't think time is the culprit. These same people are unfocused and drag through the day, taking too long to do tasks because of their lack of focus. Then, when they go home to sleep they have a fitful night's sleep and wake up tired. This is an endless, but unnecessary, cycle for many today. *We are all given the same 10,080 minutes in a week. Some people have the time to change the world and some barely have the time to change their socks. Time isn't the issue. The real issue is having enough energy to use time effectively.*

Planning and Scheduling

Your mental, physical, and spiritual health is your responsibility, not the responsibility of your doctor, pastor, or psychiatrist. In fact, many doctors consult with me on how to eat properly and exercise effectively because medical school doesn't focus on preventative but on curative medicine. Planning your time is the key to great health and fitness, as well as success in all areas of your life.

Since everyone has the same 10,080 minutes in a week, success in life lies not in having more time but in how you use the time you are given. So the excuse that you don't have enough time to eat right, exercise, read your Bible, or do anything else that would enhance your life will not exist once you finish reading this. You will have enough time if you commit to a lifestyle that supports you instead of cripples you.

Time Blocking

There are many ways to schedule your time but the easiest and most effective way I have found is called time blocking. This can be done in many ways. You can block off whole days for certain aspects of your life or you can break each day down into blocks of time. I use the latter because I find it more effective for me.

First, define the most important things that you need to get done. Then put them into time blocks. What this does is allow you to put the most important things into your schedule and make that time non-negotiable. You schedule the appropriate time to get things done. Everything else gets scheduled around these "must do" items. Below is an example of how you may block off your day.

Monday	
Time	
6:00–7:00 AM	Cardio
7:00–9:00 AM	Prepare for and travel to work
9:00–11:00 AM	Paper work
11:00–12:00 PM	
12:00–1:30 PM	Lunch meeting
1:30–3:00 PM	Return calls
3:00–4:00 PM	
4:00–5:00 PM	Prepare for tomorrows phone conference
5:30–6:30 PM	Gym
7:00 PM	

Below is an example of a simpler one, like the one I use. As anyone who knows me can attest, I don't like a lot of structure. I always "hard" schedule the things that are important.

Monday	
Time	
5:00–6:00 AM	Cardio
7:00–10:00 AM	Write
10:30–11:30 AM	Gym

I do my cardio workouts first thing in the morning. For years we did our whole workout at that time. But, due to our changing lifestyle and that of our children, we started to lift weights in the late morning before lunch. This is our "lunch break." We use a schedule that works for us and supports our lifestyle.

Cathy sets up the coffee pot the night before and puts it on an automatic timer. Cathy has more energy at night than I do. Being a morning person, I get up very early, jump out of bed, and pour us our coffee. This works for us and we have been doing it for most of our 28 years of marriage. She loves being served her coffee; it makes her feel loved and I like to be the one who speaks her love language. A little later we enjoy breakfast together. Cathy and I have busy lives with lots of demands, so this gives us time in the morning together when we can talk and be together at the beginning of each day. If we did not make time for the important things in our lives, we would never be able to find the time to fit them in. We take the time to plan our lives which allows us a lively, passion-filled, and energetic life. Find out what works for you.

Partners

Cathy is my training partner in the gym; she encourages me and spots me if I need a little help. This a good picture of how partners, friends, and family are there for one another. Cathy is more than my spotter in the gym; she is my best friend and spotter in life. I would not be writing these words if God hadn't chosen such an incredible bride for me. Cathy and I have a group of couples that we meet with every Sunday before service for some teaching and sharing of our lives so we can pray for each other during the coming week. In addition, our pastor, Chad Harvey, takes a very active role in supporting us and praying with us about important decisions in our lives. His guidance is always sound, biblical, well-thought out, and direct. Pastor Chad doesn't believe in beating around the bush and we are blessed to have him in our life. These people are spotters for our lives.

Several years ago our kids were under our care, but now it seems they are there for us every bit as much as we are there for them. They intimately know what others would never know or even guess. They know just when to pop over, give a call, or send an encouraging email. They have become our spotters and true partners. Of course, we are there for them and that is one of the joys of being a parent. All four of our wonderful kids know just how to "spot us" with their special gifts while still leaving us with our parental dignity. My son Jim is there with a caring call, a funny joke, or will pop over to help us with something just at the right time. John is in the military now, but his calls are frequent and caring and

and when he, Jocelyn, and the kids are in town they come over to see if we need any work done around the house. This also gives us time to play with our grandchildren. Jessica is probably the most reserved of our children outwardly, but she is a tiger on the inside. Jessica pops over for lunch a few times a week to see how we are and when our car died she gave us hers. She is an incredible daughter who has turned into an outstanding young lady. Jacqueline, who is still in high school, is an light-hearted joy. She never met a person she couldn't talk to or make feel special in some way. She is growing into quite an amazing young lady.

All of our children have special gifts that could have only come from God. We are so blessed that even though we have failed them in some ways as parents—me, in particular, as a hard driving dad—they still love us and are the most important part of our lives. They are our main team of spotters. They represent the good that God wanted to come out of my life. They will achieve the things I could only dream of. No one is self-made. We all have spotters and we must be humble enough not only to accept the spot but to be thankful that they are there for us.

Sand, Mucus, or a Pearl—Your Choice

An oyster opens its shell to yawn and a little speck of sand slips in. Try as the oyster might, it can't get rid of the sand regardless of how irritating it is. The oyster is left with no other choice but to secrete a mucus-like substance to protect itself. Over time this substance builds up around the sand and hardens. The end result is a pearl. If the oyster was able to stop this process at anytime, it would have had either a piece of sand stuck in it or a piece of sand covered in mucus. Either scenario doesn't sound like fun if you are an oyster. The oyster is given no choice; it goes through the process of being irritated by the sand until a valuable pearl is born.

Much like the oyster, we have things that God allows into our lives to irritate us. I don't care how much you incorporate the physical, mental, and spiritual disciplines in this book or any other book into your life—irritants come. They often slip in without notice but eventually they start irritating us. We have a choice: Do we let it remain as sand to constantly irritate us? Do we cover it with a little bit of mucus so we can avoid it? Or do we let it do its job and produce a pearl in our life?

Many people never experience the pearls that life has to offer because they let the irritants stop them. God's will is for you to grow through the irritation into the person he knows you can be. Being physically, mentally, and spiritually fit is very important and I am not minimizing that. I want you to know that sand will come into your life regardless of what you do, but it is there to make you grow.

Much like lifting weights is an irritant to your muscles that makes them get larger and stronger, irritants in our lives help us grow in areas we may not be willing to face. Fortunately, God loves you enough to strategically allow those grains of sand into your life. One word of caution: if you run away from the current irritation, God will just allow it to follow you.

Many years ago I was struggling with some things at the church we were attending. I called my good friend Ross Paterson for some valuable insight. He told me, "Mate, if you leave that church God is going to have these issues follow you until you are willing to face them. He loves you that much. So why go to another church and mess it up because you are running from God's refining fire. Stay there, work through it, and see what the Lord has for you." I am saying the same to you. Face your fears and deal with them so you can become the person God has designed you to be. Plus, why go mess up other people's lives running away from God's refining fire.

Just as I look to mentors like Ross for words of wisdom in times of need, I think there is wisdom in looking at the lives of others to see what they are doing so you can learn and grow. That is the purpose behind this next section, "Positive Fitness Interviews." Not one person on this list has the perfect lifestyle for you because we are all unique, but by reviewing the lifestyle choices and priorities of others I feel you can get some valuable insight into how to best design your lifestyle to empower your life.

Chapter 16

Positive Fitness Interviews

In this section I will introduce you to some real people with real lives. I asked all of them a series of questions without any leading, so the responses are spontaneous and genuine. Their responses reveal how they prioritize certain important aspects of their lives. In addition, no one in this section is my protégée. There are a couple here to whom I gave a good nudge to put them on the right path, but they have done all the work. This section is 100% for you to see the real lives of real people. No hype, no back patting, no sales pitch. Just real lifestyles of real people, just like you and me.

This is deliberately not a before and after section. I am very tired of "transformation" photos. It is difficult to know for certain if the pictures are doctored in some way or shot in reverse order. Also, with weight loss contest before and after photos, I often wonder if the contestants stayed in good shape after the motivation to win a contest ended. A few of the people in this section have made dramatic personal transformations and for that I applaud them, but I also know they have gone on to live a healthy lifestyle that inspires others. This group represents varied lifestyles, but they all have their priorities in place and are fit and vibrant. In other words, they have real lives with real families, real jobs, and real responsibilities.

Ed Brantley and Heba Salama are a wonderful couple. They started their health and fitness journey on a national television challenge to lose weight. This challenge turned into a passion to help and inspire others. Even though they have demanding careers, they choose to share their story wherever they go. They are living examples of what is possible when you passionately pursue your purpose. Ed and Heba truly are the BIGGEST WINNERS!

Leanne Yager Nealey lost weight and got into great physical shape while living a well-balanced lifestyle. I am good friends with Leanne and her husband Tim and I know for a fact they both have their priorities in order and are diligent in every area of their lives. I have been with them at public events, where we were all working, and have been with them in more personal settings; I can honestly say they are the same in season and out and always a lot of fun. Consistently balancing God, family, and business, in that order, while helping to improve the lives of those around them is their hallmark. Leanne is a busy wife, mom, and business owner. She stays in top shape because she has made it part of her lifestyle.

Cathy and I watched **Kristy Tyndall** transform herself from being a little out of shape into a fitness competitor. She is a wife, mother, and has a full-time career as a nurse anesthetist. Kristy has a lifestyle that supports her life.

David Lyons is a very good friend of mine. David owns Lyons Entertainment which has been creating, developing, and producing original programming for the TV and film industry. David also has multiple sclerosis and has decided to fight back by going against some of the advice of his doctors; he uses exercise and nutrition to stay strong. David is a very busy man, but he and his wife Kendra have a wonderful family and have designed a lifestyle that keeps them physically, mentally, and spiritually fit.

When I first met **Phil Strand** he was a typical, overweight businessman who was bound and determined not to be typical anymore. Phil wanted to get into shape for his health but also because he wanted to enjoy the fruits of a lifetime of hard work. What caught my attention with Phil was his consistency. I know if I go into the gym on Phil's cardio days at 6:00 AM that he is there and working hard. I know I will run into him at least two or three times a week in the gym if we are both in town. He is like the postal service. Rain or shine Phil is there. The result has been nothing short of astounding. He looks at least a decade younger than he is, has the energy of a man half his age, and is extremely effective in the business world. Phil is an inspiration to those who know him.

This is a great group of people. All have taken different paths but through review of their lifestyles you will see patterns emerge. Consistency in eating, consistency in working out, consistent sleep patterns. Sure you will see variations, which is why I picked such a diverse group, but you will see a pattern of a structured lifestyle with discipline and consistency at the core. Nothing fancy here, just the implementation of core principles on a consistent basis.

Ed Brantley and Heba Salama Ed Brantley: professional chef, chef instructor, food educator; age 34. Heba Salama: women's body image speaker, photographer, author; age 33.

❖ What time do you get up in the morning? *Heba: I am usually up between 8:30 AM and 9:00 AM.*

Ed: I'm up anywhere from 5:00 AM to 8:00 AM, depending on my schedule that day (I teach at a culinary school).

What are the morning habits or rituals that you have?

Heba: I always make the bed before I do anything, eat breakfast, and then head straight to workout.

Ed: I shower, head off to work, or to work out, and then eat afterwards.

What time do you go to the gym? How do you fit your workouts into your week.

Heba: I usually get to the gym between 9:00 AM and 11:00 AM in the morning.

Ed: I go around 3:00 PM or 4:00 PM or may do some exercise classes in the evening. This all depends on the day's schedule.

What kind of workout routine do you follow? *We do a lot of classes—yoga, bootcamp, TRX. We do classes 5 to 6 days per week. We are also training for races so we normally do another 4 days of running mixed in with our other workouts.*

How long are you in the gym when you work out?

Heba: I don't work out in the gym at all anymore. I always take classes or go running. I don't have any interest in exercising inside on the machines, unless it is in a class environment.

Ed: I work out for about 30 minutes on the elliptical machine. I will then work out with weights for about 45 minutes, followed by a quick two mile run on the treadmill.

Do you do cardio with weight training or at a separate time?

Heba: Usually all mixed together.

Ed: I keep it separate.

How do you make eating healthy convenient? Do you eat out, bring meals with you, etc.? *We try to plan a week in advance for at least 4 dinners at home, and all lunches at home. We go out about 3 times per week, depending on our schedule. Since Ed is a chef, we never have a problem asking for exactly what we want when we go out—healthy eating is a way of life for us now!*

How do you make time for your family, social life, and other activities? *Our family and friends are totally on board with our way of life. Often our social activity includes Heba taking a yoga class with a friend or going running with someone—we are lucky that all of our friends are also healthy eaters, so dinner parties are much more fun and easy now!*

What time do you get to bed at night? *Heba: around 11:00 and Ed anywhere from 10:00 PM to 1:00 AM—he is not a regular sleeper.* ❖

Leanne Yager Nealey 44 years old, owner of All That Glitters Studio & Boutique, "All That Glitters . . . Is a Heart of GOLD!" national & international trainer, health/ beauty & home spa specialist

❖ What time do you get up in the morning? *6:00 AM weekdays, 9:00 AM (ish) weekends.*

What are your morning habits or rituals? *Rush my 14 year old to school and breakfast on the run.*

What time do you go to the gym? How do you fit your workouts into your week? *I like the evening classes better so I can get all my business and errands done throughout the day. I would rather finish my business then go sweat it out and shower at end of the day rather than taking all morning to work out and get ready.*

What type of workout routine do you follow? *I do cardio dance 3-4 times a week—2-3 evenings and Saturday AM classes. I try to go to the gym once a week for weight training.*

How long are you in the gym when you work out? *Cardio dance is a one-hour class and about 45 minutes if I'm doing weights.*

Do you do cardio with weight training or at a separate time? *Separate times.*

How do you make eating healthy convenient? Do you eat out, bring meals with you, etc.? *I usually eat out—when I eat at home I tend to cheat and cut corners to be fast and easy. I find that I can eat better protein out than trying to please everyone at home.*

How do you make time for your family, social life, and other activities? *My family IS my social time. We have a blast all together! I am very involved with helping women market themselves better in all areas of life and create better self-esteem, so we are all over the place all the time with family, business, and hanging with friends. I incorporate family into business and mix friends with business time as well. I am all about networking all areas of life together—that's how you get it all done!*

What time do you get to bed at night? *I start winding down around 10:30 but never really get to bed until around 12:00 AM.*

Feel free to add anything else that you feel is relevant. *I have found that if I MOVE MORE than what any task really takes, I BURN MORE. I love to dance, so I love to Bee-Bop in the car and I find that simple ribcage-rolls and calf raises in the car are just a few great ways to keep my fitness goals in front of me. I make simple choices everyday—like apple or fries, grilled or fried, and several times I have to make the choice to choose wisely. I mess up a lot too, but I am making changes in my life and I have to be accountable to myself to take control again every day. I think one of the biggest things I do is to ask for help in prayer. I include God in everything I do throughout the day. I choose to see him in all things. So I ask him to please guide my steps and tongue so that everything I say and do will be glorifying to him. To allow me to be a blessing in other people lives each day and to move his hand mightily in my life and show me what he has done that day. I want to be an instrument for him in all areas of my life and encourage others to do the same. Many days I have to ask him to lead me not into temptation and for me, that's FOOD. He says, "Knock and the door shall be opened, ask and you shall receive"—I believe it!* ❖

Ken Huff 58 years old; played football for the University of North Carolina, Baltimore Colts 1975–1982, Washington Redskins 1983–1985; member of the North Carolina Hall of Fame, owner of Ken Huff Builders

❖ What time do you get up in the morning? *6:00 AM*

What are your morning habits or rituals? *One hour of cardio on the elliptical machine 5 or 6 days a week.*

What time do you go to the gym? How do you fit your workouts into your week? *4:30 PM , after work.*

What kind of workout routine do you follow? And how do you arrange the workouts throughout the week? *4 days a week working each body part once a week. Once you have a routine it is easy to maintain and I actually feel guilty if I don't do it.*

How long are you in the gym when you work out? *An hour and a half.*

Do you do cardio with weight training or at a separate time? *I do cardio first thing in the morning.*

How do you make eating healthy convenient? *I eat a healthy breakfast at home. When eating out for lunch or dinner, I am sure to eat something nutritious. As the day goes on, I decrease my carbohydrates and only have protein and vegetables in the late afternoon and evening.*

How do you make time for your family, social life, and other activities? *It is a matter of scheduling your day and prioritizing what's important. I schedule time for the important things in my life.*

What time do you get to bed at night? *11:00 PM*

Feel free to add anything else that you feel is relevant. *Physical fitness is an important part of my life; it keeps me fit for outdoor adventures such as backpacking, mountain climbing, sky diving, and scuba diving. I love to work with the Special Olympians and have just started to work with the Wounded Warriors Foundation to honor those heroes for their sacrifice for our country. The first trip will be a hike up to the summit of Mount Kilimanjaro and we hope to turn this into an annual event to various locations to bring recognition to these well-deserving men and women.* ❖

Kristi Frank, celebrity, diet & fitness expert from NBC's 'The Apprentice' & Featured on 'Oprah,' 'The Today Show,' MSNBC, and 'The View.'

❖ What time do you get up in the morning? *I love the quietude and power of early morning. I am at my most creative early so I'll set the alarm or wake up on my own at 4:30 or 5 am when I'm writing or working on a big project. Sleeping in is 7 :00 AM for me!*

What are the morning habits or rituals that you have? *Coffee! (with almond or soy milk) That, and some stretching to wake up my body and brain. I love waking up to that. Then I get my priorities in order for the day on a list—so I can cross them off one by one. And, of course, then make sure my son is fed a healthy breakfast and off to school.*

What time do you go to the gym? How do you fit your workouts into your week.

Gym time for me is mostly in the winter. After so many years in the gym, I love exercising outdoors. It clears my head and challenges me. My favorite workout is a hike up a mountain trail, a long beach walk or a rock 'n roll yoga class! When I travel for media or appearances, I make sure to work out, like running up a couple flights of stairs or doing high kicks or yoga in my room.

What time of workout routine do you follow? *I just started to train with the Kinesis machine. It's amazing! Usually, I'll do 20–30 min on that machine, 3–5 times a week and then sometimes do free weights on my own. As I get older, I'm seeing how important weight training is!*

How long are you in the gym when you work out? *I'll do cardio for at least 30 min 5-6 days a week, or hop into a spin or yoga class. Usually I'll take an hour outside in the summertime. When my son (he's 6) comes home from school we are always on the go. His favorite? Jumping on the trampoline, skiing, or riding bikes. My kiddo never stops moving.*

Do you do cardio with weight training or at a separate time? *I usually do cardio and weight training in the same session, although my cardio-driven brisk walks three seasons a year are separate from weight training.*

How do you make eating healthy convenient? *Seven years ago I found a new way of eating that totally transformed my body. It allows me to eat as much as I want without counting calories or worrying that I'll gain weight. I follow 3 simple keys to eating and made it easy for anyone to follow. I named the program 'Kristi Frank's get Slim & Fit Fast' and I'm about to launch it online. It represents what I've learned through the years as both a health and fitness advocate as well as an organic restaurant owner . . . I just had to find the time to write it all down.*

Do you eat out, bring meals with you, etc? *I always have food in my purse. I carry my greens, protein shake in a bag, raw almonds or sunflower seeds and my vitamin packs with me always! Healthy eating can be easy on the go, but you have to be prepared and I never allow myself to grab junk unless it's something I plan and choose to splurge.*

How do you make time for your family, social life, and other activities? *When I became a mom, my whole life changed. My family became my first priority and I realized that I needed to take care of my physical and mental health so I can be the best possible role-model and woman I can be for my boys. It's challenging to fit in everything, but with the help of my husband we make it work well.*

What time do you get to bed at night? *I would love to go to bed by 9:00 or 10:00 PM! Normal time is 10:30.* ❖

Jeff Yager 45 years old, Crown Ambassador—Amway Global.

❖ What time do you get up in the morning? *7:00 to 8:00 AM*

What are your morning habits or rituals? *Most mornings I exercise on the treadmill, have breakfast and read the Bible. It doesn't always work out that way but I make my best effort.*

What time do you go to the gym? How do you fit your workouts into your week? *I hired a trainer to work with me in the office gym.*

What kind of workout routine do you follow? *Weights three times a week, if I'm in town; but it's hard to do on the road.*

How long are you in the gym when you work out? *30- 60 minutes*

Do you do cardio with weight training or at a separate time? *After weight training or in the morning.*

How do you make eating healthy convenient? Do you eat out, bring meals with you, etc? *I'll have a sandwich or salad for lunch, dinner at home when in town.*

How do you make time for your family, social life, and other activities? *My kids are home schooled so our schedule is more flexible for dad, since mom schools the kids. I take the kids with me on special trips, ball games, etc.* ❖

Jennifer Nicole Lee 36 years old, bestselling author, motivational life coach and super fitness model. Jennifer's story has been featured on "The Oprah Winfrey Show."

❖ What time do you get up in the morning? *I get up at 4:00 AM, so I can get about two and a half hours of writing and work in before my hubby and sons wake up. It's so quiet then, and I am my best creatively when I am not distracted. I love then to wake up my family with a great big healthy breakfast.*

What are your morning habits or rituals? *I always work in the morning when my energy is freshest. Then I wake up my family, fix breakfast, and get them off to school or camp. Then I workout around 9 or 9:30, either at my home gym or a fitness center (I love Powerhouse Gyms), and then work some more after my workout. You can catch me any moment on HSN, or at a photo shoot, book signing, or a celebrity appearance.*

What time do you go to the gym? *I usually arrive around 10:00 am, once the early morning traffic has left. I also train whenever I can. If I have a window of time open, I grab it and workout!*

How do you fit your workouts into your week. *I follow my JNL FUSION method, which is in my newest book* The Jennifer Nicole Lee Fitness Model Diet. *It's a two-day/one-day split, where I go two days on with weights, and one day off. It helps me stay on track and train just right, without overtraining.*

What kind of workout routine do you follow? *Out of frustration of needing max results in minimum time, I created my method called JNL Fusion, and it's a two day on, one day off split.*

How long are you in the gym when you work out? *One hour max. If more than that, I wasted my own time. I use a Gym Boss timer to help me keep my fast pace with little to no rest in between. I also love to do our amazing Ab Circle Group X Classes here at Powerhouse Gym. They are amazing, because in 20 minutes you have burned a lot of calories and tightened up your entire mid-section like nothing ever before!*

Do you do cardio with weight training or at a separate time? *Yes, I do cardio at the same time, it's my trademark JNL FUSION technique, where I am able to get the best of both worlds—to burn ugly fat, while building and toning sexy feminine muscle. I do six circuits of 30 second intervals; for instance a shoulder press for 30 seconds, followed by a 30 second blast of speed rope. Then I repeat this circuit two more times.*

How do you make eating healthy convenient? *I always eat breakfast like a queen, lunch like a princess, and dinner like a pauper. Then I always have my BSN shakes post workout, and also after lunch.*

Do you eat out, bring meals with you, etc? *I always have my protein shakes ready to mix, bring portable snacks with me, and also at restaurants ask for no salt and no oil on my meals. I often will order grilled chicken or fish with a side of asparagus.*

How do you make time for your family, social life, and other activities? *I always am with my hubby or kids! They are my foundation. I never forsake my family time for anything! You must make it a priority, and do things together. We play golf, bike ride, travel, go to the beach. We live a very active lifestyle, and I often joke that parenthood is a full time sport!*

What time do you get to bed at night? *In bed by 10:00, lights out by 10:30. Nothing like good old fashioned beauty sleep! Rest and relaxation is the yin to the yang of working out. Since you actually are building muscle and repairing your body while at rest, I aim to get my Z's! Lastly, I want all to know that if "busy" is your middle name, like mine, if you want a super healthy lifestyle, it's possible! You just have to want it!* ❖

Mitch Gaylord 1984 Olympic Gold Medalist, motivational speaker and fitness celebrity.

❖ What time do you get up in the morning? *Having two young ones in the house gets me out of bed far earlier than I would normally want to get up. I'd say between 6:30 and 7:30 AM. Just depending on when they decide it's time to take on the world. My nature is to sleep in—I'm very much a night owl by nature.*

What are the morning habits or rituals that you have? *Rituals start with my morning cup of coffee that, I must say, has become sacred. I can't tell you exactly why, but it just makes me feel centered and ready to move forward.*

What time do you go to the gym? *In my past training days for the Olympics, I peaked from 2:00 PM to 6:00 PM and that has never left me. As much as I try to work out in the morning hours, (when kids are in school) I feel the most energetic in the afternoon hours. Funny thing is, that the afternoon time is just not viable for workouts, which puts me in the gym during the morning hours—go figure! Once I get there (the gym) and start to pump the blood and oxygen, all is good and I am energized and motivated! Sometimes the hardest thing for people to do is just start moving and let the rest take care of itself. Somehow it always does.*

What type of workout routine do you follow? *I generally try to go really hard and then take an easy day, then push it again. So mostly my workouts are 5 to 6 days a week with three of those days pushing it pretty hard and the other two to three days taking it a bit easier with swimming, stretching, or light cardio.*

How long are you in the gym when you work out? *Rarely more than an hour. Mostly forty five minutes to an hour.*

Do you do cardio with weight training or at a separate time? *I do all sorts of variation when it come to strength training and cardio. Sometimes it feels like (especially circuit training) that it's all happening together. I usually use some sort of cardio to warm up on strength training days, and then for the lighter days, it's mostly cardio (swimming, treadmill, outdoor running or stairs).*

How do you make eating healthy convenient? Do you eat out, bring meals with you, etc? *My wife and I love to cook, so we try our best to make meals at home. (By the way, we've found it usually tastes better and is better for you.)*

How do you make time for your family, social life, and other activities? *I have a very limited social life. Family comes first and if we do want to be social, it's usually at our home or friends homes that are raising kids as well.*

What time do you get to bed at night? *10:30 to 11:00PM only because I know I need to get up early in the morning. In my old days it would be 12:00 to 2:00 AM.*

Feel free to add anything else that you feel is relevant.

Nowadays, people have to know that if you want a healthy, energetic life full of vitality and well being then fitness has to be a major part of your lifelong commitment. The big shift mentally for people that I come into contact with is changing from "having" to work out, to "wanting" to work out. When that change occurs, people make it part of their lives.

Parents need to realize that their children are watching/learning from them each and every day. There's no greater lesson we can teach our kids than the importance of health and wellness. ❖

Terri Trespicio 37 years old, Senior Editor at *Whole Living* magazine, a Martha Stewart publication, and host of "Whole Living" on Sirius XM radio

❖ What time do you get up in the morning? *Around 7:30 AM. I try for earlier, but it just doesn't happen.*

What are your morning habits or rituals? *I love to get up and first thing, roll out my yoga mat and just stretch and breathe. I find this an incredibly calming and energizing way to wake up—it sort of lets you wake up mind and body together and it feels terrific. If I'm feeling particularly productive, I'll jump rope for a few minutes, or do some other more vigorous exercise. But I always try to end this mini morning session with a few minutes of sitting, eyes closed, breathing. Just to clear my head for the day and start from a place of calm. Of course, there are some days when I roll out of bed and it's a shower-and-morning-news kind of day. But I love how I feel when I've had the chance to move a little first thing.*

What time do you go to the gym? How do you fit your workouts into your week? *I'm sort of "eh" on the gym. I go in phases. I psych myself up by saying I'm just going to bang out 25 minutes of intense exercise. I don't want to be there long, especially when I don't get there on a weeknight until close to 8 PM. I make myself this compromise: I'll go and work hard, but will get it done quickly. So, I bring my jump rope and will park myself somewhere by the hand weights and alternate between jumping intensely for a minute or more to doing some weight/resistance stuff. The point is this: I don't stop moving for 25 minutes. Intervals, speed, intensity, and then a few minutes in the steam room and a shower and it's all worthwhile. I wish I got there twice a week, but I'm lucky if I get there once. So I complement my home routine with yoga or other similar-type classes at a studio near me.*

What type of workout routine do you follow? *The thing that kills me about workout regimens is that I bore easily. I can't stand the tedium and tend to do my best when it's spontaneous and varied. So I loathe a schedule. None of this "back and traps today, quads tomorrow" stuff. I can't take it. It bores me before I even start. I'd rather just move like crazy, sweat, stretch, push myself, and then call it a day.*

How long are you in the gym when you work out? *From the minute I walk in til the moment I leave, an hour—not longer than that if I can help it, and if it is longer it's because I dried my hair.*

Do you do cardio with weight training or at a separate time? *I like intervals— all at once, mix it up.*

How do you make eating healthy convenient? Do you eat out, bring meals with you, etc? *I think it's important to make a distinction between "convenient" and "simple." I tend to eat simply but as far as convenience foods go (things you pick up that someone else made, or things you nuke or add water to and stir), I try to avoid them. Convenience foods often leave me feeling disappointed, unsated. I've seen the biggest change to my body and energy when I stop buying processed food and instead, buy food that needs to be processed—by me. I was never into cooking because it seemed so time consuming; but then I realized how delicious it was and how empowered I felt by feeding myself healthy, nutritious food. And while it may not be convenient to buy a root veggie, peel it, cut it, and roast it, it's not exactly hard to do. So I pick foods and recipes that get me psyched up to eat, and I make it and plan for the day ahead. It's not hard at all. Throw some rice in the rice cooker, cook up some lentils, keep some ready-to-eat foods on hand—lots of delicious, fresh stuff—and you won't want "convenience" foods again. My best advice: buy food that goes bad. And eat it before it does.*

How do you make time for your family, social life, and other activities? *I'm single and don't have kids, so I have a considerably lighter load on that side of things. But I work a lot, and so I make sure I don't just stay at work—because I could. And that wears you down mentally, physically, spiritually. I make sure I have plans to see friends and colleagues who inspire and motivate me. And there's only one way to make those dates happen: book them. Also, I don't make plans with people I'm not excited about seeing. Life's too short.*

What time do you get to bed at night? *Not early enough. I'd love to be in bed by 10:30 PM, lights out. But I tend to linger until 11:30. It's also worth noting that I'm an inveterate napper, and I know when I need one. This is the key to my mental health. I jealously guard nap time on the weekends, and I believe it carries me. It's the best sleep I get all week.* ❖

Shawn Phillips, best-selling author, business leader, and internationally respected expert in the area of health, fitness, and human potential. Shawn was instrumental in the creation and evolution of the company, EAS, the world's leader in performance nutrition. Shawn is the CEO and founder of Phillips Performance Solutions, LLC, where he's pioneered the world's first performance fast food, Full Strength™.

❖ What time do you get up in the morning? *Whenever I want! Ha ... kidding. I am a 6:00 AM guy ... love to be earlier but this works.*

What are the morning habits or rituals that you have? *Ideally ... morning rituals are the foundation of life. How we begin the day sets the tone for the day. Head into your day compromised physically, mentally, and emotionally and you begin in a deficit. Trying to recover sucks the energy that I could use for getting stuff done—for winning.*

In the morning, I like to begin my day with a gratitude practice. Just pick three things in my life that I'm grateful for and write them down. It's a five-minute practice ... don't dwell on getting it right.

Then I like to sit in meditation for 11 minutes. It's enough to get centered and calm and serves as pre-workout centering practice too.

Then I train in the morning, have my coffee, and hit it. With two young children, there's no fantasy that I'm going to train in the evening or during the day.

What time do you go to the gym? How do you fit your workouts into your week? *I train in the mornings ... I don't "fit it in." I fit life in around the workouts. It's not long ... 40 minutes except on weekends when I can really take more time and enjoy the workouts more.*

I also ride a mountain or road bike during the riding seasons and that's another activity that can take more time but I usually keep it to two 1.5 hour training rides during the week and a weekend 3-4 hour ride.

What kind of workout routine do you follow? *My physical routine varies through the season as I present in "Book 3" of* Strength for LIFE *... a concept I call "The Seasons of Strength." This allows me to alter the emphasis and adjust the supporting components to meet the specific demands of the season. It's a sort of periodization where I emphasize strength and muscle in the winter months and move towards a cardio/endurance power for cycling season.*

How long are you in the gym when you work out? *At most would be 60 minutes ... least is 30 ... usually somewhere in the 40 minute range.*

Do you do cardio with weight training or at a separate time? *I tend to use cardio to get warmed up on the strength days in the morning but have separate full-on cardio sessions. I don't usually stack them.*

How do you make eating healthy convenient? Do you eat out, bring meals with you, etc? *I am a big proponent and believer in the nutrition shake movement ... a convenient, nutritious way to fully nourish your body. The problem is that most companies these days have confused weight loss shakes and protein shakes with nutrition shakes ... they are not the same. I have at least one and usually two of my Full Strength nutrition shakes every day. Full Strength is not a protein shake, it's an integrated food ... a near perfect meal that gets me on top of life, fast.*

Nutrition is not just about calories, it's about balancing the powerful, dynamic nature inside your body ... when you master insulin, you master all your hormones and energy to boot. It's job #1.

Otherwise, I am prepared ... both with healthy choices of foods around me and with the knowledge and freedom to make wise choices. A well nourished body and mind has the freedom to choose the right foods more often than not. That's the win ... always. That's strength.

How do you make time for your family, social life, and other activities? *I think people confuse fitness with life. Fitness is not a life, not even a decent replacement for a life. It's fitness in the service of life, not in place of. We do what we do to live strong and free ... not to be chained to a dumbbell.*

Life is the first order, then me, familly, and the rest. Me first because when I am not healthy, strong and energized I am cheating everyone, my family and my world included. A stronger me, for a stronger us, for a stronger world.

What time do you get to bed at night? *I am a night owl ... I like staying up late and writing, escaping from the demands of the day. That said, as I get on in maturity I find it more challenging and less wise to compromise my sleep ... so the target is 11:00 PM which bends towards 12:00 AM, but let's say 11:30 PM is my average. Sleep is very important for so many reasons which I would love to share here ... but you know them.*

Thank you for this opportunity . . . I appreciate every opportunity to add value for people and inspire their abundant health and vibrant energy. ❖

Myra Caffarey 42 year old mother of two.

❖ What time do you get up in the morning? *I get up at 4:45 AM (about three days a week). If my husband is traveling I get up at 6:30 AM (about two days a week).*

What are your morning habits or rituals? *If I get up at 4:45, I get dressed, eat, and am at the gym by 5:30 AM. I'm back home by 6:45 when I pack lunches for my husband and kids, eat and take kids to school; after drop-off I may do 30 minutes of cardio.*

What type of workout routine do you follow? *Currently, I lift weights three to four times a week, 30 minutes of cardio six times a week, and try to get in a boot camp/high intensity style of workout once a week.*

How long are you in the gym when you work out? *I allow myself 45 minutes of weight training, and no longer. I have realized that it's easy to socialize way too much in the gym.*

Do you do cardio with weight training or at a separate time? *I have a high metabolism (which hasn't always been that way), so I have to separate weight training and cardio with a meal.*

How do you make eating healthy convenient? *I make our diet easy by preparing certain things in bulk once a week. We eat almost the same thing every day, we just switch out the carbs or proteins. In my fridge you will almost always find cooked chicken, fish, meatballs, boiled eggs, cooked quinoa or rice, various salad items, and avocado. My husband takes a cooler to work. If he travels, I freeze his food and he packs it in his suitcase. We do eat out about once or twice a week. I know the restaurants where the chef will accommodate my diet. If a chef is willing, he can usually come up with some gorgeous fish or grilled meat with a salad or complex carb and oil.*

How do you make time for your family, social life, and other activities? *I like to work out early—the earlier the better—so the rest of my day is free. I also try to choose activities with my friends and family that are active. For example, my husband and I have a date night once a week when we take ballroom dancing; the tango is a great workout and it's a bonding time for us without the kids.*

What time do you get to bed at night? *I like to go to bed early. My bed is my sanctuary and I like to be there by 9:30 on the average night.*

Feel free to add anything else that you feel is relevant. *I know for a fact that the most important thing I can do to keep my life in order is to pray and praise God for the many blessings he has bestowed upon me. If I am not praying and thanking God then my schedule goes, my diet goes, my workouts go, my kids get irritable, and it's a downward cycle from there. I try hard to keep God in everything I do. I tell myself, "It's not about me, but about glorifying God." I also have a good schedule and a diet based on blood sugar stabilization. I worked out for years and ate what I thought was healthy. You know, "plenty of fruits and vegetables," but that doesn't work for me. I need a balance of protein, carbs, and healthy fat. Yes, I go off my diet sometimes and I definitely have a cheat or what I call a refuel day. And last but not least, I must have the support of my husband Mark and kids Adam and Luke. We all play together, eat together, laugh together, and praise God together. Amen.* ❖

David Lyons Executive Producer, Lyons Entertainment; age 51.

❖ What time do you get up in the morning? *6:30 AM.*

What are your morning habits or rituals? *I shower, eat, and take the handfuls of vitamins and supplements for my training.*

What time do you go to the gym? How do you fit your workouts into your week. *The workout times vary depending on my work load, but usually I get to the gym after my first meal. Since I am training for The MS Bodybuilding Challenge, my workouts are part of a four to six day routine. Working out is part of my lifestyle.*

How long are you in the gym when you work out? *I work out for at least an hour for bodybuilding each training day and then a half hour for cardio.*

Do you do cardio with weight training or at a separate time? *Due to having multiple sclerosis, cardio is very difficult to do, period. There is no way for me to do cardio before or after my regular workout. The fatigue and pain is too hindering. So I work in the cardio hours later or on off days.*

How do you make eating healthy convenient? Do you eat out, bring meals with you, etc? *I don't allow junk food in my house and I make healthy choices when*

I eat out. It's really not that difficult if you are a disciplined person and have goals to achieve.

How do you make time for your family, social life, and other activities? *There has to be down time from your training and work. You just have to make that part of your routine just like training and eating healthy.*

What time do you get to bed at night? *I try to get to sleep by midnight. MS has made sleep a difficult achievement. Between the pain I experience and the numbness, I wake up several times at night and never really have a "good night's sleep." I am running on maybe five hours of solid rest.*

Feel free to add anything else that you feel is relevant. *When I hear people say they have no time to stay in shape or eat healthy, I shake my head. You do not have to be a bodybuilder or enter fitness-related contests to stay healthy and fit. If someone like me, with MS, can endure training and dieting for bodybuilding competitions at over fifty years old, then no one has an excuse unless hindered by something that makes it impossible. I live in a constant state of pain, fatigue, and MS-related symptoms that make working out extremely difficult. I understand that not everyone has the determination, discipline, and faith in God that I have to overcome this debilitating disease, but healthy people making excuses for not taking care of their bodies is just not in my line of thinking.* ❖

Jeff Skeen 46 years old, CEO/Partner of health club chain

❖ What time do you get up in the morning? *The times vary depending on the day and my schedule: Mon and Fri—6:30 AM*

> *Tues and Thurs—4:30 AM*
> *Wed—5:00 AM*
> *Sat—7:00 AM*
> *Sun—8:00 AM*

What are the morning habits or rituals that you have? *Exercise (lift/cardio), eat breakfast, feed my children, and spend time with Jesus Christ through prayer and Bible study*

What time do you go to the gym? How do you fit your workouts into your week? *I workout at home or in the gym first thing in the morning. I try to exercise 5 days per week and if I don't work out in the morning, I find it is very hard to fit it into my schedule.*

What kind of workout routine do you follow? *3 days per week I do cardio and 3 days per week I lift and then do cardio. I arrange my workouts in the following manner:*

Mon/Fri—30 to 45 min of cardio

Tues/Thurs/Sat—1 hour of lifting and 30 min of cardio

How do you make eating healthy convenient? *Since I run a company, there are many days I have lunch meetings. When I eat out, I try to select menu items that fit my health goals. On the days I don't eat out, I pack a lunch. As for snacks, that I have two times per day, I keep either a bag of unsalted almonds or protein bars in my desk.*

How do you make time for your family, social life, and other activities? *I make sure that during the week, I spend time with my wife and children in the mornings before and after work and then on the weekends. If I have an unusually hectic week, I will put schedule reminders in my calendar to make sure that I have time with my family especially when it comes to events that my wife and children want me to attend. Also, I try to make sure that during the week I have lunch with someone I am mentoring so that I am investing my life back into another person's. As for social life, my wife is in charge of our calendar and she and I make sure to coordinate with each other. Sundays are set aside as a day of rest in which my family spends time together enjoying all that Jesus Christ has blessed us with. To ensure that this day is sacred, I make sure that everyone I work with knows that Sundays are off limits for work. Also, I do my very best to make sure that I don't travel on the weekends, and, if I do, I am home for Sundays.*

What time do you get to bed at night? *The time I get to bed somewhat depends on what time I have to be up in the morning; however, I make sure that I get at least five hours of sleep. On the weekends, I try to treat myself to eight hours of sleep.*

Feel free to add anything else that you feel is relevant. *Most importantly, I make sure that everything I do reflects the order of my priorities: God, family, health, work.* ❖

Renee Frasca 51 years old, set designer and stylist.

❖ What time do you get up in the morning? *Most mornings I am awake by 7:00 to 7:30 AM.*

What are your morning habits or rituals? *I stay in bed for about half hour to pray and organize my thoughts. After that I reluctantly get out from under the covers and start my day. The first thing I tend to are the pets—a little social interaction with them and feeding. Second, I check e-mails to see if anything needs tending. Then my breakfast and reading over the list of to-dos from the night before, making adjustments where needed. I find being flexible is very important. I also make sure I call my mom.*

What time do you go to the gym? How do you fit your workouts into your week? *I try to get there by 10 AM. I like to go Monday through Friday. Five days is ideal but no less than three.*

What kind of workout routine do you follow? *I work with a trainer two times a week for 30 minutes each. We work a weight routine: one day large muscle groups and one day small muscle groups. The other days I do cardio or yoga. I stretch every day and do ab work.*

How long are you in the gym when you work out? *45 minutes to one hour*

Do you do cardio with weight training or at a separate time? *Separate*

How do you make eating healthy convenient? Do you eat out, bring meals with you, etc.? *I don't keep junk in the house. I don't drink soda or eat processed meals. That's half the battle of eating healthy. When I cook I make enough for leftovers. It's just as easy to grab that as it is a bag of chips. I shop every couple of days for fresh food. I prefer to eat at home so I do that before I leave the house for the day or night. I'm not a snacker. When I'm hungry I stop, sit down, and eat. I eat small amounts all day long. When I eat out I have what I like. I eat until full, and then take home the rest. I love dessert. I don't make it a taboo so I'm not tempted to overdo it. I also don't have large portions. Sharing with someone is fine with me.*

How do you make time for your family, social life, and other activities? *My social life takes place in the evenings. I try to wrap up my work day by 7 pm. I see friends and family after that. Weekends, of course, work on a different schedule.*

What time do you get to bed at night? *11:00 to 11:30 PM*

Feel free to add anything else that you feel is relevant. *I move all day long. I don't sit much and I don't turn on the TV until the evening. When I cook I'll listen to the news and then some shows later on. I multi-task. Cooking dinner is also the time I do laundry. If you stay flexible you can make the time for a workout. I just incorporate it somewhere into my day. If I miss a few days in a row I really feel it. It's good motivation to get right back into it. I don't let my weight fluctuate more than a few pounds. Don't sit, don't make excuses, and don't make it a chore to live healthy.* ❖

Henry Dabish 30 years old, CEO Powerhouse Gyms International

❖ What time do you get up in the morning? *8:00 AM*

What are your morning habits or rituals? *I like to read something from my minute meditation first thing in the morning, do about ten minutes of cardio while I read a book, and then do about 30 minutes of weight training four to five days a week. I always have my breakfast in the morning with at least 20 grams of protein to start the day and pack one healthy meal for work.*

What time do you go to the gym? How do you fit your workouts into your week? *If I don't have time to knock out the workout in the morning, I will do so after dinner.*

What type of workout routine do you follow?

Day 1: Chest, shoulders, triceps

Day 2: Legs and cardio, 20 minutes

Day 3: off day

Day 4: Back, biceps, and abs

Day 5: Kettle bell workout with Powerhouse Gym Head Personal Trainer Guy Monarch

Day 6: Off day

Day 7: Start over

How long are you in the gym when you work out? *30 minutes to an hour.*

Do you do cardio with weight training or at a separate time? *Usually five minute warm up prior to lifting weights and then afterwards for 15 to 20.*

How do you make eating healthy convenient? *I pack a healthy lunch and for the meal that I have out I am pretty good about getting deli sandwiches. Wheat bread, turkey, no dressing. If I go to a restaurant I will get grilled chicken or salmon with healthy sides.*

How do you make time for your family, social life, and other activities? *There is always a juggle between family, working, and having somewhat of a normal social life. I think if something is a priority then you will make time for it. I make sure that I make time for all of these things.*

What time do you get to bed at night? *Usually by 1:00 AM.*

Feel free to add anything else that you feel is relevant. *I think it's important for people to take care of their health with proper exercise and nutrition. Everyone has days when they are dragging and I have noticed that for me those days are typically days when I didn't work out first thing in the morning or at all. Getting the blood flowing to your muscles and the deep breathing that goes along with exercising is the best stress reliever available in my opinion.* ❖

Kaytee Ruliffson MMS, PA-C

❖ What time do you get up in the morning? *Depends—on work days 7:30 AM, if no work, then I enjoy a great sleep in—till 10 or 11 am even!*

What are the morning habits or rituals that you have? *I am not a morning person, so the rituals come later—my morning consists of getting dressed and making time to eat a big, delicious breakfast. If I am not working, I like to get up slowly, take care of a few things around the house that have been put off during the week, and then go get in some good gym time.*

What time do you go to the gym? How do you fit your workouts into your week? *This is very sporatic depending on my schedule—I always prefer to go in the middle of the day when it is not busy so I can run the gym. I like to super set and always be moving and during this time allows me to do this easily and freely without dealing with an overcrowded gym. Sometimes I have to go at the busy time—5–6 PM, and I have to choose my workout wisely on those days.*

What type of workout routine do you follow? *Unfortunately I don't have an extremely consistent schedule, however, usually I make it 3-5 times a week depending. I always lift weights, breaking it up to different areas of the body each day, and have recently added short cardio intervals in between exercises .*

How long are you in the gym when you work out? *1-2 hours; but when I go is different almost every day!*

Do you do cardio with weight training or at a separate time? *WITH! I do not enjoy cardio unless it is an activity with other people. Like bike riding, going on walks, throwing a frisbee, etc. So combining it within my workouts and trying to continue to move with little rest between sets helps me do this.*

How do you make eating healthy convenient? Do you eat out, bring meals with you, etc? *I eat great on work days, I bring my lunch and snacks which allows me to avoid eating unhealthy food and have no other options except for what I have packed; and am never tempted to order out with the others because I have my own food with me. Occasionally having a nice meal out is delightful, but even then, my choices tend to lean more towards healthy. My flaws: not enough water, and I like a good beer or glass of wine or two.*

How do you make time for your family, social life, and other activities? *This is an extremely important aspect of my life and I will rearrange whatever I have to, to incorporate it—work is not everything. Exercise is very important to keep me sane, so I either try to plan it so I get this done and spend the rest of my time with those people and having fun—or with the people who enjoy an active lifestyle. I try to plan activities that can incorporate time together doing something healthy and active together.*

What time do you get to bed at night? *I am a night owl—there are times when I wish I could go to bed early, but usually it is never earlier than 11.*

Feel free to add anything else that you feel is relevant. *Having Jesus in my life helps keep my stress levels manageable. Before I knew him I was high stress and not healthy in my mind—body was good but my mind not so good. God has allowed me by his grace to maintain a very active lifestyle.* ❧

Johnathan Zamora, The Fit Chef. Lost over 170 Lbs.

❧ What time do you get up in the morning? *Between 6–7 AM, depending on the workout I have planned for the day. If I choose to do my workouts in the afternoon, then usually around 7 AM.*

What are the morning habits or rituals that you have? *I throw on my earphones and play some music. It helps me ease into the day and gather my thoughts. I usually have my gym clothes laid out and ready for me to get into—then it's off to the gym.*

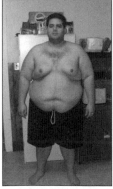

What time do you go to the gym? *If I have weight training or cardio only, I'll arrive around 7:30 AM—and I don't spend any more than 45 minutes for these workouts at the most. When I complete weight training and cardio, then I'll arrive around 6:45 or 7:00 AM.*

What time of workout routine do you follow? *I love weight training and the way I feel after completing a hard workout—it supercharges you to face the day and really gets your metabolism firing. I typically train with weights 5 times per week, with cardio thrown in the mix around 3 or 4 times a week. It's a challenging routine, but the results are well worth it, plus I enjoy pushing myself physically.*

How long are you in the gym when you work out? *My weight training sessions last between 35-40 minutes, with cardio lasting between 30-45 minutes.*

Do you do cardio with weight training or at a separate time? *I like to complete my weight training first because my muscles are fresh and ready to go. I complete cardio after weights and it really gets my heart pumping. I like to vary the types of cardio workouts, since doing the same thing over and over can sometimes get boring. I alternate between running, stair climbing, elliptical or cross trainer.*

How do you make eating healthy convenient? Do you eat out, bring meals with you, etc? *The importance of healthy eating cannot be underestimated. With two young kids and family commitments, the daily schedule can get quite hectic—so being prepared is essential to our success. Having enough healthy food in the house to prepare a few meals ahead of time is really important. Depending on our schedule, sometimes I'll prepare some grain salads or marinate some protein foods. My wife will cook a couple of meals to have enough on hand for the next few days. This way, no matter what unexpected event may come up, at least we know we've planned for success. It plays a huge role in keeping motivation high.*

I am lucky enough to live close to my office—so the daily trip home for lunch is a real treat. My wife and I are committed to providing healthy foods for ourselves and family so we eat home-cooked meals about 95% of the time. I do bring my morning and afternoon snacks with me to the office—even though the vending machine is two floors above me. I feel much better knowing that I'm eating foods that will help keep me healthy and fit versus junk foods. All it takes is a couple of extra minutes to throw something quick in my bag and I'm ready to go.

We do on occasion eat out at restaurants and enjoy doing so. My wife and I decide before arriving if we are choosing to eat a "cheat meal" or eating clean. This way our mindset is in the right place before we look at the menu which helps prevent unwanted over-indulging. If possible, we will examine the menu before venturing out and look for the lean eating options that are available. Luckily, most restaurants today are very accommodating and will do their best to prepare a menu item to your preference. This makes staying on track easier than having to rely completely on willpower.

How do you make time for your family, social life, and other activities? *Our family is very close and we try to take advantage of the time we can all spend together. We usually designate Sunday as our "family day," making time to eat dinner together and enjoy each other's company. These days, it seems everyone is trying to run around and get the most done—since it's like the work never stops (laundry, errands, practices, parties, play-dates, etc.). Once a week, we'll have friends over to hang out and enjoy ourselves, maybe share a meal. These get togethers are an easy way for us to de-stress and enjoy the company of others.*

What time do you get to bed at night? *Around 11:00–11:30 PM is when we call it a night. After the kids are in bed, my wife and I like to catch up with each other and hang out. It's really a nice way to end the day. Even though we are both busy, we enjoy having that time together which really reminds us of how lucky we are—and that's a very comforting thing.*

The most important thing we can do to ensure success is decide to be successful! Often, we look at the outward circumstances that surround us and at that point we are faced with a choice—you can choose to accept the limitations that are placed on you or choose to carve your own path and decide to be as successful as you want to be. The choice is yours . . .what will you decide? ❖

Tom & Dawn Terwilliger Tom 52 years old, best-selling author, international speaker and former Mr. America. Dawn 38 years old, Psychological Kinesiologist, sport and fitness model, Mrs. Metropolitan

❖ What time do you get up in the morning? Tom: *I generally rise between 5:30 and 7 depending on whether or not I am training that morning. On weekends I let myself catch a few more Zs and wake up between 7 AM and 8. Dawn: During the week I get up at 6:30 AM and on the weekends between 7 AM and 8 AM.*

What are your morning habits or rituals? *Tom: First thing I do is drink between 6-8 oz of water, and then I turn the kettle on for some green tea. I shower, brush teeth, and get dressed while sipping on the tea. Then I have a bowl of steel-cut oats with walnuts, pecans, and honey. Dawn: First hour nearly every day, within the first twenty minutes upon waking, I drink ½ liter of water and sip another ½ liter over the next 40 minutes while I get myself ready for the day (1 liter total within one hour). Also during this time I check emails and review what's on the daily schedule.*

What time do you go to the gym? How do you fit your workouts into your week? *Tom: I generally arrive at the gym by 7:30 AM. I have to make it a priority so that I don't allow all the other stuff to get in the way. It can be tough at times getting up early to work out if I haven't allowed myself enough sleep the night before, but that doesn't happen often. Dawn: I like getting my weight training done first thing in the morning even though my body clock prefers the evening when I'm stronger. I weight train 3 times per week. Cardio: I run one mile after weights (8-10 minutes) and run or speed walk with our two schnauzers in the evenings 30-60 minutes depending upon weather and/or schedule. If the weather is just too nasty, I ride a spinning bike at home during a favorite TV show. Weight training is easy to schedule because it's first thing but I have to have my alarm set on my phone to remind me to STOP what I'm doing and get out there with the pups and have some fun.*

What kind of workout routine do you follow? *Tom: Three days a week I start the workout with 50 minutes of strength training followed by about 15 minutes of cardio on the elliptical, treadmill, or, if I just trained legs, the recumbent bike. The fourth day, which is actually in the middle of the week, I practice JKD, a form of mixed martial arts, for about two hours. Dawn: Weight train 3 times/week. Regardless of the routine it is usually very intense as I am quite competitive with myself and my training partner. We usually train Tuesday, Thursday and Friday. Cardio 6 times/per week.*

How long are you in the gym when you work out? *Tom: I try not to stay in the gym too long. Based on experience I know that after 50-70 minutes my body starts to shut down production of testosterone at that point making recovery much more difficult. With a little mild cardio I can push it to 90 minutes, but that is it. Plus, after 30 years it gets a little boring to do any more. Dawn: Weight training sessions simply cannot go longer than 50-60 minutes . . . because there is nothing left!*

Do you do cardio with weight training or at a separate time? *Tom: I do cardio following my strength training three days a week for 15-20 minutes for two reasons. 1. We know that following the strength-training session the body is in a glycogen depleted state, leaving primarily fat for fuel (which is what we want to burn during cardio). 2. The last thing I want to do is have to go back to the gym later the next day just for cardio, so I do it while I'm already there. Dawn: I would prefer to do cardio immediately after weight training, but normally my schedule doesn't permit.*

How do you make eating healthy convenient? *Tom: It would be inconvenient to eat unhealthy in my house. For example, my wife and I were watching a movie the other night and I really had a craving for something chocolate, but I knew I would have to go out to get it. So instead I made us a delicious chocolate protein shake to satisfy my craving. Eating healthy is simply a matter of forethought and planning. If I know I am going to be away from the house for a few hours, I always bring the food I need to keep me from stopping at Mickey Dee's place for some fries. It begins on the weekend by preparing some things in advance—several chicken breasts, some sweet potatoes, and other things I need like almond butter, seven-grain bread, hard-boiled eggs, and protein powder. Occasionally I'll stop for a bite out but will take the time to think in advance about what I might be able to get that's healthy and where I can get it.*

Dawn: There is always food (and water) in my bag in the form of a protein shake, low sodium V-8, protein bar, fruit (banana or apple), or mixed nuts . . . needed for post workout or many hours away from the office. Eating healthy is convenient because I know the outcome—predictable (I don't have time for a headache or feeling sluggish). I know that with eating good, nutritionally dense food I will be hungry in about 2-3 hours. I know how I will feel within those 2-3 hours and that I took care of "ME." Tom and I have a few goodies (chocolate chips or Twizzlers) on movie nights and one "anything goes" meal a week. We eat out occasionally.

How do you make time for your family, social life, and other activities? *Tom: Social life? I guess you could say living and eating healthy, going to the gym, and getting plenty of outdoor Colorado activities is my social life. Spending my free time with my wife and two dogs is a big part of that. I can't say that I schedule time for it, but I always make time for it by being consciously aware of its importance in my life and the lives of the people I'm close to and love. Another important factor is that all my friends—the people I socialize with—are also into being healthy and active, so we combine the social interaction with outdoor activities and healthy dining. Dawn: Huh . . . social life???? Tom and I are two high driven, ambitious individuals. I think we are extremely fortunate to be able to work along side one another and still remain married (14+ years). We enjoy each other's and our friends' company while doing something active.*

What time do you get to bed at night? *Tom & Dawn: Not early enough! We try to hit the hay about 10:00 PM and almost always catch a funny TV show to help us relax and fall asleep with a big, dumb smile on our face. We try to get a minimum of 7–8 hours of sleep—but it's not always easy.*

Feel free to add anything else that you feel is relevant. *Tom: I have programmed into myself a fitness, weight, and energy level set point determined not by nature but by desire. If I feel, see, or sense that I have fallen below that set point, I kick on the heat and bring the temperature back up. Anyone can do it with enough focus and a little discipline. I believe it takes as much or more energy to complain or feel negative about how unfit or out of shape you are as it does to not let it happen in the first place. Dawn: Being healthy and in shape is a choice. It is my number one value because all else would crumble without out this structure. I love a degree of uncertainty, mystery, and adrenalin but this is one area of my life that I need consistency and predictability ❖.*

Steve Holman 52 years old, Editor in Chief of *Iron Man Magazine*, author of more than 20 books on bodybuilding, weight training, and nutrition.

❖ What time do you get up in the morning? *I wake up every work day at 5:30 AM—without an alarm.*

What are your morning habits or rituals? *I drink half a glass of orange juice, one cup of coffee, and a large bowl of high-fiber cereal with a whey-casein-protein shake poured over it.*

What time do you go to the gym? How do you fit your workouts into your week? *I train at 10 AM four days a week. Luckily, I work for a bodybuilding/fitness magazine, and half of our warehouse is a gym. The publisher encourages employees to train, which helps.*

What type of workout routine do you follow? *I hit the weights four times a week for an hour to an hour and a half—Monday, Tuesday, Wednesday, and Friday. Most body parts get trained two to three times a week directly or indirectly. Also, I run a couple of miles once or twice a week, no other cardio usually.*

How long are you in the gym when you work out? *I try to keep it close to an hour.*

Do you do cardio with weight training or at a separate time? *I run a few miles on the weekend or on my off day from the gym (usually Thursday).*

How do you make eating healthy convenient? *I bring my lunch to work as well as two ready-made protein shakes. I usually eat close to the same thing each day—small protein-based meals six times a day.*

How do you make time for your family, social life, and other activities? *Making working out a part of my work day helps me have more time for family and socializing.*

What time do you get to bed at night? *I'm in bed by 10 PM. almost every night.* ❖

Melissa Bathory

❖ What time to do you get up in the morning? *7:00 AM everyday*

What are your morning habits and rituals? *I wake up, make coffee, and while my coffee is going I do 15 minutes of meditation and stretching. Next, I may go for a 20 minute jog. After that, I turn my computer on and start my day. I like to fit the gym in first thing in the morning also.*

What time do you go to the gym? How do you fit workouts into your week? *Normally I like to go to the gym after I do my morning jog. I know that I can do cardio in the*

gym, but I like to run through my beautiful neighborhood. If I can't make it into the gym first thing in the morning, I do what needs to get done and then go about 10:00 AM. I have chosen to make working out a priority in my life, so I make sure to fit it into my daily routine.

What kind of workout routine do you follow? *I do two days of yoga-Pilates-spin classes, two days of weights, and one to two days of hiking in Runyon Canyon.*

How long are you in the gym working out? *I normally go anywhere from two to three hours. Hiking is normally one and a half hours.*

Do you do cardio with weight training or separate? *I do light cardio (my morning jog) with weights. But on the days I do spin-yoga-Pilates classes, I don't do cardio before.*

How do you making eating healthy convenient? *I love to cook at home! I'm the baby of a Polish/Italian family and grew up cooking. I have made a lot of adjustments to my family's recipes to make them healthier. I have also started hosting weekly dinner parties for my neighbors. They love my healthy cooking. I also try to make it to our local farmers market to get fresh, locally grown fruits and veggies.*

How do you make time for family and social life? *Even though I don't have much family in Los Angeles, my fiancée and my friends are considered my new family. I love hanging out with my fiancée, who has a very positive and uplifting attitude. Making time for him is a daily priority for me. I have taken my social life to another level. Instead of meeting my friends out for drinks, I have set up weekly dinner parties and group outings (Hiking and going to the beach, for example). Living in LA, there are a million fun things to do outside all year round.*

What time do you get to bed at night? *That's an easy one! Almost every day my body knows when it is 10 PM and I know it's time to go to bed. For special events, I'm up until 1:00 AM. I always try to think of how I want to feel the next day.*

Feel free to add anything else that you feel is relevant. *My life throughout the years has been very busy—moving 21 times, having a fiancée, planning a wedding 2,500 miles away, working for a worldwide company, starting up my own business, working out, cooking, entertaining friends and family, and making our house a home. But I always make sure to take the time to take care of myself!* ❖

Doug Brignole 51 years old, international bodybuilding champion, biomechanics expert, author, and fitness spokesman.

❖ What time do you get up in the morning? *I usually wake up around 6:00 AM, but it depends on the appointments I have for that day.*

What are your morning habits or rituals? *The first thing I do in the morning, after I get dressed, is have a protein drink and take my nutrition supplements.*

What time do you go to the gym? How do you fit your workouts into your week. *I usually do my own workout in the evening, around 8:00 PM. I work primarily as a trainer, and typically take clients between the hours of 7:00 AM and 6:00 PM. Of course, I have time between client sessions, which allows me time to run errands, do e-mails, or work on other projects (like writing articles for* Iron Man Magazine, *or working on my next book).*

What kind of workout routine do you follow? *I workout five days a week: Monday, Tuesday, Thursday, Friday and Saturday. I take off on Wednesday and Sunday. I have a three-way split routine (primarily weights). Day One is chest, back, and arms. Day Two is shoulders. Day Three is legs and abs. So I just rotate the workouts on those five days. I typically do very little cardio work in the off-season. But starting 12 weeks before a contest, I do 20 minutes of cardio (high intensity) after each of my weight training workouts.*

How long are you in the gym when you work out? *My workouts generally last between an hour and a half, and two hours.*

Do you do cardio with weight training or at a separate time? *As mentioned above, I usually do cardio beginning 12 weeks before a bodybuilding competition and very little, if any, in the off-season. However, eventually I will move away from a bodybuilding emphasis and more toward an over-all fitness emphasis, perhaps with a focus on training for a sport like surfing or mountain climbing. This would likely result in workouts that are primarily cardiovascular, with much less emphasis on weight training.*

How do you make eating healthy convenient? *Naturally, the diet is very important to me. I have a high metabolism, so my difficulty (as ironic as this may seem) is to keep weight on. If I miss a meal during the day, I'll lose a pound or two of muscle that same day. I have found that the best way for me to stay on track with my meals is to make my own, in semi-large quantities (sufficient to last a few days). In other words, I always have rice, vegetables, and chicken (or pork) pre-cooked in the fridge. Then, when meal time comes up, I just open the frig, scoop out (or chop) some of each, add some dressing (soup or other flavoring), heat, and serve. Dinner is usually pasta, along with veggies and chicken or beef. I try to eat four meals per day, plus my morning protein drink.*

How do you make time for your family, social life, and other activities? *I tend to be a workaholic, and given my busy schedule (working ten hours per day, and working out two hours per day), I have—so far—decided to stay unmarried. However, I do have a girlfriend (who is very understanding, and very busy herself), and we always spend Sundays together. And, assuming my career evolves the way I'm anticipating it will, I hope to create some passive income (by way of product manufacturing, publishing, and online sales), so that I can free up additional time and create better balance in my life.*

What time do you get to bed at night? *I usually go to bed around midnight, which results in only about six hours of sleep per night. I rarely get more than seven hours of sleep in a given night. I suppose I'm lucky that way. I'm not one of those people who must have eight hours of sleep to function well. But I'm excited about life and excited about my projects, so sleep does not interest me as much as accomplishing goals does. I'm usually raring to go in the morning, and reluctant to stop working in the evening.*

Feel free to add anything else that you feel is relevant. *Can busy people stay in shape? Frankly, I think most in-shape people are the busy ones. Whether you have a full-time job and a family or not, getting in shape requires a degree of organization. Organized people tend to be achievers (or over-achievers). It's not that being busy helps you get in shape so much as it is that busy people have what it takes (the right attitude, the skills, ambition) to coordinate their lives, to include a well-orchestrated fitness program. There's a limit to how much a person can do in one day. That's why it's important to treat one's life like a business, ensuring that it's well managed and designed to survive and thrive.* ❖

Danielle and Rich Perrotta The couple that trains together stays together. Danielle lost 80 lbs and Rich lost 50 lbs! Danielle, 27, therapeutic teacher, and Rich, 27, Customer Account Representative.

❖ What time do you get up in the morning? *Danielle & Rich: 6:45 AM.*

What are your morning habits or rituals? *Danielle: Juice fresh greens for breakfast, make fruit salad for breakfast and a hearty salad for lunch, and prepare protein shakes for the day. Rich: Begin with a prayer, stretch, and drink a protein shake. Both of us pack our gym bags at this time or the night before.*

What time do you go to the gym? How do you fit your workouts into your week? *We are a couple that trains together. We are usually at the gym Monday-Friday, 6-8 PM. On the weekends we work out in the early afternoon.*

What type of workout routine do you follow? *Weights five to six times a week: Monday chest, Tuesday back, Thursday legs, Friday shoulders, Saturday biceps, Sunday triceps. We also will throw in two bicep/tricep exercises during large-muscle-group days.*

How long are you in the gym when you work out? *Two to three hours. Yes, this may seem like a lot, but during 6-8 PM we are allotting extra time for sharing equipment. This is prime time for most people to be at the gym.*

Do you do cardio with weight training or at a separate time? *We follow weight training/free weights with cardio each work out. Aiming for 45-60 minutes each time. Danielle: I love training with the V-tec weight vest.*

How do you make eating healthy convenient? Do you eat out, bring meals with you, etc? *Danielle: I follow a special dietary routine (eating mostly raw, vegan foods). Rich and I prepare meals ahead whenever possible, and have protein shakes readily available. We eat out once a week and make a habit of getting to know the waitstaff and chefs at our favorite restaurants. I always explain my dietary needs before ordering and have been accommodated each time I do this. Rich: Cooking meals ahead of time, choosing meals that do not take a lot of prep time in the kitchen, buying proteins in bulk, and stocking up on my leafy green vegetables.*

How do you make time for your family, social life, and other activities? *"The couple that trains together stays together." We enjoy being active together and introducing our friends and family to our way of life. We jump at the chance to cook healthy versions of our favorite, traditional Italian-Greek foods and inform our loved ones of the simple changes we make to save the calories. Often you will hear, "The family must all eat at the table together—no matter what." We add to this thought by exercising together before and/or after meals. It is considered quality time and this positive mindset keeps things exciting.*

What time do you get to bed at night? *10 PM on the weekdays, 11 PM on weekends.*

Feel free to add anything else that you feel is relevant. *Danielle: As a woman, before I met John, I would have considered myself a slave to the cardio machines. I was not eating enough and had hit a plateau and wanted to get fit for our October wedding. Since I am a teacher, I had the summer months to train hard; that's when I met John Rowley and he changed my life by opening my eyes. He introduced me to drinking protein shakes (1-2 grams of protein per body weight) throughout the day. He explained that I was eating very healthy but was starving my muscles by depriving my body of protein and doing too much cardio. He would oversee my workouts and make sugges-tions for me to adjust my posture or turn my wrists for an extra push, and he always pushed me hard. Training with John has changed me physically, but most importantly, his coaching and friendship has given me confidence and mental strength to push through the walls. He is a testament of great character and a blessing to both Rich and me!* ❖

Dov Baron 53 years old, grandfather of 4, international speaker, bestselling author, and president of Baron Mastery Institute.

❖ What time do you get up in the morning? *5:30 -6:00 AM*

What are your morning habits or rituals? *Meditate and workout with cardio and weights*

What time do you go to the gym? *Before 7:00 AM*

How do you fit your workouts into your week. *The only way I can fit them in is by going before my workday starts.*

What type of workout routine do you follow? *Cardio and weights 3-4 times per week.*

How long are you in the gym when you work out? *A half hour per workout*

Do you do cardio with weight training or at a separate time? *Together*

How do you make eating healthy convenient? *It's not convenient, but eating lousy is not an option. I am in tune with my body enough to recognize the often instan-taneous negative consequences of not eating healthy.*

How do you make time for your family, social life, and other activities? *Thank goodness I have a schedule and have someone else to run it—that's how I get time for both. What's important to me is to make sure I am fully present with my friends and family during the time we have together.*

What time do you get to bed at night? *11:00–11:30 PM* ❖

Kristy Tyndall 35 years old, wife, mother, certified reg-istered nurse anesthetist

❖ What time do you get up in the morning? *At 4:07 AM. The odd number plays tricks with my mind so I only hit snooze once (maybe twice). I leave for the gym by 4:40 AM.*

What are your morning habits or rituals? *I fall out of bed and brush my teeth before I leave for the gym.*

How do you fit your workouts into your week? *If I am working during the day, I go to the gym before work. As a Certified Registered Nurse Anesthetist, my schedule varies and if I work nights I hit the gym sometime during the day.*

What kind of workout routine do you follow? *I work out five to six times per week. I do one day of straight cardio and at least one day of plyometrics. The rest of the days I focus on one or two body parts and do some sort of high intensity cardio afterwards.*

How long are you in the gym when you work out? *I try to keep my workouts no longer than 75 minutes. That includes weights and cardio.*

Do you do cardio with weight training or at a separate time? *I usually do cardio after my weight training. If the weather is nice, I sometimes add an evening run.*

How do you make eating healthy convenient? Do you eat out, bring meals with you, etc? *Planning is key. I don't allow myself to get hungry. I keep a pack of tuna and protein powder in my locker at work. If I am heading out to do errands, I throw an apple and a few almonds in my purse. Life happens and I will eat out (unless I am prepping for a contest). I just make healthy choices and try to keep it clean.*

How do you make time for your family, social life, and other activities? *Because I choose to make time for myself when my husband and son are sound asleep in the wee hours of the morning, I have time in the afternoons to spend with them.*

What time do you get to bed at night? *I try to have the lights out no later than 9:30. Sometimes I make it to bed by 8 PM.* ❖

Kris Gethin 36 years old, Deputy Editor, Bodybuilding.com.

❖ What time do you get up in the morning? *5:00 to 6:00 AM*

What are your morning habits or rituals? *Re-evaluate my FLOW chart (which stands for Fixed, Limitless, Opportunities and Weaknesses), eat 12 egg whites with pineapple, blueberries, Greek Yogurt, and one cup of oats. 30 minutes later I will go for a 20-minute run while listening to my iPod.*

What time do you go to the gym? How do you fit your workouts into your week? *I train around 5:00 PM so I can fit in two to three meals before bed. I don't schedule my workouts for the week, I schedule my week around my workouts.*

What kind of workout routine do you follow? *I generally train for two days and then take one day off. I will train two body parts per workout and I will follow a program that I designed called the Dramatic Transformation Principle (DTP). It allows me to choose only one compound exercise per body part, but the intensity and rep-range produces a significant amount of muscle gain while burning fat.*

How long are you in the gym when you work out? *Around 60 minutes when training upper body muscle and around 80 minutes when training legs.*

Do you do cardio with weight training or at a separate time? *I generally do my cardio at a separate time—in the morning after breakfast.*

How do you make eating healthy convenient? *I cook my food in bulk and then separate into Tupperware containers for a couple of days worth, and I always take meals with me in a cooler. I have protein shakes and protein bars with me at all times, just in case.*

How do you make time for your family, social life, and other activities? *I use weekends for my social life. I don't switch off completely though—eating healthy and staying active is part of my life. I feel that I have more confidence, more energy, and am more mentally relaxed when I take care of myself. Some people may say it's selfish, but I see it the other way around, especially if I am a better person to be around and more attractive to my wife.*

What time do you get to bed at night? *I try to get to bed around 10 PM.* ❖

John Lepak. 36 years old, Powerhouse Gym International, Vendor and Marketing Department

❖ What time do you get up in the morning? *Having a newborn and a three year old does not allow me any day of the week to "sleep in." I am usually up around 7 AM at the latest.*

What are your morning habits or rituals? *I always open my eyes and thank God for my health and pray for his strength and guidance that day. Then I spend time with my daughter in the kitchen while making breakfast.*

What time do you go to the gym? *I work out before work each day. People always say that I have it easy because I can get dressed in the gym and then come down stairs to the office. That's just a form of negativity and I will not hear it. I began working out in the mornings because I read that Arnold Schwarzenegger used to train at 5:00 AM before he had to start his days at 6 AM in the army. I can honestly say that I have a much more productive day when I train in the morning.*

What kind of workout routine do you follow? *I like to train with weights and light cardio on occasion. I boxed for many years, and that's the best form of cardio I ever experienced. I will usually shadow box for a few rounds in the group-ex room and that is my cardio.*

How long are you in the gym when you work out? *Usually one hour. You can honestly get in and hit it good in 30 minutes as long as you focus. You are there to train, not socialize.*

Do you do cardio with weight training or at a separate time? *I was taught that you should do your cardio after you weight train if you really want to burn body fat.*

How do you make eating healthy convenient? *Easting healthy is really just re-training your taste buds. I used to eat junk food at night—I mean, eating a whole bag of Doritos on the couch. Now keep in mind I used to box at 147 pounds and train in 100 degree heat, so I never gained a pound. Well, one day I looked at my waist and was like WHOA! My wife gave me the best advice ever, "Eat in moderation." So I just started eating a small bowl of junk food rather than an entire bag. I can honestly say that helped the best. People fail too often with "diets" because they fall back into their old habits. This way, you can still have some of your favorite snacks and foods but just not over do it.*

Do you eat out, bring meals with you, etc? *I bring my food every day! First of all, just add up how much you spend eating out each day and you might be shocked. If you need to get out of the office, just go sit outside and eat to get a change of scenery. I also found it's great to cook your food on a Sunday and pack your lunch for a couple of days. Then you're also not tempted to eat a pizza at lunch and be all tired when you get back to work.*

How do you make time for your family, social life, and other activities? *Family. That's what it's all about. I used to rip and run on the road for most of my life. I came off the road one time and woke up on the couch all jet lagged and worn out to see my daughter take her first step. It was that moment that changed my life. And I called my friends Darryl Francis and Mike Tyson. Mike said to me, "Stay home, brother. Don't come back out on the road. Your life changed today!" Mike was right. I have not gone back on the road since. I start each day spending time with my family at home and end each day the best I can by putting my children to bed. Weekends I always make sure to do a family activity.*

What time do you get to bed at night? *I like to get to bed by 10 or 11 on week nights. The problem is that is when my brain starts clicking and I usually end up lying awake brainstorming until very late most of the time.*

Feel free to add anything else that you feel is relevant. *Everyone is busy these days. Everyone says how busy they are and do not have time to go to the gym. It's all just an excuse. Stop making excuses and take action. Once people do, they will find this is the nucleus that will help them make changes in all aspects of their lives. It's about so much more than going to the gym to work out. Getting into the gym has really made an incredible impact in my life. Ironically through getting my body together, it has helped me get my mind together and because of that I am in a great place both physically and spiritually.* ❖

Crystal West 46 years old, attorney, personal trainer, model, and motivational speaker; hold's three current world records in pull-ups.

❖ What time do you get up in the morning? *I get up at 4:00 AM every morning. If I sleep in it is usually until 5:00 or 5:30. At first I thought this would kill me, but you do get used to it. I make coffee and get on the computer and respond to any correspondence, business matters, and fan mail, and then head to the shower. I have a quick breakfast before I leave the house at 5:45.*

What are your morning habits or rituals? *I train clients sometimes non-stop between 6:00 AM and 1:00 PM, and then often in the early evening hours as well. Sometimes, however, I get breaks in my training day. I have a slot that is not filled, or someone calls in sick. I take advantage of that time to get in some cardio, either elliptical or the treadmill. If I continue to get breaks I will do more cardio or run errands.*

What time do you go to the gym? How do you fit your workouts into your week? *If it is a day when I am going to teach boot-camps in addition to my personal training, I will sometimes get a workout in between clients. I can get shoulders and abs done in 45 minutes if need be.*

What kind of workout routine do you follow? *My day is always flexible and subject to change, so each evening I plot the likely times I will have to train the next day. I train six days a week and do cardio seven days a week. I also have to carve out three days a week where I get at least two hours to train on my pull-ups. I currently hold three world records: Two are open women's world records and one is an age division record (over 40). (The current open women's record is 36 consecutive pull-ups, and the current women's open record for most added weight is 189 pounds inclusive of body weight, so 79 pounds one rep pull-up.)*

How long are you in the gym when you work out? *I would say that my weight training each day is between 45 minutes to three hours. I train full body but emphasize back, shoulders, and biceps since this is what helps me the most with my pull-ups.*

Do you do cardio with weight training or at a separate time? *I always do at least an hour of cardio per day. I try to do it with my weight training, but if I can't I always fit it in somewhere. I think of cardio like flossing, just something that needs to be done for my health—it takes a little longer (than flossing) is all.*

How do you make eating healthy convenient? *I eat healthy by planning ahead. If I know I will be in the gym working, I will have snacks with me always. Raw almonds, a banana, an oatmeal packet, protein bar, etc. In my opinion it is crucial to plan ahead. I only keep healthy food in my home, so I rarely go off the rails with food or portions.*

How do you make time for your family, social life, and other activities? *I make time for friends and family in the evening. I sacrifice television so that I have time to be social. I rarely watch TV and quite frankly don't miss it.*

What time do you get to bed at night? *I end up going to bed around 9:30. I simply must have that much rest to perform the way I do. I get teased about my early hours, but I just smile and keep accomplishing my goals.*

Feel free to add anything else that you feel is relevant. *I am convinced that people can fit a lot more into their lives than they do by cutting out extraneous activity. I am currently in training to break other pull-up records in a variety of time frames. I seek to show others that nothing is impossible if you have a goal, if you make a plan to reach that goal, and if you are consistent in your actions and determined in your beliefs. Ultimately my wish is to inspire and motivate others to live their lives without limits.* ❖

Pat Teague 47 years old, Community Sports Chaplain at Crossroads Fellowship, former NFL linebacker with the Tampa Bay Buccaneers after graduating from N.C. State University as an All-ACC linebacker.

❖ What time do you get up in the morning? *Between 6-6:30 AM*

What are your morning habits or rituals? *Take a shower, do sit-ups, pray, drink 16-20 ounces of water, eat a whole-grain breakfast or shake. Read the Word and pray some more. Listen to worship music, a teacher, or Christian radio to get my mind set to "tune in" to God's voice, not the world's voice (Rom. 8:6, Rom. 12:1-2, Ps. 1).*

What time do you go to the gym? How do you fit your workouts into your week? *After I drop the kids off for school typically, or during lunch time if I have a break-fast appointment.*

What kind of workout routine do you follow? *Weights three times a week, cardio on the other three days, and typically rest on Sundays.*

How long are you in the gym when you work out? *35-55 minutes*

Do you do cardio with weight training or at a separate time? *Ten minutes warm-up cardio before weight training*

How do you make eating healthy convenient? Do you eat out, bring meals with you, etc? *Breakfast and dinner are usually at home. My wife buys healthy items for us. Breakfast: high fiber, multi-grains. Lunch: usually eat out, making wise choices with salads, protein, and veggies. At dinner, I eat high protein, veggies and fruit, and lay off the breads.*

How do you make time for your family, social life, and other activities? *God, family, friends. We attend church regularly and host a class. We see friends there and make arrangements to be with them. I have regular date nights with my wife. I make it a priority to spend time with each of my three children. I make a priority to lie down with them at night; I start with the youngest and end with the oldest (since they like to stay up longer). We read the Bible together and then pray together. After that they open up and chatter away. I hug them and tell them I love them and encourage them genu-inely, telling them something they are doing right. Then we talk about areas to improve (sometimes that happens when we are reading the Word—because the Holy Spirit is working on both of us!). We have a family devotional at supper on a regular basis. We make it a priority to eat supper together regularly. Josh McDowell said, "Rules without relationship breeds rebellion." We have an annual family vacation and another in the fall if budget allows. During the day, I call buddies to check on them and text scriptures to them as the Holy Spirit puts on my heart for them. Also, we will arrange lunches or breakfasts to talk, laugh, and encourage one another .*

What time do you get to bed at night? *Too late! 11:30 PM -12 AM. It's hard to get everything done. After the children are in bed, Sheila and I get to talk and spend time together. We wrap up different tasks we didn't finish during the day. I usually read and study the Word before I go to bed.*

Feel free to add anything else that you feel is relevant. *Matt. 6:33, "Seek first the Kingdom of God and His righteousness and all things will be added unto you."* ❖

John DeFendis 53 years old, founder and director of the Ultra Fit Weight-loss Program; weight loss, health, and fitness expert; life coach; International Fitness Hall of Fame Recipient 2007; former Mr. USA; motivational speaker and author

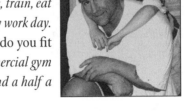

❖ What time do you get up in the morning? *I get up at 4:45 AM.*

What are your morning habits or rituals? *Get up, get online, do my email correspondence for two hours, train, eat a healthy Ultra Fit Breakfast, and then attack my work day.*

What time do you go to the gym? How do you fit your workouts into your week? *I built a commercial gym on my home premises and I train for an hour and a half a day in the mornings.*

What kind of workout routine do you follow? *I train on a four day on and one day rest regimen with only strength training but at a pace that effectively works my cardiovascular system.*

How do you make eating healthy convenient? *I get up and prepare my meals for the day and take them with me or I eat out at restaurants that I can depend on for healthy meals.*

How do you make time for your family, social life, and other activities? *Time Management*

What time do you get to bed at night? *I lie down to watch the 10:00 news and usually fall asleep watching television about 11:00 PM or midnight.*

Feel free to add anything else that you feel is relevant. *It's all about time management and the relentless pursuit of one's goals. Apathy causes us to fail. Apathy destroys our goals and replaces productive time with wasteful time. It's all about the will to be the best that God made us to be and to be RELENTLESS!* ❖

Suzanne Graban 26 years old; MBA student at the University of Tampa, and intern at SHAPE magazine.

❖ What time do you get up in the morning? *I am not an early riser. I wake up between 8 and 9 AM usually.*

What are your morning habits or rituals? *I eat the exact same breakfast every morning, and it is the meal I look forward to most: egg white omelet with mushrooms, onion, green pepper, and a tiny sprinkle of cheese (my guilty pleasure). Then, I either have half a grapefruit or an orange. I was never one to skip breakfast. I could eat this meal five times a day and never get sick of it!*

What time do you go to the gym? How do you fit your workouts into your week? *I usually hit the gym in the evening. I am back in grad school now, so I have to work around my class schedule, but it's usually 5 or 6 PM.*

What type of workout routine do you follow? *On average I am in the gym four days a week. I do a mix of cardio and weights every single time. As soon as I get to the gym, I do about 20 minutes of cardio: always intervals of some type, be it on the treadmill, elliptical, or stepmill. Then, I will concentrate on one body part each day for lifting: legs, shoulders, back, arms. I mix in abs every few days. If I am not at the gym, I will do abs at home. Since I am a student, I am doing a lot of walking around campus, so I count that towards some of my cardio.*

How long are you in the gym when you work out? *One to two hours, depending on what I am working (leg days take me about two hours). And, if I know I have a lot of time to spare, I will chit chat between sets.*

How do you make eating healthy convenient? Do you eat out, bring meals with you, etc? *I love to cook so I try to do that as much as possible. I cook clean meals so then I don't feel as guilty if I go out to eat with friends every once in a while. It's fun to think of new things to make and to throw food together and see how it turns out. I cook with a lot of lean turkey, fish, and veggies. I also pack lunches and snacks when I am at school. Convenience is an important factor. No matter how many times I tell myself I am going to wake up early and pack a lunch, it doesn't happen. So once or twice a week I will make three or four lunches and snacks at a time. Then I just wake up, grab it out of the refrigerator, and I am out the door.*

How do you make time for your family, social life, and other activities? *School is #1 right now. But typically I try hard to get lots of work done during the week, while working out and eating well. Then, I set aside the weekends for friends and family and feel good about letting loose a bit.*

What time do you get to bed at night? *Usually around midnight. The night time is when I unwind, catch up on TV or reading, and also do some extra studying.* ❧

Tom Venuto natural bodybuilder and author of *The Body Fat Solution*

❖ What time do you get up in the morning? *I usually get up by 7:00 AM, sometimes earlier if I'm training for a contest or event and I want to get an extra workout in early.*

What are the morning habits or rituals that you have? *I use bodybuilding-style nutrition which calls for multiple small meals a day. That seems challenging for busy people, but it's easy when you prep your food in advance. First thing in the morning, I cook and prep all meals for the day and pack them in containers or foil so they're ready when I need them. My entire food prep ritual only takes about 45 minutes.*

I also meditate in the morning. I have a tendency to allow myself to get stressed due to having so many irons in the fire, but the quiet time in the morning works wonders for keeping me de-stressed, calm and focused. I'm convinced it's good for your body, mind and spirit.

What time do you go to the gym? How do you fit your workouts into your week. *Over the years I've gone to the gym at all different hours of the day and night and I sometimes change my training time to accommodate a training partner. But my best training time is mid to late morning because that allows me to fully wake up, be fully alert, and to get a couple of meals in me (and some coffee!) before I hit the gym (the gym is usually almost empty then too!).*

What kind of workout routine do you follow? *I do my weights on a 4 day split with a day just for legs, a day for back a day for chest and biceps and a day for shoulders and triceps. I usually work calves and abs twice a week. I use a two days on, one day off schedule. The day off after every two days of training gives me plenty of recovery time and each major muscle group gets worked once every six days.*

My cardio varies depending on my goals at the time. For maintenance and general health and fitness I do three days a week of cardio work, usually for about 30 minutes. Sometimes I go longer if I want to do a long walk or something light, sometimes I might do a bit shorter, like 15-25 minutes if I'm doing something more intense like sprint work, intervals, hill or stair running and so on. When my goal shifts to getting leaner as it does before competitions, I progressively increase my cardio up to as often as 6-7 days a week and as long as 45-60 minutes per day.

How long are you in the gym when you workout? *Weight training workouts are usually about an hour. Sometimes a little more, sometimes a little less but almost always in the 45-75 minute range. I think the popular rule about keeping workouts to an hour or less is a solid one, but there's no magic amount of time that guarantees you results. I prefer to think in terms of results, not time. With high intensity workouts, you can get the same or better results in less time, but I'm willing to put in whatever time investment is necessary to reach my goals. I believe in efficiency but not in short cuts.*

Do you do cardio with weight training or at a separate time? *Both ways. It depends on my schedule and how I feel. Doing them separately I believe is ideal if for no other reason than you are fresher and have full energy reserves (whatever you do last always gets the least energy). But sometimes I do the cardio right after lifting because it's convenient to do it all at once.*

How do you make eating healthy convenient? Do you eat out, bring meals with you, etc? *I make most of my own food. I've learned how to cook healthy in bulk and have learned how to make food that travels well so I can take food with me, even on planes, road trips and so on. It's all about planning in advance. Most nutrition mistakes are made from lack of planning and from not thinking ahead.*

How do you make time for your family, social life, and other activities? *Being an entrepreneur always juggling multiple projects, I have to block off the free time in advance or my workaholic tendencies would have me living in the office. My solution is to schedule a lot of free days where there's no business work allowed whatsoever, not even business reading or checking email. This is hard to do at first when you've been a compulsive over-worker, but it gets easier when you realize that the off time is what turns on your subconscious and rejuvenates your body and mind so you're more creative and efficient when you go back to work. In that sense, you actually become more productive and more successful by working less and spending more time with friends and family.*

What time do you get to bed at night? *Usually no later than midnight, but I've been known to get caught up in a good book or a business project and read or work until the wee hours of the morning.*

Feel free to add anything else that you feel is relevant. *I believe that if you look at fitness not just as something you do in your life, but as your lifestyle itself and if part of your sense of identity relates to health and fitness (for example "I am an athlete" or "I am a body-builder") then all the struggle to stay healthy and in shape goes away because you'll always act automatically in congruence with your identity. When you live the fitness lifestyle and see yourself as a "fitness person," all the behavior and action necessary for great health and fitness just comes naturally.* ❖

Phil Strand 63 years old, SAS Director, Performance Management. SAS has been voted by *Fortune Magazine* as the #1 company in the U.S. to work for, for a second year in a row. SAS is the leader in business analytics software and services.

❖ What time do you get up in the morning? *Most days I am up at 6 AM. On cardio days, MWF, I am up at 5:30 AM.*

What are your morning habits or rituals? *MWF, cardio-30-60 minutes: shave, shower, dress for work (locally or travel). I always eat breakfast—usually oatmeal and a protein shake (when with customers it is more elaborate).*

What time do you go to the gym? How do you fit your workouts into your week? *Time at the gym varies, due to work/travel schedule; I usually work out at mid-morning to noon or around 2-4 PM. My workouts always fit into my week, even when traveling. I usually don't work out one day a week.*

What kind of workout routine do you follow? *I usually do weights five to six days a week; when I do cardio (MWF) it is early in the morning and I return to the gym to do weights.*

How long are you in the gym when you work out? *About one hour or 75 minutes at most.*

How do you make eating healthy convenient? *Most of my eating is healthy; breakfast at home or at a hotel, but healthy. I bring a lunch with me to work. Only potential for less healthy eating is when I am traveling and eating out with clients.*

How do you make time for your family, social life, and other activities? *My children are grown and out of the house, so it is only my wife and me. Our nightly routine is always dinner together, then watching TV, reading, or some other social event together.*

What time do you get to bed at night? *I am in bed by 9 PM and fall asleep by 9:15-9:30 PM at the latest. Occasionally when we are out on a Friday or Saturday evening I am in bed by 11 PM at the latest.*

Feel free to add anything else that you feel is relevant. *I think it is essential to keep a focus on your health and well-being, including eating right and ensuring a workout routine combining cardio and weights. Socialization and communicating with others (family and professionals) is critical for mental stimulation and growth. I think having a strong faith background and living your faith also contributes to your overall health.* ❖

Gary Gruber 40 years old, chiropractor.

❧ What time do you get up in the morning? *5:30–6:00 AM*

What are the morning habits or rituals that you have? *Take the dog for a walk while I'm doing a prayer walk. If not, then read the Bible or something educational.*

What time do you go to the gym? How do you fit your workouts into your week? *Workouts are during lunch hour for 45 minutes—this way I don't have to take away from time with the family or stay late after work*

What time of workout routine do you follow? *Weights 4 times per week and cardio at home or early morning. This way I can listen to something on the computer or simply be home with the family.*

How long are you in the gym when you work out? *45 minutes—and do a lot of supersets for muscle intensity and time efficiency.*

Do you do cardio with weight training or at a separate time? *With weight training—to save time.*

How do you make eating healthy convenient? *I Usually make food during the weekend and will bring to the office during the week.*

How do you make time for your family, social life, and other activities? *By getting up early to walk the dogs, do paperwork, etc, after they go to bed and exercise during lunch hour.*

What time do you get to bed at night? *No specific time—when I'm tired, which is usually 11:00.*

Ginny Huff

❧ What time do you get up in the morning? *Gym mornings—6 AM. Chiropractor mornings—6:45.*

What are the morning habits or rituals that you have? *I am NOT a morning person! The best I can do is roll out of bed and put on whatever I picked out the night before. If I'm going to the gym, my bag is already packed & sitting by the bedroom door.*

What time do you go to the gym? How do you fit your workouts into your week. *Classes that I want to attend are put on my calendar weekly. Usually it's 7 AM on Tuesday and Thursday for my favorite spin class and misc classes at 5:45 PM Mon, Tues, Wed, and Fri after work. Saturday is swim practice* at 8:30 AM and Sunday, if I feel up to it, is kickboxing after church. I have made friends in these classes and gotten to know the instructors, so if I miss a day I know I'll be asked about it! Accountability. If my after work schedule won't allow me to go to a 5:45 PM class, I know in plenty of time to rearrange a few things so I can at least get in a few mile run sometime during the day.

What kind of workout routine do you follow? *I really need to do better at this on my own. If I'm not training for a race (running or triathlon) I just do whatever I feel like that fits in my day! If I am training, I follow a suggested schedule. Weights/cross train once a week, stretching/yoga once a week, cardio 5 days a week. I get my weight training in during a Monday "total conditioning" class. Several days a week I do have to do back to back workouts: run then yoga, swim then run, bike then run. Deciding which days to do what workout is easy some days. Tuesday and Saturday, swim practice is scheduled. Tuesday and Thursday mornings and Wednesday and Friday afternoons, spin class/cycle club is scheduled. Long runs have to be on Saturday mornings for me because I want to get them over with and on with my weekend!*

How long are you in the gym when you work out? *I'm at the gym as long as class/practice is—usually and hour to an hour and a half per class/practice. If I do have to stay after to run on the treadmill on my own, it's only another 20-30 minutes.*

Do you do cardio with weight training or at a separate time? *I do cardio/ weights at the same time during a weekly total conditioning class. Other than that, I use my body weight to tone muscles. Example: just a pull set while I'm swimming or running hill repeaters.*

How do you make eating healthy convenient? Do you eat out, bring meals with you, etc? *I do ok with eating healthy. Grocery stores have great salad bars now, so I do that almost every day for lunch. Lots of spinach with a little lean protein keeps me going the rest of the day. I keep whole wheat english muffins with natural peanut butter, yogurt, and no salt added almonds at work for breakfast and snacks. Dinner... not as good! It's usually a "meal in a box" or something from the freezer. I do always have microwavable frozen veggies on hand. If you can't have fresh, it's the next best thing. For the most part, I do NOT keep junk in the house. I can't trust myself! I keep apples, bananas, and I do have Goldfish for snacks.*

How do you make time for your family, social life, and other activities? *Friends and family are the priority. They go on the calendar first. My gym time fills in around that. If I miss a day in the gym, no big deal. My priorities are the people that would cry at my funeral. But, the people I care about in my life know how important gym time is to me and respect that. If I need to be late or leave early, they understand.*

What time do you get to bed at night? *Between 10 and 11 PM.*

Feel free to add anything else that you feel is relevant. *For me, gym time is ME time. It has to be on your calendar, just like any other appointment you can't miss. Respect yourself and your health enough to tell people you're busy if they want to meet during your gym time. You can always meet before or after. Accountability helps a lot. I got to know other "regulars" as well as my instructors so I know if I skip class, I'll be missed. Not only will I be missed but I'll miss out on seeing people I enjoy spending time with.*

Ira & Sheree Grady Ira: North Carolina State Highway Patrol; age 38. Sheree: Director of Marketing; age 38.

❖ What time do you get up in the morning?

Ira Grady: I normally get up every morning around 8:30.

Sheree Grady: I get up every morning between 8:30 and 9:00 AM.

What are the morning habits or rituals that you have? *Ira Grady: The first thing that I do in the morning is check my work emails. Right after doing so, I try to eat a complete breakfast while catching up on the news. Sometimes, due to work demands, my breakfast may consist of protein shakes and bars. These are convenient, healthy, and easy to eat when I am on the go.*

Sheree Grady: My morning routine consists of first making sure that my husband and I eat breakfast. Some days are more hectic than others, so that's why I try to keep breakfast items that that are quick and light, and can be taken with you.

What time do you go to the gym? How do you fit your workouts into your week.

Ira Grady: My work hours are from nine to five, with every weekend off so I normally go to the gym around 7:00 PM during the work week. This might seem late to most, but I find myself to be the strongest, physically at this time of the day.

Sheree Grady: On the weekdays, I will try to go to the gym around 5:30–6:00.

What time of workout routine do you follow? *Ira Grady: My goal is to go to the gym at least 5 times a week. During each workout I primarily focus on one body part.*

Sheree Grady: I try to workout 2 to 3 times a week. My workouts are combination of weight training and cardio (group classes).

How long are you in the gym when you work out? *Ira Grady: On average, my workouts last about two hours.*

Sheree Grady: My workouts vary between one to two hours.

Do you do cardio with weight training or at a separate time? *Ira Grady: Over the years, my workout routines have changed. I have incorporated cardio into my weight training routines by integrating high intensity interval training techniques into each session.*

Sheree Grady: Over the last two years, I have found myself enjoying group exercise more and more. If I am unable to attend group classes, I will either train with my husband when he goes to the gym around 7:00 or workout at home utilizing high intensity interval training routines.

How do you make eating healthy convenient? Do you eat out, bring meals with you, etc?

Ira Grady: In my line of work, I am always on the go; making it very hard to stick to a schedule for meals. When I have the opportunity to grab a bite to eat, I try to select meals that are fast and convenient; however, I do my best to remain conscious of eating meals that are healthier for me.

Sheree Grady: Eating healthy is a bit easier for me than it is for my husband. Since I work from home at least three times a week, it is much easier for me to eat lunches that are healthier.

How do you make time for your family, social life, and other activities? *Since my wife is also into staying fit, it adds to the amount of time we spend together because we often are able to workout together. On the weekends, we find time to exercise and hangout with family and friends.*

What time do you get to bed at night? *We usually go to bed around 11 PM.* ❖

You may listen to some of these interviews by visiting http://positivefitnessinterviews.com/

Chapter 17

The Lifestyle Restoration Cycle

Your *Why*

Know your why and the what and how
will take care of itself. —John M. Rowley

Your "why" in life is your purpose in life. This is the time to put in a little work and define why you want to do what you are setting out to do. Knowing your *"why"* will make it so much more powerful as you go about implementing the principles in this section. This section is the culmination of the entire book. You did this for the end of each section, now I want you to do this for every area of your life. Knowing why you are doing something, instead of just doing it, is probably the most energizing revelation you can have.

Step 1

Write down *why* you want to achieve things in your business and personal life. Next to each *why*, on your list, write a brief paragraph defining why you are committed to achieving the result you are after.

1 _____

_____

_____

2 _____

_____

_____

3 _____

_____

4 _____

_____

5 _____

_____

Step 2

This is where we put the plan together. Take the above list and put together an action list of things you would need to do to achieve them in your life. Formulate your plan. Remember that it is easier to put a plan together once you know why you are doing it.

_____

_____

_____

_____

_____

_____

Step 3

For each step in your plan, write down one or more habits you will need to develop and the disempowering habits you will need to get rid of in order to support your ultimate outcome. Imagine if you exchanged six limiting habits for six empowering habits every year. In five years, that would be 30 empowering habits that you do without effort and 30 disempowering habits that don't hinder you any longer. Do you think your life would be different?

Master your habits or they WILL master you!

List of Disempowering Habits

1 _____

2 _____

3 _____

4 _____

5 _____

List of New Empowering Habits

1 _____

2 _____

3 _____

4 _____

5 _____

List Which New Empowering Habit Will Replace The Old Disempowering Habit

(For Example: Replace sleeping in with having quiet time with God.)

1 _____

2 _____

3 _____

4 _____

5 _____

Congratulations! You just defined your fourth lifestyle restoration cycle! You found your *why*. You put a *plan* together. Then you identified disempowering *habits* that you are going to replace with empowering habits on a regular basis so they become part of your *lifestyle*, hence closing the loop on The Lifestyle Restoration Cycle. Developing powerful habits in every area of your life will change your life.

Now go to http://habitfoundry.com to supercharge your habits. We will check in with you daily by email to see how you did the day before. You can either "Go solo" or "Join a Group" of people who are working on a similar goal as you.

Afterword

The Barna Group recently released a study on teen role models. The expected names found their way into the list: Obama, Jesus, Oprah, LeBron James, and Lady Gaga. However, parents, grandparents, teachers, siblings, and coaches found their way to the top of the list. When asked what it was about these top-tier individuals that caused them to be elevated to the realm of "heroes" and "role models," one word aptly described the overarching traits: Integrity.

The word "integrity" is powerful but misunderstood. Instead of describing a list of moral do's and don'ts, the word describes someone who is "integrated"; that is, one's value system is part of the practical warp and woof of one's everyday lifestyle. A person of integrity doesn't segment his or her life into isolated parts, acting one way in one setting and another way in a different setting. With integrity, one part impacts the whole.

What you have just finished reading is John Rowley's attempt to coach you into leading a life of integrity. He has encouraged you to bring the physical, spiritual, and mental components of your life into an integrated whole. Too often motivational books focus on the mental to the exclusion of the physical and spiritual, the spiritual books treat the spirit in isolation from the physical and mental, and the physical books help us acquire healthy bodies but leave us with weak minds and spirits. Not this book. This book is passionate about seeing every dimension of your life developed to its fullest.

If John has put you on the path of integrity, then this book has served its purpose. May you live a healthy, long life. May you stay positive, focused, and goal-oriented. May you find peace with God through his Son, Jesus Christ. And after you have begun implementing the principles found in this book, may your friends, spouse, children, co-workers, teammates, and supervisors say without hesitation, "That, without a doubt, is a person of integrity!"

Chad Harvey
Senior Pastor
Raleigh First Assembly of God
Raleigh, North Carolina

Recipes for Success

As I stressed throughout this book, you must take responsibility for what you eat. But that doesn't mean it can't be tasty! This section provides recipes that taste good and that are healthy, although some may require some tweaking. I am not a fan of some of the ingredients, but I know that if you deprive yourself too much you won't stick to your healthy eating plan. So *pay attention to the ingredients*; if something in one of these recipes doesn't fit your health goals, then omit that ingredient or replace it with something else. For example, some of the recipes call for sugar or brown sugar; so either take that out or use the recipe for a Victory Meal. You can replace bread crumbs with spelt bread crumbs or gluten free bread crumbs. I didn't change these recipes from the originals provided by the chefs because I want you to think your way through the process from day one. My goal for this book is to teach you how to make wise decisions and form healthy habits.

Chef Dean James Max

Chef Dean James Max is the "King of Seafood." I met Dean at the 2010 Great American Seafood Cook-Off in New Orleans. Chefs from 15 states competed against one another to see who the best of the best was. They came armed with their favorite seafoods from their own states, cooked them before the live audience, and served them to a panel of judges known for their seafood, cooking and presentation expertise. The featured ingredients included fish and shellfish from the Atlantic Ocean, Gulf of Mexico, Great Lakes, Pacific Ocean, and even some freshwaters in a couple of landlocked states.

Left to right:
John Rowley, Dean Max, and Ewell Smith

At the end of the fierce competition and delectable food presentation, Chef Dean Max was crowned as the 2010 American King of Seafood. He is chef at 3030 Ocean at Marriott Harbor Beach and Spa Resort in Fort Lauderdale. Below are some recipes that Dean wanted to share with you to help you on your quest for health and fitness. If you are ever in Fort Lauderdale, stop in to visit Chef Dean and tell him John sent you!

Rare Wahoo with Tangerine Citrus Bowl

Serves 6

Wahoo:

3 lb. Wahoo loin
2 Tbs. Japanese Togarshi

Cut the Wahoo into long log shapes, which have a 1-inch diameter. Season them with salt and togarashi and wrap them in plastic wrap and then foil. Sear them in a dry sauté pan on all sides for 10 seconds. Remove and cool them immediately in the refrigerator. Keep chilled until serving.

Citrus sauce:

6 tangerines (halved and juiced with shells reserved)
1 grapefruit (segmented and diced)
1 orange (segmented and diced)
1 lime (juiced)
1 Tbs. chopped cilantro
1 Tbs. fish sauce (optional)
1 red Thai pepper (minced)
1 avocado (smashed)
1 lime (juiced)
1 Tbs. sesame oil

Cut the tangerines in half and carefully scoop out the flesh. Keep the tangerine halves and use to serve the appetizer. Squeeze the tangerine juice in a sauté pan and mix with the juice of the grapefruit, orange and lime. Add the thai pepper to the juice and reduce it down over a medium heat by 2/3 thirds its volume. When the reduction has cooled, add it to the segments of orange and grapefruit, cilantro, fish sauce. Mix the smashed avocado with the lime juice, sesame oil, and salt to taste. Place the avocado at the bottom of each tangerine shell and arrange two thin slices of the wahoo on top. Spoon some of the citrus sauce over the fish and serve with a small fork.

℀ Spicy Tuna Tartar with Pickled Daikon ℀

Serves 6

Juice:
2 Tbs. soy sauce
2 Tbs. sesame oil
1 Tbs. chili sambal paste
1/2 cup grapeseed oil

Mix the ingredients together and keep chilled.

Pickled Daikon:
1/2 cup rice wine vinegar
2 Tbs. sugar
1 Tbs. salt
1 bay leaf, 1 tsp. Peppercorns, 1 tsp. Cloves
1 whole daikon root

Bring all the ingredients except the daikon root to a boil and chill. Peel and slice the daikon. Put the slices in the cold pickling juice for 30 minutes. Drain the daikon from the juice and keep cold.

℀ Lime Aioli ℀

1 egg
2 limes
1 tsp. mustard
2 sprigs cilantro
1/2 cup grapeseed oil

Add all the ingredients to the blender and on a slow speed drizzle in the oil until thick. Season with salt and pepper

Tartar:
1 lb. sushi grade tuna
1 Tbs. chopped chives
1 shallot (grated)

Dice the tuna into small cubes. Mix in the chives and grated shallot. Season with the soy juice above to your desired taste. Place the tuna in molds and present on the plate. Fan the Daikon around the tuna and serve with lime aioli. Garnish with a small salad greens.

Wine Selection: Trimbach, Pinot Gris, Alsace, 2000

Grilled Swordfish with Tempura Squash

Serves 6

Block Island Swordfish:
6 each 7 oz filets of sword
6 Tbs. extra virgin olive oil
Salt and cracked black pepper
5 Tbs. lemon oil (Manicaretti brand)
5 Tbs. chopped chives (minced)

Rub the swordfish with the olive oil and seasoning. Grill over a high heat for 3 minutes on each side. Drizzle with lemon oil and top with chopped chives.

Tempura squash

1 cup flour
8 oz. soda water
Pinch of baking soda
1 Tbs. sea salt
12 squash blossoms
2 cups canola oil

Whisk together the flour, water, baking soda, and sea salt. Heat the oil in a small deep fryer to 350 degrees. Dip the squash in and fry them for 2 minutes. Drain them on paper towels and season with fine salt.

Lemon Aioli

5 lemons (zested and juiced)
1 Tbs. dijon mustard
1 tsp. saffron powder
2 whole eggs
Salt
Grapeseed oil (approx. 2 cups)

Combine all ingredients in blender except oil. Blend until smooth and strain through chinois strainer.

Spinach:
1 large bunch spinach or spicy greens
2 lemons juiced
4 Tbs. extra virgin olive oil
2 Tbs. butter
1 tsp. minced garlic
salt and pepper

To serve: Sauté the butter, olive oil, and garlic for 1 minute. Add in the spinach and wilt for a couple of minutes. Add the lemon juice and season the spinach with salt and pepper.

⤫ Grilled Shrimp with Arugula and Cauliflower Salad, ⤫ Beet Vinaigrette

Serves 6

Shrimp:
12 each jumbo shrimp (peeled and deveined)
Zest of the lemon below
3 Tbs. Extra virgin olive oil
salt and pepper
4 Tbs. parsley julienne
Season the shrimp and grill them until done on a open flame. Finish them with the parsley and serve while warm.

Beet Vinaigrette:
2 medium red beets (roasted whole until tender)
1 lemon (juiced)
1 tsp. dijon mustard
3 Tbs. sherry vinegar
1/4 cup grapeseed oil
1/4 cup extra virgin olive oil

Puree all the ingredients until smooth. Season with salt and pepper.

Salad:

1/2 pound arugula

1 head cauliflower (trim into small florets)

4 Tbs. olive oil

1/2 cup toasted pine nuts

1/2 cup golden raisins (soaked in sherry vinegar)

1/2 cup crumbled goat cheese

Roast the cauliflower with the olive oil, salt and pepper in a 350 degree oven until golden brown in a large oven skillet. Remove the skillet and while still very hot add in the pine nuts, raisins with a couple tablespoons of the vinegar, and then the arugula. Toss this mixture to slightly to wilt the arugula and then put in the goat cheese to let it slightly melt. Season with salt and pepper.

To serve:

Place down a couple of big spoonfuls of the beet vinaigrette in the serving dish and put the salad on top of the vinaigrette. Top with the shrimp.

❧ Sweet Pepper Grouper Barbecue, Peanut Corn Salsa ❧

Serves 6

Grouper Marinade:

2 lbs. fresh grouper filets

1 yellow onion

1 Tbs. grapeseed oil

1/4 cup rice wine vinegar

1/4 cup ketchup manis (also called Kecap manis)

1/2 cup brown sugar

1 spicy chili (scotch bonnet or Serrano)

2 green onions (chopped)

1 small knob ginger (juiced)

1/2 cup roasted red peppers (peeled and diced)

1 Tbs. chili sambal

1 Tbs. paprika

2 cups water

Sauté the onions in the oil until nicely browned. Add the brown sugar and let it melt. Add the ginger, chili, paprika, and let it cook for one minute. Add the vinegar, spicy pepper, red pepper, green onions, and water and reduce at a medium heat until the mixture has thickened. Grill the grouper over a medium high heat and apply the marinade. Move the grouper to the upper rack and cook until almost completely firm. Brush on some more of the sauce and serve warm or chilled.

Peanut Corn Salsa:
8 ears of corn (boiled or grilled, 8 minutes)
1 bunch green onions (diced)
1 cucumber (peeled, seeded, and diced)
1/2 cup diced roasted peppers
1 cup roasted and chopped peanuts
1/4 cup rice wine vinegar
1/2 cup olive oil
2 Tbs. chopped cilantro
1 lime juiced

Remove the corn from the cobs and toss the corn kernels with the other ingredients. Season with salt and pepper.

Garnish:
2 heads of Romaine lettuce
2 limes (juiced)
4 Tbs. extra virgin olive oil

Slice the romaine hearts into 3 large wedges. Marinate the romaine with the lime and oil. Season with salt and cracked pepper and grill it for 3 minutes on each side. Re-apply some lime, salt, and olive oil to taste.

Ahi Tuna Coconut Ceviche

Serves 6

Tuna:
1 pound Sushi grade ahi tuna (blood line out)
Trim and cut tuna into smaller workable portions. Slice tuna into thin strips and small dice.

Coconut Sauce:
1 can coconut milk (unsweetened)
1 Serrano pepper
2 Tbs. ginger

1 tsp. fish sauce
1/4 cup sugar
1 lime

Dice the peppers (keep seeds if you like it extra spicy) and ginger. Add to the pot with the coconut milk, sugar, and fish sauce. Bring to a boil and immediately turn down to a low simmer for about 10-15 min. Take off the stove and let sauce completely cool. Strain and refrigerate.

Ceviche Mix:
1 bunch cilantro
1 Serrano pepper (seedless)
1 bunch green onions
1 Red bell pepper
Chop the cilantro; thinly slice the bell pepper and Serrano peppers. Slice the green onions and combine all the ingredients together.

Crispy Yucca
1 yucca
2 cups canola oil

Peel and grate the yucca on a box grater with the larger grate. Fry the Yucca until crispy and season with salt and pepper.
To Serve: Serve the ceviche on an Asian spoon with crispy yucca on top.

❧ Dill Crusted Halibut with Spring Vegetable Succotash ❧

Serves 6

Cooking the Halibut:
6 each 7oz. halibut filets
1/2 lb. butter (room temperature)
1/2 cup bread crumbs
2 Tbs. chopped dill
2 Tbs. grated fresh horseradish
Zest of one lemon
1 cup white wine
1 garlic clove (smashed)
1 cup water

1/2 cup smoked tomatoes (if using sun dried, add them in with the wine and water when baking)
1/2 cup cream

Mix the butter with the bread crumbs, dill, horseradish and lemon zest. Season with salt and pepper and coat the top of each halibut filet with some of the crust. Place the fish with the crust side up in a buttered baking dish. Add in the garlic, wine, and water, and bake the fish for 10 minutes, or until just cooked medium rare. They will carry over as you finish the sauce. Add in the smoked tomatoes and reduce about 1/2 cup of liquid is left. Add in the cream and puree. Season with salt and pepper.

Succotash:
6 ears of corn (boil on the cob for 6 minutes, cool and cut off the kernels)
1 cup of shelled fava beans (blanched and peeled)
1 bunch white asparagus (peel and blanch)
1 cup English peas (shelled and blanched)
2 Tbs. butter
1 Tbs. extra virgin olive oil
1 lemon juiced

Warm the butter and oil in a pan. Add in the vegetables and warm them throughout. Finish with a touch of salt and the lemon juice. Serve immediately.

Crispy potato cake:
3 russet potatoes
1/2 cup chives (minced)
1 tsp. minced garlic
Salt and cracked pepper
3 Tbs. extra virgin olive oil
2 cups grapeseed oil (canola can be substituted)

Roast the potatoes in the oven at 350 degrees as if you are going to bake them, but only for 10 minutes. Peel them hot and shred them on a box grater. Mix the potato with the chives, garlic, olive oil, salt and pepper. Press them in a mold and cover them with plastic until needed. Fry the potatoes in the oil at 350 degrees in a small pot until crispy. Serve immediately.

To serve: Place the Halibut on plate with the sauce next to it. Place the vegetables in the sauce and set the crispy potato next to it.

❧ Citrus Cured Salmon, Crispy Oyster Mushroom Salad, ❧ Goat Cheese, Raspberry Vinaigrette

Curing the Salmon:
One 3lb. side of wild king salmon (with the skin on but bones removed)
1 bunch basil (chopped)
1 bunch cilantro (chopped)
1 orange (zested with juice)
1 orange (sliced)
2 lemons (zested and juiced)
2 limes (zested and juiced)
8 each garlic cloves (smashed)
1/2 cup white sugar
1/2 cup brown sugar
1/2 cup rum
2 Tbs. whole black peppercorns
1/2 cup kosher salt

Combine the herbs, zests, garlic, sugars, peppercorns, and salt. Coat the fish with all the wet ingredients—rum and citrus juices. Sprinkle the dry rub equally over the flesh of the fish. Put the fish on a baking rack over a baking pan. Place in the refrigerator, covered, for 48 hours. Remove the salmon and brush off all the ingredients. Cut thin slices of the salmon before serving.

Crispy oyster mushrooms:
1 lb. oyster mushrooms (cut off the root)
1 cup flour
8 oz. soda water
1 Tbs. salt
1 Tbs. white pepper
Pinch of cayenne
1 tsp. baking soda

Mix the flour, salt, baking soda, pepper and cayenne in a bowl. Whisk in the soda water until combined. The batter should coat your finger when you dip it in the bowl, not running off too quickly. Toss the mushrooms in the batter and fry at 350 degrees in a deep fryer or large pot with canola oil. Remove when the mushrooms are golden brown and crispy. Season with fine sea salt.

Raspberry Vinaigrette:
1 Tbs. dijon mustard
1/4 cup raspberry vinegar
1 lime (juiced)
1/2 cup grapeseed oil
1/4 cup extra virgin olive oil
Salt to taste

Whisk the mustard in a bowl with the vinegar and lime juice. Drizzle in the oils and taste for acidity. If you like it more bright, just use a touch less oil and more vinegar.

Serving:
1 lb. mixed greens
1 cup goat cheese
1 large radish (sliced)
1 pint fresh raspberries

Toss the salad with the goat cheese, radish, vinaigrette, mushrooms and strawberries. Serve with two slices of the cured salmon.

❧ Grilled Octopus Salad with Tomatoes and Arugula ❧

Serves 6

Court Bouillon
Yields: 1 Gallon

This stock is simply a flavorful broth in which to cook lobsters, shrimp, and other seafood items. We tend to make the flavor much too intense to drink as a soup since it will need to leave its impact on the item being cooked.

2 cups onions (chopped)
1 cup leeks (chopped)
1 cup carrot (chopped)
1 cup celery (chopped
1 cup fennel (chopped
1 garlic bulb (halved)
6 sprigs of fresh thyme, tarragon, and parsley
2 Tbs. black peppercorns

2 star anise (substitute fennel seed)
4 Tbs. sea salt
Zest and juice of 2 lemons
1 cup dry white wine
1 1/2 gallons water
Marinade:
1 Tbs. red pepper flakes
3 Tbs. fennel seed
Zest of 2 lemons
Salt and cracked pepper
1/2 cup extra virgin olive oil

Bring the above ingredients to a boil in a large stockpot. Add in the cleaned octopus and bring the liquid back to a boil. Turn down to a gentle simmer and cook for 30 minutes. Remove the pot from the heat and let the octopus cool in the liquid. Remove the octopus when cool and trim any excess fat off the tentacles. Cut into individual pieces. Mix with the marinade ingredients and refrigerate overnight. Grill on each side for 2 minutes and serve warm.

Lime Vinaigrette:
2 limes (juiced)
1 lemon (juiced)
1 tsp chili garlic paste
1/2 cup olive oil
Whisk the above ingredients and adjust for salt and lime. Store in the refrigerator.
1 bunch arugula
3 vine ripe tomatoes

To assemble: Arrange slices of tomatoes on each plate. Toss the arugula with the lime vinaigrette and place on each plate. Top with the grilled octopus and drizzle with basil oil.

2 Sisters Recipes

This section is a special treat for me. www.2sistersrecipes.com is a cooking blog created by two sisters, Anna Petralia and Liz Venditto. The girls were raised by Italian immigrant parents in my neighborhood and we all went to high school together in Long Island, New York. They are not chefs by profession, but they can make dishes that would make you think they went to a culinary school for training. They got their kitchen skills from their Mom, Maria Venditto, who is a wonderful cook and received her informal training from a famous chef who lived in her building in Capri, Italy.

Anna and Liz created a blog to record and share their mother's Italian recipes while creating some of their own. Check out www.2sistersrecipes.com for some tasty dishes from our neck of the woods! Enjoy and Buon Appetito!

Grilled Shrimp with Arugula Salad

Serves 3-5

1 lb. medium or large size raw shrimp
5 oz container of Baby Arugula—organic
5 Tbs. of extra-virgin olive oil
1 lemon—juiced
pinch of oregano
pinch of fresh parsley, chopped
pinch of garlic powder
sea salt and fresh ground pepper
cooking oil spray

Peel shrimp clean. Rinse well a few times and drain. Heat a nonstick skillet on high heat for grilling. Lightly spray cooking oil. Add the shrimp. Sprinkle sea salt and fresh ground pepper over the shrimp. Grill shrimp for 3 minutes on each side, or until medium pink.

In a large mixing bowl, add the baby arugula, olive oil, half the lemon juice, oregano, garlic powder and parsley. Sprinkle sea salt and pepper. Mix well. Transfer to a serving platter. Add the grilled shrimp on top. Drizzle remaining lemon juice on top and serve!

✎ Basa Livornese ✎

Serves 4-6

4 cloves of fresh garlic, finely chopped
1/2 large onion,chopped
5 Tbs. Extra Virgin Olive Oil
3 lbs. Basa or Swai fish filets
2 Fresh Ripe Tomatoes—diced
1 Box of Frozen Artichoke Hearts, 9 oz
1/4 Tbs. Red Pepper Flakes
2 Tbs. Capers
A handful Black Olives-pitted
A handful Green Olives with pimento
1/2 cup of Chicken Stock
1 tsp. Sea Salt
1 tsp. Black Pepper
Handful of Italian Parsley for garnish

On low heat **sauté** garlic and onion in a deep pan with olive oil for a few minutes, until garlic is golden brown only. Onions will continue to cook slowly along with other ingredients. **Lay** the fish filets flat on top of garlic and onions. Add **diced** tomatoes. Break all olives in half and **sprinkle** around pan evenly. **Add** 1 box of frozen artichoke hearts.

Add capers, sea salt, black pepper, red pepper and chicken stock. Garnish with Fresh Italian Parsley. Cover and simmer for 5 minutes on high heat. Transfer to a serving platter and serve.

✎ Baked Branzino ✎

Serves 2-4

2 small Branzino's (about 1 lb each)
Extra virgin olive oil
4 garlic cloves- sliced
1 lemon—sliced
1 cup of flat leaf parsley
1 Tbs. of dried rosemary
1/2 cup of white wine
1/2 Tbs. of sea salt

1/2 tsp. freshly ground black pepper
1/4 cup of lemon juice

Rinse fish, pat dry. Line a baking pan with foil wrap and spray with cooking oil. Place fish onto pan. Stuff the cavity of each fish with some garlic slices, 2-3 lemon slices, and some parsley. Sprinkle the fish with salt, pepper, and rosemary. Drizzle extra virgin olive oil inside the cavity and over the fish as well. Bake at 400 degrees, uncovered for 5-10 minutes. Turn the fish over and bake another 5-10 minutes. Add the wine and lemon juice. Turn the oven to broil, and broil the fish for 4- 6 minutes, until the skins blister. Take the fish out and with a fork, place it inside the center of the cavity and flip it open. Remove the spine of the fish and some large bones, and place it onto a serving dish. Drizzle some olive oil and lemon juice onto the fish and serve!

Grilled Salmon Over Balsamic Salad

Serves 2-4

2 small Salmon steaks
1 lemon—squeezed
3 Tbs. Extra Virgin Olive Oil
3 Tbs. Balsamic Vinegar
2 tomatoes—chopped
1- 2 cups of fresh arugula
1 celery stalk—chopped
1/4 cup of red onion—chopped
1 garlic clove—minced
1 Tbs. of fresh basil—chopped
pinch of dried oregano
salt & pepper to taste

In a platter, lightly salt and pepper the salmon steaks. Add some lemon juice and drizzle olive oil over them. Set them aside to marinate for about 1/2 hour. In a small bowl, whisk together the garlic, basil, oregano, balsamic vinegar, and olive oil. Add salt and pepper to taste.

In a salad bowl, add the chopped tomatoes, celery, red onion, and arugula leaves. Pour the dressing over salad and mix well. Refrigerate the salad for about 1/2 hour. Grill salmon on an outside grill for about 10 minutes. If you prefer salmon to be rare, then grill them for less time. Spread the salad onto a serving platter. Place the salmon steaks on top of the tomato balsamic salad and serve !

↝ Simply Baked Chicken ↜

Serves 6-8

2 lbs. of Chicken cutlets, cut in half for portion control
2 cups of Whole Wheat Bread Crumbs
1 cup of Extra Virgin Olive Oil
1 Tbs. Fresh Italian Flat Leaf Parsley
1/2 tsp. Salt
1/4 tsp. Black Pepper
1/2 tsp. Garlic Powder
1/4 tsp. Cayenne Pepper or Ground Red Pepper

Mix all dry ingredients in a bowl. Rinse all chicken cutlets in a Zip lock bag. In one bowl, dip the chicken in olive oil. In a separate bowl, dip the chicken in the dry ingredients mix until covered on both sides. Place in a 9 x 13 baking pan. degrees. Turn once after 7 minutes and continue to bake for 7 minutes. Depending on the thickness of the chicken it may need to cook a little more or a little less. Enjoy with a side salad and some veggies.

↝ Chicken Rollatini with Pesto and Mozzi ↜

Serves 2-4

One package of Chicken Cutlets, about 4-5 Chicken Cutlets
1/4 cup of Olive Oil
1/4 cup of Plain Bread Crumbs
1 small fresh Italian Mozzarella
1 small (4.2 oz) jar or container of Pesto Sauce
Olive oil cooking spray
garlic powder
fresh ground pepper

Rinse chicken cutlets. In a small dish, add the olive oil for dipping. In another plate, add the plain bread crumbs. Take each chicken cutlet and dip into the oil, both sides, and then gently into the bread crumbs. Lay them flat onto a plate. Spread 1 Tbs. of pesto sauce onto each cutlet. Cut a small piece of mozzarella and place in the center of each cutlet. Roll up the cutlet (no need for toothpicks).

Place them with seam side facing down onto a baking dish. Spray with olive oil on top of cutlets. Sprinkle fresh pepper and garlic powder onto each cutlet. Bake at 450 degrees for 15 to 20 minutes (depending on the thickness of the cutlets). Serve Immediately!

⊷ Chicken with Arugula and Wine ⊶

Serves 2, but you can double the recipe for family portions.

2 Tbs. of Olive oil
3 Garlic Cloves—sliced
1 medium container of Baby Arugula (washed and dried)
4 thin Chicken Cutlets
6 Sun Dried tomatoes (not in oil)—chopped
2 Tbs. of Capers (rinsed)
1 cup of Dry White Wine
1/4 tsp. Garlic Powder
salt and pepper to taste

In a non-stick skillet, heat oil and add the sliced garlic and sauté until golden on both sides. Add the entire container of baby arugula, turning while cooking to mix with olive oil. Once the arugula is sauteed (to a slightly darker green) and reduced in size, push arugula to one side of skillet. Place the chicken cutlets into the skillet and grill them for a few minutes until golden on both sides. Add the capers, sun dried tomatoes, and the white wine. Add salt, pepper, and garlic powder and simmer for a few minutes until the wine has reduced a little. Enjoy!

⊷ Mom's Roasted Low-Calorie Asparagus ⊶

Serves 6

1 bunch of fresh asparagus (about 30)
2 Tbs. of bread crumbs—unseasoned
1 Tbs. of Parmesan cheese
1/4 tsp. of garlic powder
4 Tbs. of olive oil
salt and pepper to taste

Cut the ends off the asparagus (about 2 inches from bottom of stems).
Steam the asparagus for 5 minutes. Use baking pan lined with foil wrap for fast cleaning. Spray cooking spray onto foil. Lay the asparagus in a single row on

the baking pan. Sprinkle bread crumbs, grated cheese, salt, pepper, and garlic powder. Drizzle olive oil over them. Bake at 350 degree oven for 15 minutes.

✑ Sweet Potatoes with Mascarpone Cheese ✑

Serves 4-6

4 large sweet potatoes
2 oz. of Mascarpone Cheese (you can find in any gourmet or Italian specialty market)
2 Tbs. of sour cream
1/2 tsp. salt

Using a potato peeler, and peel the skins off from sweet potatoes. Cut into small chunks and add to large pot of water. Bring to boil. Boil potatoes for about 20 minutes, or until they are soft. Drain all potatoes from pot using a colander. Add mascarpone cheese, sour cream, and salt. Use a hand mixer on high speed to blend and puree.

Johnathan Zamora

Johnathan Zamora is a culinary nutritionist and professional chef. Graduated from Johnson & Wales University, a world-class culinary institution, Johnathan has spent over a decade working alongside award-winning chefs and industry leading professionals. His role as a food and nutrition authority allows him the unique position to blend culinary arts with present day nutrition theory. Mainly, Johnathan responds to his clients' needs for healthy, satisfying meals that provide fuel for athletic performance, weight loss and general wellness. Johnathan has also overcome obesity, having lost over 170 pounds by using food and regular exercise as a means to naturally and safely transform his body and health. He practices in New York State and currently offers private in-person and web-based nutrition consulting for a wide range of clients including athletes, bodybuilders, and fitness models with a variety of health and wellness goals. To learn more, visit www.fitchefnutrition.com

✑ Turkey Taco Salad ✑

Serves 4

1 lb. Ground Turkey meat
6 ea. Taco shells, baked

1 pkg. Taco seasoning
4 cups Mixed lettuce (romaine, red leaf, etc.)
1 ea. Tomato, red ripe, diced
1 cups Cheddar cheese, shredded
Taco sauce to taste

Heat oven to 450 degrees.
In a heavy skillet over medium high heat, brown meat and cook through. Mix in seasoning and reduce heat to low. On a sheet pan, arrange one layer of foil and place taco shells upside down on sheet pan. Bake for 5 minutes or until slightly browned. Arrange lettuce in bowls and add 1/4 meat, 1/4 tomato, 1/4 cheese and taco sauce to taste.

Nutritional Information:
486 Calories; 30g Protein, 23g Carbohydrates, 31g Fat

﹌ Western Griddle ﹌

Serves 1

1/2 cup Egg whites
1/2 cup Black beans, canned
1/4 cup Corn Niblets, canned
1/4 cup Yellow Onions, chopped
1/4 cup Salsa Verde
1/4 cup Shredded Cheddar Cheese
1 Tbs. Parsley, chopped
1 tsp. McCormick's Season All
Salt and Pepper, to taste

Coat a small pan with cooking spray, and add corn, onions, and beans. Heat until onions are translucent and corn is browned. Add eggs to vegetable mixture and add season all. Cook until eggs are bright white and cooked through. Add salsa verde and mix well. Add cheese to eggs and heat until cheese is melted. Remove from heat. Sprinkle parsley and add salt and pepper to taste.

Nutritional Information:
375 Calories; 29g Protein, 40g Carbohydrates, 11g Fat

Seafood Salad Sandwiches

Serves 1

2 oz. Fresh crabmeat, shredded
2 oz. Cooked shrimp, tails removed, de-veined, chopped
1 Tbs. Light Mayonnaise
1 cup Coleslaw mix, no dressing
1 Tbs. Red onion, diced
1 ea. Whole wheat club roll
2 ea. Tomato slices
2 ea. Pickle spears
Old Bay seasoning, to taste
Pepper, to taste

In a medium bowl, combine the first five ingredients and mix well. Add seasonings to taste. On club roll, layer seafood salad, and then top with tomato slices. Serve with pickle spears.

Nutritional Information:
470 Calories; 34g Protein, 55g Carbohydrates, 12g Fat

The Eye Opener Smoothie

Serves 1

1/2 cup Vanilla yogurt, nonfat
1 cup Black coffee, brewed
1 Tbs. Chocolate syrup
1 Tbs. Peanut butter
1 scoop Chocolate protein powder
3 ea. Ice cubes

In a blender, combine all ingredients and blend for 1 minute or until smooth consistency is reached.

Nutritional Information:
300 Calories; 31g Protein, 23g Carbohydrates, 10g Fat

✍ Avocado Salad with Tomatoes and Red Wine Vinaigrette ✍

Serves 1

1 cup Romaine lettuce, chopped
1 cup Fresh spinach
1/4 ea. Avocado, sliced
1 ea. Tomato, red ripe, cored, cut into wedges
1/2 cup Cucumber, peeled, sliced into rounds
1 Tbs. Bacon bits
2 Tbs. Red Wine Vinaigrette

In a medium bowl, combine all ingredients and toss well. Keep refrigerated until ready to eat.

Nutritional Information:
275 Calories; 9g Protein, 23g Carbohydrates, 16g Fat

✍ PEACH GREEN ICED TEA ✍

Serves 6

6 each Green Tea Bags
6 cups Cold Water
2 each Ripe Peaches, pitted and sliced
1/2 cup Honey

Place tea bags in teapot or pitcher. Place sliced peaches in saucepan, add water, boil, and then pour mixture over teabags. Steep 6 minutes, add sweetener, allow to cool, and serve.

Workouts for Every Level

How to Pick the Right Weight

If you have never lifted weights before you may have some questions. It is not uncommon to wonder if you are using the correct weight, how many reps (short for repetition) you should do, and how many sets of reps are you to do for a given exercise. For best results in the least amount of time, you want to lift a weight that allows you to complete only 8 to 12 repetitions. When you use a weight that is so heavy that you can complete less than 8 reps, you are getting more into strength training. Once you go beyond 12 reps, you are more into endurance training. I suggest you stick with the 8 to 12 rep range because you will get stronger and this is the best rep range for building muscle. This gives you the best bang for your buck.

When you get to the gym, choose a weight for a given exercise and if you can easily do 20 reps, you are lifting way too light. Add more weight until you can do more than 8 reps, but not more than 12 reps. As you get to the 12th rep, you should be struggling and unable to get the 13th rep. When you can do more than 12 reps with that weight, it is time to increase the weight for that exercise. Your strength will go up and as it does you'll add more resistance weight. Make sure you can do 8 reps and stay with this weight until you can complete 12 reps again. It is that simple. Each of the below routines will give you great results. I have categorized them into beginning, intermediate, and advanced routines as a baseline guide. Intensity is the main ingredient that separates a novice from the advanced lifter. I know many advanced athletes that use a routine similar to the beginner routine but they lift very hard and heavy. If you have never worked out before, I suggest you start with the beginner routine until you feel comfortable advancing, and then go onto the intermediate and advanced schedules. As I stated earlier in the book, consistency is the key ingredient to getting the results you want, which is why I have given you so many options.

I change my routine every few months. I use one of the advanced routines and when I start getting bored or if I feel my body needs a change I will switch. Normally it isn't my body needing a change because the body doesn't get bored; it is my mind needing a change. Keep in mind that these workouts are just guidelines to get you going in the right direction. If you don't like a certain exercise, find ones that you do like. Now let's look at some training schedules that will give you great results.

Old Reliable: The Perfect Routine

I listed this workout earlier in the book and I also have it in the advanced section below. If you want to start off with a routine that you can grow with as you get stronger this is it. This is the routine I used on a group to bring them from fat to fit in a few months. I was able to monitor their intensity and not push them until I knew they were ready. This routine is used by beginner, intermediate, and advanced athletes alike. The more advanced the higher the intensity. This is a great all around routine that you can use to get into great shape.

Aerobic Training

On non weight training days, do thirty to forty five minutes of aerobic training. First thing in the morning would be best. If you can't do it in the morning, schedule it for the best time that is good for you, but don't skip it.

Resistance Training

You will train with weights three times a week, preferably with a day between each training day. For example, you can train Monday, Wednesday, and Friday or Tuesday, Thursday, and Saturday. Rest sixty to ninety seconds between each set. A *rep* is one complete motion of the exercise. A *set* is a group of the quantity of reps suggested.

Monday or Day 1 (Chest, Shoulder, Triceps and Abs)

Chest Press	3 sets of 8–12 reps
Incline Chest Press	3 sets of 8–12 reps
Shoulder Press	3 sets of 8–12 reps
Lateral Raise	3 sets of 8–12 reps
Triceps Press Down	3 sets of 8–12 reps

Lying Triceps Extension	3 sets of 8–12 reps
Crunch	3 sets of 10–20+ reps
Reverse Crunch/ Leg raises	3 sets of 10–20+ reps

Wednesday or Day 2 (Legs and Abs)

Leg Extension	3 sets of 8–12 reps
Leg Press	3 sets of 8–12 reps
Leg Curls	3 sets of 8–12 reps
Standing Calf Raises	3 sets of 8–12 reps
Crunch	3 sets of 10–20+ reps
Reverse Crunch/ Leg raises	3 sets of 10–20+ reps

Friday or day 3 (Back, Biceps and Abs)

Pulldowns	3 sets of 8–12 reps
Seated Rows	3 sets of 8–12 reps
Hyper Extensions	3 sets of 8–12 reps
Curls	3 sets of 8–12 reps
Preacher Curls	3 sets of 8–12 reps
Crunch	3 sets of 10–20+ reps
Reverse Crunch/Leg raises	3 sets of 10–20+ reps

BEGINNER LEVEL

Aerobic Training

Twice a week do, twenty minutes of aerobic training, either first thing in the morning, immediately after your workout, or on your non-weight training days.

Resistance Training

Do the prescribed workout two or three times a week, resting sixty to ninety seconds between each set.

Monday and Thursday or Monday, Wednesday and Friday

Squat	2 set of 10–12 reps
Lunge	2 set of 10–12 reps
Chest Press	2 set of 10–12 reps
Incline Chest Press	2 set of 10–12 reps
Pull Down	2 set of 10–12 reps
Row	2 set of 10–12 reps
Shoulder Press	2 set of 10–12 reps
Lateral Raise	2 set of 10–12 reps

Triceps Press Down	2 set of 10–12 reps
Curl	2 set of 10–12 reps
Crunch	2 set of 10–20 reps
Reverse Crunch	2 set of 10–20 reps

INTERMEDIATE LEVEL

Aerobic Training

Three to five times a week, do twenty to thirty minutes of aerobic training, either first thing in the morning, immediately after your workout or on your non-weight training days.

Resistance Training

Do the prescribed workout every other day, if you want to workout on the weekends. Or you can opt for Monday, Wednesday and Friday. Four days per week is popular by doing Monday, Tuesday, Thursday and Friday. All work well; it's just a matter of which you like best. Whichever plan you choose, just make sure you rest sixty to ninety seconds between each set. The workout below is described as Monday and Thursday and Tuesday and Friday, as well as "Day One" and "Day Two." If you are working out with weights every other day, just alternate between the "Day One" and "Day Two" workout.

WORKOUT 1
Monday and Thursday (Day One)

Squat	2–3 sets of 10–12 reps
Leg Extension	2–3 sets of 10–12 reps
Leg Curl	2–3 sets of 10–12 reps
Standing Calf Raise	2–3 sets of 10–12 reps
Biceps Curl	2–3 sets of 10–12 reps
Seated Biceps Curl	2–3 sets of 10–12 reps
Triceps Press Down	2–3 sets of 10–12 reps
Lying Triceps Extension	2–3 sets of 10–12 reps
Crunch	2–3 sets of 10–20 reps
Reverse Crunch	2–3 sets of 10–20 reps

Tuesday and Friday (Day Two)

Chest Press	2–3 sets of 10–12 reps
Incline Chest Press	2–3 sets of 10–12 reps

Pull Down	2–3 sets of 10–12 reps
Cable Row	2–3 sets of 10–12 reps
Shoulder Press	2–3 sets of 10–12 reps
Lateral Raise	2–3 sets of 10–12 reps
Crunch	2–3 sets of 10–20 reps
Reverse Crunch	2–3 sets of 10–20 reps

WORKOUT 2
Mondays (Chest, Shoulder, Triceps and Abs.)

Chest Press	3 sets of 8–12 reps
Incline Chest Press	3 sets of 8–12 reps
Shoulder Press	3 sets of 8–12 reps
Lateral Raise	3 sets of 8–12 reps
Triceps Press Down	3 sets of 8–12 reps
Lying Triceps Extension	3 sets of 8–12 reps
Crunch	3 sets of 10–20+ reps
Reverse Crunch	3 sets of 10–20+ reps

Wednesday (Legs and Abs.)

Leg Extension	3 sets of 8–12 reps
Leg Press	3 sets of 8–12 reps
Leg Curls	3 sets of 8–12 reps
Standing Calf Raises	3 sets of 8–12 reps
Crunch	3 sets of 10–20+ reps
Reverse Crunch	3 sets of 10–20+ reps

Friday (Back, Biceps and Abs.)

Pulldowns	3 sets of 8–12 reps
Seated Rows	3 sets of 8–12 reps
Curls	3 sets of 8–12 reps
Preacher Curls	3 sets of 8–12 reps
Crunch	3 sets of 10–20+ reps
Reverse Crunch	3 sets of 10–20+ reps

ADVANCED LEVEL

Aerobic Training

Four to six times a week do 30 or 45 minutes of aerobic training, either first thing in the morning or immediately after your work-out.

Resistance Training

Choose one of the prescribed workouts depending on what appeals to you and what works for your schedule. Keep in mind, the more often you are in the gym, the shorter your exercise routine will be. No matter what, rest 60 to 90 seconds between each set.

WORKOUT 1
Mondays (Chest, Biceps and Abs.)

Chest Press	3 sets of 8–12 reps
Incline Chest Press	3 sets of 8–12 reps
Decline Chest Press	3 sets of 8–12 reps
Biceps Curl	3 sets of 8–12 reps
Preacher Curl	3 sets of 8–12 reps
Crunch	3 sets of 10–20+ reps
Reverse Crunch	3 sets of 10–20+ reps

Tuesday (Legs and Abs.)

Leg Extension	3 sets of 8–12 reps
Leg Press or Squat	3 sets of 8–12 reps
Lunge	3 sets of 8–12 reps
Hamstring Curl	3 sets of 8–12 reps
Standing Calf Raise	3 sets of 8–12 reps
Crunch	3 sets of 10–20+ reps
Reverse Crunch	3 sets of 10–20+ reps

Thursday (Back and Abs.)

Pulldowns or Chins	3 sets of 8–12 reps
Close Grip Pull downs	3 sets of 8–12 reps
Low Cable Row	3 sets of 8–12 reps
High Hammer Row	3 sets of 8–12 reps
Hyper Extensions	3 sets of 10–20 reps
Crunch	3 sets of 10–20+ reps
Reverse Crunch	3 sets of 10–20+ reps

Friday (Shoulders, Triceps and Abs.)

Shoulder Press	3 sets of 8–12 reps
Lateral Raise	3 sets of 8–12 reps
Rear Delt Machine	3 sets of 8–12 reps
Triceps Press Down	3 sets of 8–12 reps

Lying Triceps Extension	3 sets of 8–12 reps
Crunch	3 sets of 10–20+ reps
Reverse Crunch	3 sets of 10–20+ reps

WORKOUT 2
Mondays (Chest and Abs.)

Chest Press	3 sets of 8–12 reps
Incline Chest Press	3 sets of 8–12 reps
Decline Chest Press	3 sets of 8–12 reps
Cable Crossovers	3 sets of 8–12 reps
Crunch	3 sets of 10–20+ reps
Reverse Crunch	3 sets of 10–20+ reps

Tuesday (Legs and Abs.)

Leg Extension	3 sets of 8–12 reps
Leg Press or Squat	3 sets of 8–12 reps
Lunge	3 sets of 8–12 reps
Hamstring Curl	3 sets of 8–12 reps
Standing Calf Raise	3 sets of 8–12 reps
Crunch	3 sets of 10–20+ reps
Reverse Crunch	3 sets of 10–20+ reps

Wednesday (Back and Abs.)

Pulldowns or Chins	3 sets of 8–12 reps
Close Grip Pull downs	3 sets of 8–12 reps
Low Cable Row	3 sets of 8–12 reps
High Hammer Row	3 sets of 8–12 reps
Hyper Extensions	3 sets of 10–20 reps
Crunch	3 sets of 10–20+ reps
Reverse Crunch	3 sets of 10–20+ reps

Thursday (Shoulders and Abs.)

Dumbbell Shoulder Press	3 sets of 8–12 reps
Lateral Raise	3 sets of 8–12 reps
Hammer Shoulder Press	2 sets of 8–12 reps
Rear Delt Machine	3 sets of 8–12 reps
Crunch	3 sets of 10–20+ reps
Reverse Crunch	3 sets of 10–20+ reps

Friday (Arms and Abs.)

Biceps Curl	3 sets of 8–12 reps
Seated Biceps Curl	2 sets of 8–12 reps
Preacher Curl	2 sets of 8–12 reps
Triceps Press downs	3 sets of 8–12 reps
Lying Triceps Extension	2 sets of 8–12 reps
Dips	2 sets of 8–12 reps
Crunch	3 sets of 10–20+ reps
Reverse Crunch	3 sets of 10–20+ reps

WORKOUT 3

(I like this one when I am short on time because I can be in and out of the gym quickly)

Monday (Legs and Abs.)

Leg Extension	3 sets of 8–12 reps
Leg Press or Squat	3 sets of 8–12 reps
Lunge	3 sets of 8–12 reps
Hamstring Curl	3 sets of 8–12 reps
Standing Calf Raise	3 sets of 8–12 reps
Crunch	3 sets of 10–20+ reps
Reverse Crunch	3 sets of 10–20+ reps

Tuesday (Chest and Abs.)

Chest Press	3 sets of 8–12 reps
Incline Chest Press	3 sets of 8–12 reps
Decline Chest Press	3 sets of 8–12 reps
Cable Crossovers	3 sets of 8–12 reps
Crunch	3 sets of 10–20+ reps
Reverse Crunch	3 sets of 10–20+ reps

Wednesday (Back and Abs.)

Pulldowns or Chins	3 sets of 8–12 reps
Close Grip Pull downs	3 sets of 8–12 reps
Low Cable Row	3 sets of 8–12 reps
High Hammer Row	3 sets of 8–12 reps
Hyper Extensions	3 sets of 10–20 reps
Crunch	3 sets of 10–20+ reps
Reverse Crunch	3 sets of 10–20+ reps

Thursday (Shoulders and Abs.)

Dumbbell Shoulder Press	3 sets of 8–12 reps
Lateral Raise	3 sets of 8–12 reps
Hammer Shoulder Press	3 sets of 8–12 reps
Rear Delt Machine	3 sets of 8–12 reps
Crunch	3 sets of 10–20+ reps
Reverse Crunch	3 sets of 10–20+ reps

Friday (Biceps and Abs.)

Biceps Curl	3 sets of 8–12 reps
Seated Biceps Curl	3 sets of 8–12 reps
Preacher Curl	3 sets of 8–12 reps
Cable Curl	3 sets of 8–12 reps
Crunch	3 sets of 10–20+ reps
Reverse Crunch	3 sets of 10–20+ reps

Saturday (Triceps and Abs)

Triceps Press downs	3 sets of 8–12 reps
Lying Triceps Extension	3 sets of 8–12 reps
Dips	3 sets of 8–12 reps
Triceps Kick Back	3 sets of 8–12 reps
Crunch	3 sets of 10–20+ reps
Reverse Crunch	3 sets of 10–20+ reps

WORKOUT 4

(Only have three days a week to work out)

Mondays (Chest, Shoulder, Triceps and Abs.)

Chest Press	3 sets of 8–12 reps
Incline Chest Press	3 sets of 8–12 reps
Flyes	3 sets of 8–12 reps
Shoulder Press	3 sets of 8–12 reps
Lateral Raise	3 sets of 8–12 reps
Rear Delt Raise	3 sets of 8–12 reps
Triceps Press Down	3 sets of 8–12 reps
Lying Triceps Extension	3 sets of 8–12 reps
Triceps Kick Back	3 sets of 8–12 reps
Crunch	3 sets of 10–20+ reps
Reverse Crunch	3 sets of 10–20+ reps

Wednesday (Legs and Abs.)

Leg Extension	3 sets of 8–12 reps
Leg Press	3 sets of 8–12 reps
Lunges	3 sets of 8–12 reps
Leg Curls	3 sets of 8–12 reps
Standing Calf Raises	3 sets of 8–12 reps
Seated Calf Raises	3 sets of 8–12 reps
Crunch	3 sets of 10–20+ reps
Reverse Crunch	3 sets of 10–20+ reps

Friday (Back, Biceps and Abs.)

Pulldowns	3 sets of 8–12 reps
Close Grip Pulldowns	3 sets of 8–12 reps
Seated Rows	3 sets of 8–12 reps
Curls	3 sets of 8–12 reps
Preacher Curls	3 sets of 8–12 reps
Crunch	3 sets of 10–20+ reps
Reverse Crunch	3 sets of 10–20+ reps

WORKOUT 4—Old School

This is a 3 days on, 1 day off routine. Or you can do it six days in a row and take Sundays off. But 3 days on, 1 day off is best for your recovery ability. This is old school training. This is the way Arnold Schwarzenegger and Lou Ferrigno trained in the movie *Pumping Iron* and I personally love the physiques from back in the golden age of bodybuilding. I know a lot of the greatest physique athletes in the world still work out this way and many are in their 50s, 60s, 70s and beyond.

Variation: You can vary this to match your schedule, lifestyle, and recovery ability. I know some who use this routine but train on Monday, Tuesday, Thursday, Friday, and Saturday. This gives you Wednesday and Sunday off. Just cycle through the 3-day split and if you miss a day for travel just pick up where you left off.

This section gives you more options of how to arrange your body parts. Simply use the exercises from the above workouts to design your own custom workout. This is where working out becomes fun.

Option 1
Day 1 (Chest, Back & Abs)
Day 2 (Shoulders & Arms)
Day 3 (Legs)

Day 4 off
Day 5 repeat

Option 2

Day 1 (Chest, Back & Abs)
Day 2 (Arms & abs)
Day 3 (Shoulders, Legs & Abs)
Day 4 off
Day 5 repeat

Option 3

Day 1 (Chest, Arms & Abs)
Day 2 (Back, Shoulders & abs)
Day 3 (Legs & Abs)
Day 4 off
Day 5 repeat

Option 4

Day 1 (Chest, Shoulders, Triceps & Abs)
Day 2 (Back, Biceps & ABs)
Day 3 (Legs)
Day 4 off
Day 5 repeat

Daily Tracking Success Forms

Daily Protein Requirements

Body	Protein		Body	Protein	
Weight	Grams	Portions	Weight	Grams	Portions
100	100	5	260	260	13
110	110	6	270	270	14
120	120	6	280	280	14
130	130	7	290	290	15
140	140	7	300	300	15
150	150	8	310	310	16
160	160	8	320	320	16
170	170	9	330	330	17
180	180	9	340	340	17
190	190	10	350	350	18
200	200	10	360	360	18
210	210	11	370	370	19
220	220	11	380	380	19
230	230	12	390	390	20
240	240	12	400	400	20
250	250	13			

Daily Meal Tracking Form

Date:	
Total Portions of Protein:	
Total Grams of Cautious Carbs:	
Total Oz. Water:	
Meal 1	
Meal 2	
Meal 3	
Meal 4	
Meal 5	
Meal 6	
Notes:	

WORKOUT LOG									
Date:									
Exercise	Set #1	Reps	Weight	Set #2	Reps	Weight	Set #3	Reps	Weight
AM Cardio									
PM Cardio									
Notes									

Get fresh. Be fit. Have fun.

The Louisiana Seafood Fitness and Health Challenge
COMING BACK STRONGER

Everyone knows Louisiana got hammered by Hurricane Katrina. The next strongest hurricane ever to the United States was Rita, which hit the western side of Louisiana one month following Katrina. Three of America's largest fishing ports were wiped off the face of the earth in one month. Then a couple years later we get slammed by Hurricanes Gutsov and Ike within a week of each other, literally shutting down the fishing business in Louisiana for a month. Katrina and Rita didn't even do that. And then the BP oil spill . . .

By default and necessity we have become experts in overcoming crises. Our fishing communities and fishermen are some of the most resilient people you will ever meet. Following Katrina, I will never forget a friend of mine in the seafood business, Eddie Gordon, who visited from South Carolina and shared his experience of surviving Hurricane Hugo. He lost his crabbing business to Hugo, and the city of Charleston was devastated. He jarred me with what he said as we were standing in front of one of our marinas with boats piled on top of boats and debris all over. He said simply, "It looks really bad now, but you will come back. Your city, New Orleans, will look better. And your fishing communities will come back stronger—in time." And he was right.

In crisis comes opportunity. It's what you do with that opportunity that matters. Will you run from your challenges or will you face them head on? As executive director of the Louisiana Seafood Board, we chose to take the challenges head on. We came back a long way and then some—right before the BP spill hit us. This time we knew exactly how to handle the crisis after having been through Hurricanes Katrina, Rita, Gustov, and Ike. We certainly didn't expect to ever deal with an oil spill the magnitude of what happened, but we also know that we will not only come back, but we will come back much stronger. I have to add that it's a privilege to be in John's book. The title *The Power of Positive Fitness* is dead on; right in line with the mindset we all must have to make it though life's challenges.

The Louisiana Seafood Fitness and Health Challenge also embodies John's wisdom and the spirit of the people of Louisiana. This fitness challenge is symbolic of much of what we have been though. There is no doubt life will wear on us at times and sometimes knock us to our knees; but if we pick ourselves off the ground, focus on the opportunities, and define what we want to achieve, we can rebuild our cities, fishing communities, and even our bodies and lives better than before. I want to challenge you to come back stronger. From personal experiences I know we can.

Note: John is proud to be an expert and judge for the Louisiana Seafood Fitness and Health Challenge. You can find out more at http://www.seafoodfitness.com/

Change YOUR Habits—Change YOUR Life!

HabitFoundry.com will automatically take you through the life changing Lifestyle Restoration Cycle.

What could you do daily to improve your life?

Imagine if you just replaced one dis-empowering habit with one empowering one.

If you did this every month for a year that would be 12 dis-empowering habits that you broke and 12 empowering habits that support your life.

Welcome to Habit Foundry! Many have said it takes 21 days to form a habit. I think that works for smaller habits, but to make permanent lifestyle changes that really transform your life, it can take a bit longer. 21 days, 30 days, or 60 days—no one really knows how long it takes because that is individual. What I do know is that it takes consistency and that is what HabitFoundry helps you with. I chose 30 days simply because it gives a full month and then if you are solid in the foundation of this new habit you can start a new one. It simply fits on the calendar better.

This is be an online tool that will change your life forever!

A foundry is a factory that produces metal castings. Metals are cast into shapes by melting them into a liquid, pouring the metal in a mold, and removing the mold material or casting after the metal has solidified as it cools.

Habits are the foundries that "cast" our life!

Empowering Habits lift our lives to incredible heights.

Dis-empowering Habits destroy our lives.

Habit Foundry will help you cast new habits on an ongoing basis so you can live the life of your dreams, with just 3 simple steps.

3 Simple Steps

Step 1: Name the challenge.

If you could do one thing every day that would change your life for the better, what would it be?

Step 2: Check your email.

We'll ask you daily by email if you were successful the day before at doing that one thing. From within the email, just click "yes" or "no," and we'll do the rest.

Step 3: Succeed for thirty days.

Do that one thing you've committed to doing. If you skip a day before succeeding for 30 days straight, we'll start you back at day one. Succeed for 30 days in a row, and you can enter monitoring mode. But by that point the action should seem second nature.

Habit F☼undry

To sign up, go to HabitFoundry.com. Oh, I almost forgot to mention—it's FREE!

Bibliography

Unless otherwise noted, the Bible is quoted from the New International Version.

Chapter 1

1. http://www.cdc.gov/vitalsigns/adultobesity/

Chapter 5

1. Psalm 118:24
2. Matt. 6:26-27
3. Numbers 23:19
4. http://articles.orlandosentinel.com/2008-05-25/news/lbard25_1_panzarella-rehabilitation-medicine-nervous-system

Chapter 6

1. http://barbaracorcoran.com/

Chapter 7

1. http://quotations.about.com/od/stillmorefamouspeople/a/MichaelJordan1.htm
2. http://www.innserendipity.com/paradigm/matson.html

Chapter 8

1. Philippines 4:8
2. Proverbs 28:19

Chapter 10

1. John 10:10
2. Ephesians 2:10
3. Jeremiah 1:5
4. Joel 2:25A ESV
5. Matt 10:30

Chapter 11

1. Genesis 39:1-2
2. Genesis 39:3 NAS
3. Romans 8:31b
4. James 2:19
5. Ephesians 1:18-20
6. John 8:7
7. John 8:10-11

Chapter 12

1. Gen 12:2
2. 1 Tim 6:10
3. Matt 6:31-33
4. Matt 6:33
5. Matthew 15:32-39

6. Matthew 14:15-21
7. Heb 13:8
8. John 10:10 NAS
9. Matt 6:33
10. Psalm 1:3
11. Prov 18:21
12. Philippians 4:8
13. Matt 12:34
14. Hebrews 11:6
15. Phil 4:19
16. Romans 10:17
17. Joshua 1:8
18. Numbers 23:19

Chapter 13

1. Psalm 118:24-25 NKJV
2. Romans 10:17 NAS
3. 1 Timothy 4:7-8 NAS
4. Romans 10:17 NAS
5. Hebrews 11:6 NAS
6. http://www.famousquotesandauthors.com/authors/martin_luther_quotes.html
7. Matthew 6:5
8. Matthew 6:6
9. Matthew 6:7
10. Matthew 6:9
11. Mark 11:22-24
12. Matthew 7:11
13. Matthew 6:9-13
14. In Acts 1:8
15. http://www.youtube.com/watch?v=ZhG-tkQ_Q2w&feature=fvw
16. http://www.merriam-webster.com/dictionary/stewardship

Chapter 15

1. http://habitforge.com/
2. Nehemiah 3: 28-30

Photo Credits